What to do when your child
your child
hates school

Antonia Chitty

WHITE
LADDER
PRESS
new tricks for old dogs

This edition first published in Great Britain 2008 by
Crimson Publishing, a division of Crimson Business Ltd
Westminster House
Kew Road
Richmond
Surrey
TW9 2ND

A catalogue record for this book is available from the British library.

ISBN 978 1 905410 38 5

Designed and typeset by Julie Martin Ltd
Cover design by Julie Martin Ltd
Colour photography by Jonathon Bosley

Contents

	Introduction	1
Chapter 1	**From special needs to academic issues**	3
Chapter 2	**Social issues and school troubles**	24
Chapter 3	**Work it out with the school**	50
Chapter 4	**Changing schools**	69
Chapter 5	**Home education, flexischooling and tutors**	99
Chapter 6	**Education 11-16**	122
Chapter 7	**Education post 16**	137
	Conclusion	149

Introduction

The school years can be challenging for parents and children alike. If your child is struggling, you may have problems working out how to help. If your child is playing up or behaving badly, it can be hard to understand that they may be trying to tell you something. However, you're not alone. Your child's problem may seem unique, but there's probably another mother or father who has been through something similar. This book will help you to help your child through a range of issues. Read on to find out how other parents have helped their child cope with academic challenges, bullying and other problems at school. You will also find tips from experts and useful resources.

Where to start

If you think the school isn't meeting your child's needs, start with Chapter 1. There is lots of information to help if you want to work out whether your child has special educational needs, and how to access additional help, with example letters to make it easier to follow what can be a complex process.

If your child is struggling at school due to traumatic events such as bullying, serious family illness, death or divorce, Chapter 2 is full of useful information. Chapter 3 will help you work problems out with the school, starting with informal meetings and guiding your through more formal complaints procedures to the head and to Governors. There are also contacts if you need to go further.

If you have got to the stage where it no longer seems possible to work things out with your child's current school, Chapter 4 will fill you in on your options when changing school. From following the process to move within the state system, to explanations about all sorts of independent schools, this chapter makes it clear where to go next. And Chapter 5 takes things one step further if you feel your child needs a break from school, and you would like to look into home educating, flexischooling and tutors.

Some problems can affect children of all ages, while other issues crop up mainly at secondary school. Chapters 6 and 7 look at children aged 11 to 16 and 16-plus respectively, dealing with academic and career issues, as well as looking at online and phone bullying, racist and homophobic bullying.

Chapter 1

From special needs to academic issues

Why do children have problems with school? There's no single answer to this one as the issues vary from child to child. This chapter looks at some of the reasons children learn at different rates, how conditions like Asperger's, dyslexia and autism can affect your child at school, and the help you can get. We also examine why bright kids may have problems at school too, and how to help. See Chapter 2 for more on bullying, truancy and how events in the family can cause stress at school.

IS YOUR CHILD STRUGGLING TO KEEP UP?

Some children take longer than others to learn, or may struggle with schoolwork or behaviour. It can be hard to know when to look for more help and advice, or whether to just accept that some children learn more slowly than others. Professor Patricia Preedy has 12 years' experience as a head teacher at a beacon school and also has, among other qualifications, a Masters in Educational Management investigating how schools can work in partnership with parents. She says, "Children can have some sort of learning difficulty, which may not emerge initially. As they get older it can become evident that their peers are 'taking off' whilst they are making slower progress. This frequently becomes evident at around the age of six but may also happen at later key stages."

Things to eliminate

Firstly, it is worth eliminating physical issues such as poor hearing or sight. Ask your GP or school nurse about getting your child's hearing checked. Professor Preedy says, "I assessed an 11 year old and we were all surprised to find out that he could barely hear in one ear." Shortsightedness becomes more common as children progress through secondary school and can easily go unnoticed. All children are entitled to free NHS eye examinations. Ask friends if they can recommend a local optometrist to check whether your child might need spectacles.

If you do find your child has problems with sight or hearing, tell the teacher as soon as possible. Even if you are waiting for hearing aids or spectacles to be made up, the teacher can make sure your child is sitting in the best position for them, and take a little extra time to check they are keeping up.

Professor Preedy advocates thinking about other possible causes of delayed development, saying, "Think about whether birth problems or early childhood illnesses could have impacted on your child. A child who was born prematurely could find themselves effectively in the wrong year group. When they get older this won't have such a big impact, but at age four a few months' difference is a large proportion of your life."

Help from the school

If your child's sight and hearing are fine, ask to speak to the

SENCO, the person who is responsible for co-ordinating help for children with special education needs. They should have experience of children with a range of abilities and be able to look at your child's progress. Ask whether they think your child has difficulties, or special educational needs. Find out if your child is working at the same level as children of a similar age, or whether the SENCO and class teacher think they could do with further assessment or extra help. They may suggest devising an Individual Education Plan (see below).

If your child has special educational needs, the school has a duty to meet their needs and provide them with 'a broad, well-balanced and relevant education'. In most cases your child's education will be in a mainstream school, perhaps with outside help from specialists. For a few children a specialist school may be more appropriate.

What sort of help?

There is a staged process for bringing in more help for a child with additional educational needs, using internal and possibly external specialists. Throughout this process, the school must listen to you and your child, consult you, and take into account what your child wants. The SENCO can help you through the process. They are not there necessarily to provide all the extra input themselves, but can arrange for the help your child needs.

THREE STEP PLAN

There are official terms in England for three steps in getting your child the help they need:

1 School Action: This is the stage when you and the school decide

your child needs more help. Progress should be monitored, and if the extra support is not making enough difference you move on to...

2 School Action Plus: The class teacher or SENCO will talk to you about getting more help from someone outside the school. This could be an educational psychologist, a speech and language therapist or simply a specialist teacher.

3 Statement of Special Educational Needs: If your child needs still more help to make progress, you need to start thinking about applying for a Statement of Special Educational Needs.

ENQUIRE

In Scotland, Enquire provides advice and help for parents and young people about additional support for learning. You can call them on 0845 123 2303 or visit **www.enquire.org.uk** to download an excellent and comprehensive guide to additional support for learning in Scotland.

What can help at school

To start with, the school should offer to look at different ways of teaching that work well for your child. They may benefit from extra input from a teacher or assistant, focussing on work they find harder. Or the school may arrange special equipment which will help them meet your child's needs. The school should keep you informed about this and any other actions that they take. Their plans for your child should form an Individual Education Plan. This plan helps everyone who works with your child know their weaknesses and strengths, and which strategies work well for them. Once this is set up, book regular meetings to talk about your child's progress. You may want to meet every term or more often if issues arise.

Help at home

You will probably be able to help your child at home, alongside whatever the school is doing. Talk to the SENCO or class teacher and ask them about what you can do to help your child practise the things that they struggle with.

Outside help

The SENCO can also tell you how to get referred for external help from, for example, a speech therapist or other professional. You may find it useful to ask the local education authority about your local parent partnership service, which can provide you with help and support.

Educational psychologists

You may come across an educational psychologist if your child receives an assessment for special educational needs. The local authority employs educational psychologists to check your child's progress at school. Educational psychologist Tim Francis says, "An assessment will involve taking your child's developmental history. An educational psychologist will look at levels of reading, writing, spelling and comprehension. He then makes recommendations for an 'intervention' – in other words he suggests how best to help your child." The assessment may involve talking to other professionals involved with your child. You can also go to an independent educational psychologists and pay for an assessment.

Local education authority assessment of SEN

You can request an assessment for your child from the local authority. This assessment could lead to your child having a 'Statement of Special Educational Needs'. In Scotland you can ask for a Co-ordinated Support Plan, which is similar. According to government advice website Direct.gov, very few children actually need an assessment. The assessment is only offered if your child's school cannot provide all the help they need. The school may also ask for the assessment but should discuss this with you first. Some parents feel that their child needs a statement because their needs aren't being met, yet have to battle to get one. Senior Early Intervention Teacher Victoria Dawson says, "You, the parent, need to apply in writing which can be off-putting. Look for a template to help you."

To the Additional Educational Needs Manager
Your Local Authority

Dear *(Name)*
Re: *Your child's name (Date of birth) School*

I am writing to ask the Local Authority to carry out a Statutory Statement of Special Educational Needs for my child under the Education Act of 1996 as I am entitled to.

Or

I am writing to ask the Local Authority to carry out an assessment for a Co-ordinated Support Plan under the Education Additional Support for Learning (Scotland) Act of 2004 as I am entitled to.

Write in details of: your child's difficulties at school, other problems,

---

> *medical history and diagnosis. Write down the help your child is get-*
> *ting already, for how long each day/week, and from whom. Then*
> *explain how this is not meeting your child's need. Back this up with*
> *evidence of slow progress.*
>
> Yours sincerely

Six-week wait

It can take up to six weeks for the local education authority to decide if they will do an assessment, and they must write and explain if they decide against your request. Talk to the school about how else your child's needs can be met if this is the case. You can also appeal to the independent Special Educational Needs and Disability Tribunal.

> Richard was being home educated, due to bullying, but wanted to try school again. Mum Nicola asked for a Statement of Special Educational Needs as he has Asperger's Syndrome, to ensure that Richard's needs could be met by a new school. She says, "We got support from Families First who are there to support families experiencing difficulties, and were happy to support us in going for the statement that we felt that Richard would need to return to school. It was a little more difficult because usually statements are done through the school, with teachers' feedback etc, but we got statements from the Families First support worker and also from a local autism charity worker who had had experience with Richard attending various activities they organise for young people on the autistic spectrum.
>
> "Richard is very academically capable but struggles a bit with some of the school set-up and noise. He now has full support at school. This is really hard to get, not least because of the cost. I feel we were successful in getting

the level of support he needs. He's doing very well back at school and enjoying it for the most part. He's even been picked for the rugby team."

Professional opinions

If they do assess your child, they will get information on your child from the school, a doctor, and educational psychologist, social services if they know your child already, and any other relevant professionals. You can go to any part of the assessment with your child. You may want to suggest other people or organisations who should be involved in the assessment.

Report time

Once the information has been collected, the SEN officer decides whether to write a report. They will let you know this within 12 weeks of the start of the assessment. If the officer is not going to write a report, the local education authority should explain this decision, and how your child's needs can be met.

What is in a statement

If the local education authority decides to provide a statement of your child's needs, it will outline these needs and specify the help your child should get. It will also spell out the long-term aims for the help and the arrangements for regular short-term goals and reviews of your child's progress. The statement should also describe other, non-educational, needs and how these can be met. You get a chance to look at a draft statement and comment. Victoria Dawson says, "Once a year, you should be invited in for an Annual Review. This is your chance to review whether the statement is still meeting your child's needs."

Changing schools

As part of meeting your child's needs, the local authority will send you details of local state mainstream and special schools as well as independent schools that are approved by the Secretary of State for Education and Skills as suitable for children with SEN. You can visit the schools and check out whether they support the needs of your child. Around six in every ten children with special needs attend a mainstream school. Specialist schools may have facilities for helping children with different types of SEN, such as physical disabilities or dyslexia. You can say whether you prefer a mainstream school or special school.

The local authority has to agree with your preference as long as the school is suitable for your child's age, ability, skills and SEN. They also take into account whether your child's presence will damage the education of other children already at the school and be an efficient use of the authority's resources. The local authority does not have to fund your child at an independent school if there is a suitable state school place available.

Educational psychologist Tim Francis says, "After an assessment, most schools will implement the suggested intervention. However, a minority have no confidence, competence or interest in special needs. In this case you may want to look at the other schools available that are more supportive before starting on a fight with the school. Don't be deterred by a school's external appearance, but look inside to see how they welcome and support children with special educational needs." Tim is part of the team behind the website **www.educational-psychologist.co.uk** which is packed with articles on different topics to help you help your child.

Carolyn's son Gabriel has had developmental problems since he was born prematurely. She says, "He was late achieving all targets like walking, talking, potty training, etc. In school he was considered nice and polite but with a tendency to be easily distracted and unable to concentrate on lessons. At the junior school, age seven, his gains deteriorated. This school was more competitive and, basically, if the child was not causing problems then his needs weren't seen as a priority. My son couldn't keep up. He would come home from school pinch-faced and unable to remember what had happened on any given day.

One day he reported to me that the SEN teacher had done a very theatrical yawn when he was trying to read for her, then looked at her watch and said something like 'Come on I haven't got all day!' At the end of the year his teacher said he had only achieved about a third of where he should be over the year. I talked to the teacher, tried to get an appointment with the SEN teacher but we never managed it. I kept being told he was behind but making progress and not to worry. They didn't seem that bothered about him. He was a problem, but not a big one for them. The reality was that he wasn't improving and wasn't engaging but it wasn't until the end of the school year that they actually admitted that what they were doing hadn't worked. It was obvious that the school wasn't going to ever work for him and I had to do something drastic. I mentioned to the teacher about looking at other schools and she said she thought it was a good idea.

"I looked into private education. The local Steiner had a good reputation and I knew Waldorf Steiner education had a different perspective on child development. I strongly felt that in the right environment my son would be able to learn. There was a good feeling in the school. Location and cost played a part. They have a sliding scale of fees and I could just about manage the costs and the school is only about a mile away and as I don't drive I needed to be practical. After that visit I noticed some older kids outside the school sitting on some grass talking. They looked like kids from any school and I asked them what they thought of Steiner. Not one was sullen or rude or shy, they all said it was great and they loved it. I really didn't expect a group of teenagers to talk about their school that way.

"The emphasis on learning in a holistic way really helped my son develop an interest in learning again. There are no exams until they are 16 so there is less pressure on children and teachers to jump through arbitrary hoops. There is consistency too, with having the same teacher every year and building up that bond and trust. I think that has added to his sense of responsibility not to let his teacher or his classmates down and to try hard. He has developed a healthy competitiveness he never had before. The range of things they are doing allows him to find skills he might never had noticed. For example, he is really good at needlework and really impressed the crafts teachers with his eye for design. He has also developed a skill for storytelling and has been asked to develop a performance with his best friend for a special event.

"I really believe that an environment where being good at Art is treated as just as important as being good at maths has been really significant to him. My son, who struggled in fear with maths and English and is now considered average to the rest of the children in the class in maths and with his reading and handwriting, is for the first time making really steady, significant progress. Last week I met with his class teacher and his SEN teacher and they both are very pleased with his progress. He is happy too and enthusiastic about trying new things. He has had his normal ups and downs with friendships and schoolwork but seems to have found his niche."

SPECIFIC DIFFICULTIES

In this section, you can find out more about some of the most common causes of difficulties at school and how to help:

- Specific Learning Difficulties (dyslexia, dyspraxia, dyscalculia, attention deficit disorder)
- Autistic Spectrum and Asperger's Syndrome disorders
- Moderate Learning Difficulties
- Behaviour, emotional and social difficulties
- Gifted and talented

SIGNS OF DYSLEXIA

Children with dyslexia can be reluctant to go to school, or may have been labelled as disruptive. While there are no exact criteria for distinguishing dyslexia, there are some traits which the British Dyslexia Association lists as common to many children with the condition. In general, they will have 'good' and 'bad' days, for no apparent reason, and often confuse directional words, such as up and down, in and out. Dyslexic children will have difficulties with sequences, such as putting coloured beads into a pattern, and remembering days of the week or numbers. There may also be a family history of reading difficulties. For more detailed lists of signs to watch out for, see the British Dyslexia Association's website: **www.bdadyslexia.org.uk**.

Jennifer's son Alex seemed different from other children right from when he started nursery. She says," He didn't want to paint or draw like the other children. However, it only became a problem once he started school. We fought for years, arguing with school, the local authority and educational psychologists to have him recognised as having Special Educational Needs. His teachers just said he was being difficult or arrogant or lazy. Educational psychologists said his difficulties weren't that severe and the local authority said they didn't have any money in the budget. We had meeting after meeting with teachers: they were rarely helpful and ultimately we ended up just telling them to leave him alone. We felt they were bullying him, and his behaviour in class was getting worse and worse, yet he was still a pleasure to be with at home."

In the end Jennifer took Alex to a private educational psychologist, who identified him as having severe dyslexia. The family used the report successfully, after some battles, to insist that the local authority provided for him. Jennifer arranged for extra lessons for Alex to help him keep up. She says, "Once the local authority provision was in place he had lessons at a Special Unit. Some people thought that it would be a negative taking him out of school for this provision, but it helped him when he needed the space outside the school environment. Later he had a Special Needs Tutor who came into school to help him and they developed a very good relationship."

Alex had become ostracised from his class and one teacher concentrated on reintegrating him. Jennifer says, "This worked well. She recognised his visual spatial skills and put him as leader of a group."

"When he went to high school we persuaded them not to put him into the Moderate Learning Difficulties class, as he would cause problems with his behaviour if he was not stimulated. Although he struggled with the work he was bright. They really were not sure but we were insistent and eventually they agreed to put him into the 'top class' as a trial. He stayed there throughout school, became Head Boy and left with eight GCSEs, which he sat with maximum provision of extra time and a scribe to write for him."

The family found that the secondary school was very helpful. Jennifer says, "Although they couldn't provide a great deal in the way of tuition because of lack of resources, their attitude toward him was positive and that made a lot of difference. Ultimately, our greatest support came from the SEN co-ordinator at High School and from the local authority."

Now 23, Alex has a job he loves for a small family company who value his skills and strengths, and understand the areas where he will always struggle. He has just bought his first flat and is happily settled with his girlfriend.

DYSGRAPHIA AND DYSCALCULIA

Most people will have heard of dyslexia, but if your child struggles more with writing or maths, you may want to investigate dysgraphia or dyscalculia. Signs of dysgraphia include illegible writing and poor spelling in an otherwise bright child. Similarly, if your child finds it difficult to do mathematical calculations, and doesn't notice that they frequently reverse numbers, they may have dyscalculia. This may not mean that they are poor at all things mathematical, but could have problems with specific areas such as remembering times tables or formulas, reading and understanding maths questions, or laying out their answers in the way the teacher wants. Educational psychologist Tim Francis explains, "A child with dysgraphia may be helped if they learn to touch type and are given a laptop. A child with dyscalculia may benefit from a multi-sensory approach, like doing their sums in a sand tray or using play dough. Children with one of these conditions are likely to have dyspraxia too."

DYSPRAXIA

Dyslexia, dyscalculia and dysgraphia can be accompanied by a lack of co-ordination, known as dyspraxia. Children with dyspraxia can have problems with fine motor movement, hand-eye co-ordination and putting things in order, making activities like doing a jigsaw far more challenging than for other children. Dyspraxia can also cause problems with a child's sense of time or direction, and with their memory for lists of events or names.

ADD OR ADHD

Attention deficit disorder or attention deficit hyperactive disorder (ADD or ADHD) causes children problems with concentration. They may find it hard to sit still and be more impulsive than their classmates. Their behaviour can appear much younger than that of children of a similar age and may be disruptive in a school setting.

AUTISM

Autism can cause problems with social interaction: an autistic child may struggle to recognise other people's feelings and express how they feel themselves. Children struggle to understand people's body language and facial expressions, and may have a literal understanding of what you say. They can find it hard to make friends as a result. They lack 'social imagination', the ability to work out how other people will react or make sense of an abstract idea. This can make it hard for them to understand danger or take part in made up games and imaginative play.

Different children have different levels of impairment, so the condition is often called 'autistic spectrum disorder'. Children on the autistic spectrum may have limited speech or have apparently good language yet struggle to understand others. They will enjoy routine, almost to the point of obsession, and need preparation to deal with change. They may be extra-sensitive to light, feelings of touch, sounds, tastes or smells, or may lack sensitivity in some areas. They may have intense interests and obsessive hobbies. Autism can be accompanied by learning disabilities and difficulties in acquiring life skills. Senior Early Intervention teacher Victoria Dawson says, "You might hear the phrase, 'triad of impairment model', which covers the different areas a child may struggle with if they are on the autistic spectrum."

ASPERGER'S SYNDROME

Children with Asperger's syndrome may show similarities to those with autism, but have fewer problems with language and speaking, and may have average or above average intelligence. They can struggle to deal with change, and may therefore respond in an unexpected or unconventional way. They struggle to understand other people's body language, have different ideas about their own and other people's personal space, and as a result have difficulties in social situations. They are likely to be extremely focused on subjects that interest them, which can help if they are interested in a topic at school. Their school work can also benefit from their attention to detail, so their difficulties may not be academic but behavioural.

Suzanne's daughter has Asperger's syndrome. She has managed to work with the school so that both teachers and pupils now understand about Jordan and how her condition affects the way she behaves. Suzanne says, "Bullying began early at school. We helped Jordan by telling her about her disability from an early age, not hiding it from her, and being very open about it. We talked to the school and got them to study Asperger's in more depth. Once the teachers became more educated on the disability themselves things improved. They then went on to establish an anti-bullying scheme."

Suzanne did not need to get a statement of special educational needs for Jordan. She says, "We gave her extra tuition at home to help her keep up. Jordan is now ten and doing brilliantly. As she is nearing high school age, she is still coping with her naivety as her friends grow more mature. If your child is having problems at school, I'd say to go straight to the head teacher and educate them."

MODERATE LEARNING DIFFICULTIES

Some children may not have one specific condition but have general learning difficulties or developmental delay, usually termed 'global developmental delay'. Signs can include poor co-ordination and communication, problems with language and maths, short attention span, and appearing socially immature. Children may have extra difficulties getting organised and understanding where they should be and what they should be doing. They may appear clumsy and find it hard to remember things.

BEHAVIOUR, EMOTIONAL AND SOCIAL DIFFICULTIES

Behavioural, emotional and social difficulties cover a range of conditions, such as depression and eating disorders, and can include attention deficit disorder or attention deficit hyperactivity disorder and syndromes such as Tourette's. Children with these problems can find the way they behave makes it difficult for them to learn, and can cause difficulties, disruption and disturbances for the class. Children can be withdrawn or isolated, hyperactive and lack concentration, have immature social skills or present challenging behaviours. "The first thing to do is look for reasons behind problematic behaviour," explains Tim Francis. "Then, depending on the cause, you can take the most suitable course of action, be it family therapy or rewarding the sort of behaviour you want to encourage."

Diagnosis

If you are concerned that your child may be affected by one of the conditions above, start by talking to your doctor, health visitor, class teacher or SENCO. They can help you work out whether you child is just developing at a different rate to their classmates or whether there might be cause for further investigations.

Express your concerns to the school as soon as possible. This helps your child make the most of their time at school, and avoids them struggling unnecessarily. Older children can find it harder to change their way of learning and behaviour.

A formal identification of any condition can help you understand the sort of difficulties your child is having, and makes it easier for them to get the right sort of help. Victoria Dawson says, "Early intervention is valuable in education. Even if your child is of pre-school age, if you have concerns contact your Health Visitor who can make referrals for further investigation."

PRIVATE SCREENING

If you have the funds and don't want to wait, you could think about a private assessment by a suitably qualified teacher or a Chartered Educational Psychologist specialising in Specific Learning Difficulties. Contact your local Dyslexia Association for a list of professionals. This sort of assessment costs several hundred pounds, for which you get a written report and recommendations about the most appropriate help and support for your child's education.

The report can be taken to the school to help them establish the best ways to work with your child. Occasionally, though, the school will not automatically accept the findings of an independent report. Talk to your local authority Chief Education Officer and ask them to get the school to work with the report. There may also be interventions recommended in the report that the school cannot provide. You will have to go back to the local authority, and possibly through the assessment and statementing processes to get further resources released.

HELP AT SCHOOL

Once you have a diagnosis, or even before, ask the school about how they can help with support and special methods of teaching. Ask how the school will help your child understand their condition and equip them with ways to cope and help them learn.

IDEAS FOR HOW THE SCHOOL CAN HELP

Make sure the school finds out about your child's abilities and strengths. Ask them to build his or her self esteem by using strengths or special interests, and making sure that goals are realistic. Your child needs to experience successes in learning, so targets need to be achievable. In class, can the teacher:

- Provide extra explanations for your child?
- Break a task down into smaller, more manageable steps?
- Check your child understands what they have been told?
- Repeat information in a different way?
- Allow extra time for tasks?
- Tell you what styles of teaching work well for your child?
- Praise your child for their achievements and effort?

Your child can also benefit if there is a regular routine for lessons, so they know what to expect. Can the teacher or assistant help them to remember what they have already learnt about a subject, and go back over points if necessary before moving on? Your child will gain if you and the school can co-ordinate to help them practise key skills. Keep practice sessions short so they stay interested.

Does the school have, or can they acquire, different equipment which might help your child? This is where talking to other parents whose children have similar difficulties can help you find out what is available. Look on the net or ask your local authority about support groups.

OTHER THERAPIES

Talk to your GP about whether your child could be helped by physical, speech, or occupational therapy. The majority of these conditions are for life, but the right help at an early stage can benefit your child enormously.

SPEECH, LANGUAGE AND COMMUNICATION HELP

Your GP can refer your child for speech therapy, although there may be a waiting list. To get the most from an appointment, note down areas where you child has problems and examples of what they say, or can't say. A speech therapist can give you strategies to help your child in areas where they struggle. You may be offered regular help from a speech and language therapist.

Gifted and talented

What if your child is coping well with the work, so well in fact that they complain of being bored? Lack of stimulation can be a cause of bad behaviour. Look at the work your child is doing. You may think that their homework is too simple, and they get all the answers right in minutes. In the first place, talk to the class teacher. They may be setting work to help build your child's confidence, or feel that they need to repeat some lessons to develop an in-depth understanding of the subject.

Duty of schools

Schools have a duty to identify, stretch and challenge bright kids and track their achievement. There should be a lead teacher at every secondary school and at groups of primary schools to help with this. There is a national register for gifted children and a national programme of summer schools for children at secondary level.

How do I know my child is gifted?

According to the Government, your child needs to have 'one or more abilities developed to a level significantly ahead of their year group' to be classed as Gifted and Talented.

What sort of support should my child get?

Ask the class teacher how she or he helps each child to learn at their own rate. Look at the amount of small group work, and whether different groups cover work at different rates or levels. Some schools set up clubs or extra classes. This is not necessarily for 'more of the same' schoolwork, but may set children different sorts of problems to solve, using creative thinking skills.

Chapter 2

Social issues and school troubles

In this chapter, read about how to spot that your child may be having problems at school. Find out about causes, how family events can affect children's behaviour, and how best to help your kids. There are lots of tips from families who have been through similar experiences too.

WHAT TO LOOK OUT FOR

Children don't always tell you when they have problems at school. Sometimes you need to watch out for subtle changes. Is your child quieter than usual? Have they stopped talking about school, and no longer want to invite friends home? Do they have headaches, or appear more irritable than usual? Or do they drag their feet more than normal on the way in? Other children act up when they are struggling to deal with something. Educational psychologist Tim Francis says, "Your child is trying to tell you something when they say school is boring, or tell the teacher where to go. Children are herd animals, and don't act outside the herd unless something is wrong."

Reluctance or refusal

Children may appear reluctant to go to school. It can be hard to know whether this is simply a dislike for getting out of bed, or whether there is something more serious at the root. If they often mention a tummy ache or feel sick in the mornings, make an appointment with the GP to rule out health problems. Tim Francis says, "School refusal can be one of the hardest problems to deal with." Parentline Plus offer a 'Troubles at School' leaflet, where they advise, "Seek help as soon as you realise there is a problem … the sooner the situation is faced the easier it is to deal with."

Time to talk

Take some time to talk about school. Do this in a 'low pressure' way, perhaps while you are doing an activity together or on your way somewhere. Hopefully your child will share any concerns about school. Sometimes refusal to discuss school can indicate that there is a problem which your child is afraid to discuss.

Laura's son Alexander was very excited about starting school. She says, "He seemed to be socially, emotionally and academically ready to go and so he skipped in the door. Then, he started to have nightmares. We didn't think much of it at first and put it down to his being very tired. He continued to enjoy school. He ran to get there every day and was full of stories about what they'd done when we collected him at home time. And yet, every night before school he had a nightmare."

Alexander's nightmares changed gradually until he was waking drenched in sweat, wild with panic but unable to string together a coherent sentence. Laura says, "Sometimes he didn't recognise us and would frantically try to get away when we went to comfort him. On occasion, he was not fully awake but was trying to run down the stairs to 'get away'. He would sleep all night once he had calmed down and was unable to remember the incident in the morning. Weekends were a reprieve – he didn't have the night terrors on Fridays or Saturdays."

Laura went into school to speak to the teacher. She says, "I asked if there was anything happening in the class which might be upsetting him but she said that he was the same happy, chatty, chirpy boy we know at home. She assured us that she would keep an eye on him and let us know of any problems". Laura's next move was to read up about nightmares. She says, "I read about 'night terrors' which seemed to fit with what Alexander was going through. They occur most often in the first couple of hours after going to bed. We watched for the pattern and then each night we went to offer him a drink just before he was likely to wake up. The idea of this is to interrupt the sleep cycle. It was pretty tricky because he was not happy about waking up but I just tried to sit him up for a drink and it seemed to break the cycle."

Laura carried on with this strategy and noticed an improvement after three months. She says, "Thankfully, Alexander seems not to be affected by the night terrors. He never mentions them during the day. I had never heard of night terrors but apparently it is quite common, especially when a child faces a new challenge."

Born too late

Some children just are not ready to start school with their peers. Many local authorities now offer part-time nursery places for children from three and reception places after their fourth birthday. If all children start in September, some of those with summer birthdays may find it hard to keep up. If you have concerns about your child's readiness for school, it is still important to fill in school application forms at the same time as everyone else or you may find all the places are filled. Once you have been offered a place, request that your child starts later in the school year, and the local authority should keep their place open for them. Ask for this to be confirmed in writing, and remember that children must start education the term after their fifth birthday. If you are still unsure about school at this stage, you may want to read Chapter 5 which explains about home education.

Handling change

Your child may simply be reluctant to go to school because they are struggling with a change. This could be something expected, like starting a new school or moving up a year, or an unexpected change of teacher or class. Professor Preedy explains, "Every child starts life closely reliant on their parents or carer. It is impossible to avoid life's challenges, but there are ways to help your child mature and handle changes. Be positive, using play and stories to help your child to visualise and experience the positive benefits of change. Do not discuss your child's worries and concerns with others in front of your child."

Jo's daughter Tiffany found it strange when, on moving into Year 4, she had a male teacher for the first time. Jo says, "She was struggling with the teacher and wouldn't ask for any help. She bottled it all up and became withdrawn and then became angry with close family – mainly me as I'm the person she spends the most time with. She didn't want to tell me anything and didn't like the idea of me going into school. It took a long time to get to the bottom of it."

Jo carried on asking Tiffany about what was upsetting her, and discovered that she found it strange having a man as her teacher. She says, "I told her that she was not the only one who went through all this and it was a big step for everyone. I told her about my experiences when I was in school and she listened to stories about my school days." Jo then arranged an appointment to see the head teacher and the teacher in question. She comments, "Because Tiffany didn't want me to interfere, I went in without telling her. The school were very good, and they had a word with her but used a softly, softly approach. It was a hard few months to get through but once I went into school and they were aware of the problem she seemed better."

If your child is struggling, Jo advises, "Speak to your child and try and find out the reasons behind it. Go into school and tell them your worries and fears and also talk to other family members or friends." Tiffany is now in Year 6 and happy and confident. Jo says, "She asks more questions in school and has another male teacher this year and she likes him very much."

Learning levels

Find out as much as you can about how your child is getting on with their work. If they are disruptive in class, this can be an indication that they are either struggling with the work or finding they can complete it with ease and still have time to make trouble.

Trouble topics

When talking about school, find out how your child is getting on with their teachers. A statement that they 'hate Mr Smith' is worth investigating further. Have they been in trouble for failing to hand in homework, or disrupting class? Or is there a subject that they are struggling with? You may want to talk to the teacher in question to help your child work things out. If they are reluctant to do that it can be worth talking to the class teacher or head of year instead.

Listening ear

It is important to listen to what your child is saying. If you feel they are only telling you part of the story, ask open questions like, "Tell me more about that … ?" If they have told you about a problem, ask them what they think might help. Senior Early Intervention Teacher Victoria Dawson says, "Use open questions when you are talking to your child. Say something like, 'Tell me about school', or 'What do you get up to at break time?' Avoid leading questions, where the words in the question can encourage certain answers. A leading question could be, 'Is Mr Smith giving you a hard time?' This doesn't give your child so much scope to explain the problem from their point of view."

Tim Francis recommends listening to your child, then summarising back what you have heard them say. He says, "This helps them know you are listening. Then, keep quiet for a few minutes to see if they will share anything else."

Being me

There are many other things that can leave your child struggling to cope with the day-to-day routine of school As well as academic pressures, teens, and even pre-teens start to feel the pressures of growing up. It can be hard to cope with the physical changes and mood swings, especially if your child is going through these things earlier or later than their peers. Classmates can add to a child's concerns about their body image and relationships too. All this can add up to make your child unhappy at school and reluctant to attend.

Truancy

Older children who travel to school independently have the option of not going in at all if they are having problems, and some children may simply skulk in the cloakrooms to avoid a lesson. Usually they will try to hide this from you, so the first thing you may know about it is when you get a letter or call from the school. If your child is not attending school on an occasional or regular basis, you will face pressure from the school to get them to attend, and the possibility of a fine too. The most important thing is to find what's at the bottom of the problem. It may be that your child is being bullied, feels like they have no friends or can't keep up.

Bullying

If you are worried that your child is being bullied, find some time where you can chat about school without interruption. See if you can find a few minutes when the rest of the family is out, or take them to a café. Ask them who they hang out with at break, or what they do at lunchtime. Your child may be reluctant to tell that they are being bullied. The bullies may have made threats to keep them quiet, so if it comes out, reassure your child that they have done the right thing.

Older children may prefer to talk to a family friend or youth club leader. If you know your child has someone they look up to, why not tell the adult friend you think something might be going on, and ask them to have a chat?

Connor was eight when his mum, Carolyn, found he was having problems with bullies. She says, "The deputy head was very helpful. He checked out the situation and could see that the trouble started when Connor stood up for the under-dogs. Fights started when he squared up to any child who was behaving unjustly."

The deputy head talked to Connor and came up with some clear rules. "He told Connor that he didn't have to sort out everyone's problems. He explained that if Connor was being struck by another child, he should warn the child not to hit him again. He then said that he would understand if Connor got hit again after this warning, he might end up hitting back. I was just relieved that the deputy head stood by this promise and ensured that Connor did not get into trouble as long as he stuck to the rules.

Connor felt much better and more in control of this situation as a result. He is now in Year 7. He is a confident child, and is still incensed at unjust behaviour. I still sometimes have to hold him back as he tends to get involved with others' problems."

What is bullying?

Your child may be being hurt, or threatened, either directly or via phone messages or online. Bullying can range from name calling, to damaging your child's gear, to deliberately excluding them from conversations and activities.

Nicola's son, Richard, was subject to persistent bullying both in and out of school. She says, "Problems started when Richard was in primary school. Abuse was shouted at him in the street, even if I was present. We had bricks thrown at our house, children peeing up our gate and his arm was broken by a group of boys."

Nicola approached the school on numerous occasions, but, she says, "The school maintained that Richard was not being bullied and that he was 'playing' me. He has Asperger's syndrome, and the school called me in sometimes because he was having a 'meltdown'. They said that due to his 'difficulties with social communication' that he was 'misinterpreting horseplay', yet even other mothers expressed concern about him being beaten up at playtime."

Nicola found she was hitting a blank with the school, so phoned the local Austism Support Service. They were already involved with Richard, and she was surprised to find that they had made a recommendation that he did not go out at break-time as they had had to physically intervene as he was being beaten. She says, "I was shocked to hear this. Where were the supervisory staff at this point?"

Nicola continues, "At the same time, my younger son Erik was struggling at school, seemed distant and was classed as 'below average'. The school just suggested that we should make an effort to read to him, which was rather insulting as we have a house full of books and read to the boys all the time." Both these events led Nicola to decide school wasn't working for the boys. She decided to take them out of school. She says, "Richard had started to talk about killing himself. After deregistration he had counselling for a couple of years as his mental health had severely suffered whilst at school."

Nicola home-educated the boys for two to three years until Richard chose to try a different school in a different area part-time for a couple of months. This worked well, and he moved to attending full-time a couple of months later.

She says, "He has a Statement of special educational needs. Now he's back in school they tested him and our work at home seems to have helped. He scored very highly on the tests he took at 11, with the age-related achievement level generally placing him at around 16 years."

FACT FINDING

Start by noting down what happened and when so you can fill the school in on the facts. Again, your child may not want to tell the school. Spend some time talking through why they are worried, and how you and the school will be able to work together to help them.

TIME TO TALK

Talk to the teacher. The bullying may be news to the school. Ask about the school anti-bullying policy. Give the details of what has happened and when. Ask clearly what the school plans to do about it, when they will do this, and how they feel their actions will help to stop the bullying.

Arrange for a follow-up meeting and fix up a way to inform the school if the problem recurs. Keep reassuring your child that it is right to tell their teacher every time the bullying happens. The government information website, Direct.gov, has good information about bullying and how to handle it. Also see Chapter 6 for more on homophobic, racist and cyber bullying.

Moving house

A house move can cause children stress, just like adults, especially if it involves a move to a new school. Some children find it harder than others. Try to introduce the idea of the move gradually. Think about what you can do to help your child stay in touch with old friends and make new ones. Arrange play dates for younger kids. See if there is a club or special interest group that your child can join in your new area. This can help children of any age meet new people with the same interests.

Tanya moved house when she was 13. She says, "It had a big effect on my performance and behaviour at school. I'm sure I would have done better in my GCSEs if I had not moved schools then. My behaviour was awful. I was called in to the headmistress's office one morning and I started crying so she left the room to get some tissues and I made a run for it. I just wandered around the town until my mum and her friend caught up with me. I became depressed and resentful towards my parents.

"This went on for a while until the school took note and helped me. They were rubbish at first but after a while there was one lady who took me under her wing, listened to my problems and gave me a chance. I was taken out of mainstream school and had to go to this particular classroom every day. There were some other children there but most days it was just me and her. We played computer games, wrote a lot, and did reading. I went to that classroom for about a year or so before returning to mainstream school which was the hardest thing I ever had to do. That lady, Mrs Bell, was my saviour."

Tanya offers this advice for parents thinking about moving house when their children are teens: "I would say to parents to take into consideration what effect it would have on their children if they move schools. Once you get to secondary school it can be really tough. If your child really hates school and refuses to go, there must be a reason. Please talk to your children and listen to what they have to say and be understanding. If your child can't talk to you about it then let them talk to one of your close family friends. I always found it easier to talk to a family friend than my own parents."

Tanya has left school now, and says, "I did find it very hard to get my first job but got over that. I have very high anxiety and I think this started when we moved."

Kat and family moved house the term after her son started school. Their new home was just a few minutes from their old one, but son Alex found the move tough. Kat says, "Alex has ADHD, which meant the change in routine really affected him. He had a routine for going to school, and knew when we needed to leave and which way we would walk. Alex's behaviour was already difficult and ideally we would have preferred to have moved house during the summer holidays before he started school, but the usual delays in the house-buying process meant this did not happen."

Kat has learnt from her experience, and says, "If you are moving, try to keep your routine as simple and normal as possible. We talked about moving house, and read books about moving house. We told Alex how things would be better when we moved: he would have his own bedroom, and there would be a bigger garden. Alex was worried when we packed his toys that we were taking them away from him forever which must have been a real ordeal for him. We had to explain that the toys were just going in the garage and that he would seem them again really soon. We let him keep his favourite things in a backpack so he felt secure." Kat also suggests that it helps to take your child on visits to the new house. She says, "Let them choose wallpaper, carpets, new bedding and so on. Let them pack their own toys and keep reassuring them that nothing bad is going to happen."

Divorce

Everyone finds divorce traumatic, but it can be extremely confusing for a child who doesn't understand what is going on, and can't control it either. You can help your child by reassuring them that mum and dad both still love them. Work out what you can do to help your child feel secure when established relationships are changing. If you have to move house or change schools, try to establish a new routine with regular contact with both parents.

And when your partner is around, try to avoid direct conflict. There may be things you need to say to each other, but minimise clashes in front of the kids.

Be as honest as you can reasonably be with your children without causing them unnecessary distress. Discourage children from taking sides, and ask family and friends to focus on supporting your children rather than being partisan in front of them. You need to allow your child to talk about your partner – they will be missing their presence even if you are relieved to have them out of the house.

Children will be angry at times, frustrated and find it hard to manage their feelings. They can feel that they are not important to you any more, which can result in emotional turmoil and bad behaviour. See if there is someone outside the family who can offer support for your child. This might be a teacher, a family friend, or your GP may be able to put you in touch with a counsellor. At the same time, look at getting support for yourself so you have someone other than the children to talk to. Try to make space to vent your own hurt and anger. This could be by talking to a friend over coffee, or seeing a professional, or you might want to plan a regular trip to the swimming pool, or time for a long walk.

Rachel was 13 when her parents divorced. She says, "I was ashamed of what happened. My dad was a teacher at the school and it was a big talking point. I became quite aggressive, started to hang out with undesirable crowds, pushed the boundaries a lot, and started smoking. My marks deteriorated. Inside, I denied anything was wrong – it was the only way I could cope.

"My parents' divorce was particularly vicious: I didn't see my mum for three years. One thing the school did which helped, but perhaps not intentionally, was to send me on a work placement. It took my mind off things and got me interested in working with children with special needs, which has ended up being my career."

Rachel got divorced herself, when her son was five. She says, "It was a difficult thing to go through for both of us. Ben wet himself at school. He started to get worried whether people were going to pick him up: he felt abandoned. He would cry at anything and hit himself, calling himself a bad boy. It took time to work through this. I spent plenty of time with him, giving cuddles, reassuring him, and talking to him about it. I told Ben's school and they were understanding. Ben didn't open up to them though. They are very discreet, and will make separate appointments for my ex and me at parents' evening without me even having to ask."

Things improved for Ben when Rachel started seeing someone regularly. Rachel says, "I introduced them slowly and gradually. Ben got a male role model back in his life and feels more secure. We're both a lot happier. Ben is top of the class. He sees his dad and they have a functional relationship, and there's no more crying or wetting himself." Contact with Rachel's ex is not always easy, though, and she says, "I have to work hard to keep the relationship going between Ben and his dad. I'm not sure how long it will last though. Ben does still want me back with his dad and does get upset about that now and then."

Rachel has learnt a lot from her experiences. "Counselling helped me to move on from my own divorce," she says. "I feel I need counselling about my parents' divorce now as they still score points off each other through me and I hate it."

She has some advice for anyone going through a similar experience: "It's important to be honest with your child, but without being cruel: they don't need to know every last detail. Stick to a routine as much as you can at home, and have an honest dialogue with school about what has happened. Try to keep the child in the same school if at all possible, and both attend school concerts or parents' evening even though you may feel like you can't stand the sight of each other. I found it helpful having a friend going through the same thing and Ben found it useful to know her daughter was experiencing the same.

"Recognise that the child will react in some way, don't be angry about their reaction but just see it as the rollercoaster that they have to travel through in order to come out the other side. Don't focus on all the negatives, look at how well they are coping too and celebrate that, and remember to congratulate yourself too on how well you are doing with the situation. Most importantly, remind your child how much they are loved."

Serious illness

Ongoing health problems can cause children to miss school on a regular basis and make it hard to keep up. Tell the school as soon as you can, and keep them informed about appointments and during periods when your child can't be there. They may be able to arrange for work that your child can do from home. The Special Educational Needs Co-ordinator (SENCO) may have more ideas on how they can help. Talk to the local authority as well. There may be the possibility of a home tutor if absences are regular or pro-longed. Your child may also miss out on the social side of school. Plan regular meet-ups as their health allows.

More health issues

It can be just as hard for a child if a family member is seriously ill. They may be angry and resentful as more attention is focused on the sick child, or become quiet and withdrawn in an attempt to be 'good'. The 'well' child may also develop unexpected stomach aches or other psychosomatic illnesses as they feel understandably neglected and see that the person who is ill gets more attention.

Try to make sure that your child has time and opportunity to talk to someone, be it a teacher or friend. Some schools also have counsellors now, or can put you in touch with a local service. Make time to spend with each of your children, even if you feel all your attention should be on the sick child.

Think carefully about how much you involve your child in their sibling's treatment. Hospitals can appear to be scary places, and a visit may help defuse some of their fears. Allow that they may not want to attend every time you visit, and maybe arrange for them to visit a friend some days instead.

Hannah's sister, Alice, was born severely disabled. Alice's ongoing health problems affected Hannah for much of her time at school. She describes the effects, "I wrote a lot of stories about Alice at primary school. My grandmother took Alice as a foster child, and I was confused why she had gone away. I felt my bad behaviour was to blame, even though I later found out that it was due to my mother having depression.

In the stories I tried to explain what had happened and why Alice had left us." From age 10, Alice's' health deteriorated. When Hannah was 13, Alice was diagnosed with kidney failure. Hannah says, "Things became difficult at home. At school, I didn't think about Alice and didn't talk about her. I was ashamed of having a disabled sister because I had started to notice that people stared at her when we were out. I rarely talked about her to my friends or teachers, even though I felt stressed. Most weekends were spent visiting Alice in hospital, in a ward full of ill children. At school, I wasn't coping. My behaviour wasn't great. I was silly and didn't concentrate. Several teachers expressed concern. I was told I was in danger of failing my GCSEs and my parents were angry. I started to rebel, wore lots of make-up and dressed provocatively. This got me into trouble and made me unpopular at school."

Things changed dramatically for Hannah when, shortly before her GCSEs, Alice had a successful kidney transplant. Hannah says, "She became 'well' overnight. I felt the pressure disappear: it was like a miracle. I think it is no coincidence that I did much better than expected in my GCSEs. I stopped behaving badly and tried to become the academic my parents said they wanted me to be. Things improved for me at school and I did well. I became more popular, I was the star of the debating society and ended up winning awards. I went to university and got a good degree."

There have been long-term effects for Hannah, who says, "I have suffered with depression and I am sure part of the problem was accumulated stress from my childhood and teens. I had four miscarriages before my son was born. One of the babies I miscarried was severely disabled and this upset me terribly. I had an insight into how my parents must have felt when Alice was born. I have found strength in becoming much closer to my family. They were incredibly supportive during my illness. In a way, I think we were all shocked that I, like Alice, had suddenly become ill."

Hannah has a few things which helped her cope during the difficult times. She says, "In the early years, my grandmother helped me cope. She picked me up from Yorkshire, where I lived, and took me to stay with her. She was kind, spoiling me and helping me sleep by stroking my forehead. During my teens, rebelling gave me a sense of independence. I particularly enjoyed rebelling against my parents' wishes that I visit Alice in hospital every weekend. Now, I feel guilty but it was a natural reaction: I found visiting Alice in hospital disturbing, I was frightened that she would die."

Hannah didn't get any help from the school. In retrospect, she says, "I don't think I gave the teachers the chance to help, because I had no desire to confide in them. This is a pity, I think, because actually they were kind people and I wish I had talked to them. Even when Alice had her transplant, no one knew about it at school. I had to go in on the day she had the operation and I wish my parents had given me the day off, because I was extremely stressed." Hannah's advice for other families dealing with serious illness: "Talk to each other. Seek therapy or family counselling. Don't assume your children are coping because they won't talk about their stresses. Expect challenging behaviour. Keep your children informed and make sure you inform their school what is going on. If the school doesn't know, it can't help."

Parental illness

If you or your partner is seriously ill, this has its own effects on the child and the whole family. A child may need to help more with siblings, or look after themselves more. In some cases children take on caring for their parent. All these responsibilities can make it hard for the child at school, due to tiredness, or perhaps the thought that, relatively, school does not seem important.

Tell the school what is happening: a quick phone call can make all the difference if your older child ends up late every day as they have to drop their younger brother off. The school can also help with contacts if your child needs someone to talk to. Speak to Social Services to find out about practical help.

Dan, 15, has had a hard time coping with his mum Georgie's illness. Georgie explains, "Dan has taken the brunt of it. He has had to call the ambulance on several occasions. If I pass out he can tell the ambulance driver about what medication I am on and what I am allergic to. It is a source of heartache to me. He shouldn't have to be so capable. He has been my rock when I have been angry or when I'm ill."

The whole family moved more than 100 miles after Georgie became ill, which meant that Dan had to change schools at the age of 12. Georgie says, "He found the move from Essex hard, as he was separated from his friends, and absolutely hated it when he first got there. Nobody knew what was going on with his life and it was difficult for him to have to explain to everyone." Dan comments, "It was all just so much to cope with. I was scared and lonely. It took me time to be able to confide in a teacher."

Georgie continues, "He rebelled, smoked cannabis and drank. Basically, he got in with the wrong crowd. The school were supportive, particularly the head of year. We had to get him some counselling to help him talk through all the stuff he's been through. He used to come back saying, 'All we did was talk,' but it seems to have helped. The community police took notice too. Our local officer discovered that he was interested in joining the police and she has been around to help him keep on the straight and narrow. He still has a lot of anger inside him, which can burst out unexpectedly: the other week he punched a wall after a blow-up with a friend. He and I are very open and can talk about things, though. He has a good network of friends in and out of school, and they all come in and out of our house."

Death

If a family member or friend dies, you child may seem to take it all in their stride, but their worries can appear in different ways. Children can also be affected strongly by the death of a pet.

Younger children have little understanding of death, just as they may be unclear about the difference between today and tomorrow. They may think that the person will return. A primary school age child will be frightened by death, and probably aware that it is final. By eight or nine your child will have a clearer understanding of death, depending on their maturity and experiences. Teenagers' reactions may be more extreme as they are going through a period of strong feelings and emotions.

Fiona's children were nine, seven and four when their dad died suddenly. She says, "All of them lost confidence. The older two also found it very hard to concentrate for several months and their work suffered. Teachers were mostly sympathetic and understanding." Fiona's youngest child coped best, but became clingy at dropping-off time.

Fiona says, "The one thing that really upset me was when the whole class made Father's Day cards. His teacher confused him completely by explaining that as I now did all his dad's chores at home, I was like his dad as well as his mum, so he could do a card for me. This upset me too because it seemed to negate his dad. My children have the best dad in the world, who just doesn't happen to be alive any more. I'm not their dad. I just couldn't understand why they had to make the cards at all. Every parent in the class knew about my husband's death and they would all have understood completely if they hadn't made cards."

Fiona's eldest child's behaviour became disruptive at times: he had had intermittent behaviour problems due to Asperger's traits in the past. Fiona says, "The school didn't cope with this and responded with sticks instead of carrots, which just made his behaviour far worse. After much fruitless discussion with his head teacher I felt I had no option but to take him out of the school. This solved the problem instantly."

Problems do not always show up straight away. Fiona's middle child appeared to be happy, but more than a year later started complaining of feeling sick, especially on school days. She says, "The school were again supportive and, after we ruled out other options, recognised that this was a long-term reaction to his dad's death. He hated being away from home, I suppose in case anything happened to me unexpectedly too. The school allowed him to stay off games for a few weeks as he felt sick, and arranged some bereavement counselling for him."

Fiona concludes, "Their dad's death affected all three children very differently, and the school's ability to cope varied too. I think the loss of confidence and poor concentration would affect the majority of children in this situation, but other reactions can vary considerably and go on for months and even years."

Listening and feeling

Listen to your child and try to understand what they are thinking. Like adults, children can feel loss and grief, shock, anger and guilt after someone has died. Children will grieve, but may do so in short spurts, then appear to get on with their everyday activities. Others can put off grieving until they are emotionally ready.

Denial, guilt, anger and fear

The classic reactions after a death are denial, guilt, anger and fear, and these feelings can occur in different orders, or even all together. Your child may carry on talking about someone as if they are still alive, which can be distressing for you and other relatives. This is just part of denying that the death has happened. Children often feel guilty and wonder if they are to blame for a death.

They may feel angry towards the dead person for not being there, or towards a surviving parent, or towards their friends who have not had a similar loss. They will also worry about being different from their peers, which may make it hard to talk about how they feel when they are at school. Children may seem to go back a few stages, or become more clingy out of fear that they will lose other loved ones.

When Caroline was 18 one of her mum's younger sisters died of cancer. She says, "My aunt's death completely devastated me. It made me realise that school was really a very small part of the life cycle and after she died, learning didn't seem that important for a while and I failed all my A Levels. I think my parents expected me to get over it, but as she was one of my favourite aunts, it didn't seem possible. To add to the death, at the same time, I had been ill, and I had one teacher who seemed hell-bent on persecuting me. It all meant that I found being in the sixth form very difficult. It didn't exactly help either that I also seemed to have my finger permanently on the self-destruct button."

Although Caroline had problems at school, she also found help there. "I had one teacher who literally saved me from myself. With hindsight, I think I was so angry and didn't really have anywhere I could put it. I was technically an adult but I'd never had anyone in the family die that I was close to. On top, no one prepared me for that moment when the phone call came – it totally throws you."

Caroline suggests that if your teenager is struggling with a loss, "try and give them time and space to sort themselves out; everyone deals with loss and grief differently and there's no 'right' or 'wrong' way to do it. You just end up grieving – and then one day it just seems to stop hurting quite so much."

Helping your child

It can be very hard to help your child through grief when you have lost someone too. The things to remember are to talk to your child, to be clear and honest about the death, and to listen to them. Reassure them that there is no blame attached to them, the death is not their fault in any way, and that it is OK to have all sorts of feelings. Show them you accept their feelings, and share how you feel too. Work out how you can remember and commemorate together the person who has died. Children may want to be allowed to say goodbye, or I love you, or I miss you, or whatever else they feel they missed saying while the person was alive.

Day to day, try to provide your child with reassurance that life can go on as normal, as far as possible. Stick with usual routines as far as is practically possible. Some children may need a physical outlet for all their feelings, so build in time for activities such as riding a bike, swimming, kicking a ball around together, or going for a walk. Professor Preedy has some more suggestions: "Stories can help your child to grieve and understand their feelings. Through the story you can remember the good times and start to come to terms with the loss. Supporting your child when they lose a pet can also be an opportunity to prepare for the loss of a loved one."

Rose's father died after a short and unexpected illness at the end of the summer term. Her son, Karl, was seven at the time. Rose says, "He had a fantastic infant school teacher who completely understood what we were going through as a family. It was dreadful that I was not there to collect him from school on the last day of infants as it was quite a special leaving day." Karl then moved up to his junior school, but was unsettled.

Rose says, "He had been so close to his grandfather that the death was unthinkable. He really needed someone to understand what he was going through. The school didn't seem to make any allowances and any misdemeanour of Karl's was pounced on heavily."

Rose eventually got help for her son outside the school. "We found a brilliant group called Chums who ran four-week coping with bereavement sessions for children and adults, and that was the best thing ever. It really helped my son. I just saw a poster for it one day at the doctor's and self referred."

Karl is now 10 and has settled at school, having come to terms with his grandad's death. Rose comments, "He says that he does not think about it every day now but can think about grandad in a nice way."

From her experiences, Rose has some tips to help other families. She says, "Use the internet or read for an understanding of how a child experiences death. It can be quite different to an adult's grief. Show your feelings in front of your children. It's no use saying 'you have to be strong for the kids'. It hurts and they need to know that it is all right to cry and that you don't get over people in five minutes. Remember the deceased. On my father's birthday we have a cake and let the wind blow out the candles. His memory is very much alive all the time and my son can ask anything about what happened. We celebrate days that were special to him: we love St Patrick's and Halloween because they were important to my father."

Grief and school

It can be difficult to decide when your bereaved child should go to school. There is a balance to be struck between letting life go back to some sort of normal, and allowing your child the time and space they need. Professor Preedy says, "Going to school gives a child the chance to be a child, whereas at home they may be taking on more responsibility, especially if a parent has died." Some children may be reluctant to go to school at all, perhaps being afraid that something might happen while they are away from their family. You need to decide what is a reasonable period away from school, and when, in fact, they might be better off getting on with their usual activities. Again, listen to what your child is saying, reassure them, and talk to the school about how they are feeling.

At school children may find it hard to concentrate on the work in hand. Tell the school what has happened so they can understand if your child's behaviour changes. Sometime children can take their anger at a death out on their peers. They may start bullying, telling lies or being aggressive. This can be difficult to handle, especially if you are not feeling 100 percent yourself. Ask the teacher to talk things out with your child, as they may benefit from sharing feelings with someone outside the situation.

Sometimes it can take some help from the school to move a situation on. Professor Preedy explains, "A seven year old girl always seemed sad in class and had difficulties with friendships. She built up a close relationship with a nursery nurse, who found out that her baby sister had died some time ago. There were still lots of reminders of the baby at home but the child had not been to the funeral. She told the nursery nurse one day that she 'hadn't said goodbye' to her baby sister. With the nursery nurse's help she wrote a letter which she and her parents took to the cemetery. This enabled the parents to understand how their daughter felt and helped them all to move forward."

MORE SUPPORT

This book can only touch on some of the issues that can cause problems for your child. If you know that they are going through a traumatic life event or experience, tell the school. Ask for help, for yourself and your child. Tim Francis comments, "Talk to your child's head of year or SENCO. They may know of a local bereavement centre, or how to get some written materials or access to a counsellor. Use the referral system." You can also call the local authority children's services department, or talk to your GP if you are unsure where to start. Look on the internet or in your local library for details of help groups, as you don't have to struggle alone.

Chapter 3

Work it out with the school

This chapter looks at how to start solving problems at school. Read on to find out about your rights and how to complain. You will also find stories about how other parents have liaised with schools to find solutions.

MAKING THE PROBLEMS KNOWN

You may be worried that talking to the school may make the problem worse. Indeed, your child may ask you not to tell the teachers what is going on. In general, schools want to know what is happening and most problems are easier to solve if you are working with the school. Often, the teacher is not aware of the problem, which can make it hard to find a resolution.

What have other parents raised?

Parents bring many matters to a school's attention. A good school will want to address problems, and speaking up about a problem that your child is experiencing can help other kids. You can talk to the school about:

- The subjects your child is studying, or would like to study
- Faith and religious education at school
- Sex education
- The quality of teaching and teaching methods in general
- The standards and methods of a particular teacher
- Personality clashes between a member of staff and your child
- Too much or too little homework
- Your child's results and the way their work is marked
- Clashes with classmates, making friends, and bullying
- School resources
- Treatment of children with special needs
- How the school disciplines children

You have a right to complain to your child's school, and the school must have a procedure in place to deal with your complaints. In the first place you may be able to resolve matters with an informal chat. Professor Preedy says, "Most schools make it easy to contact the teacher. A lot of issues, like falling out with a friend, can and should be dealt with as soon as possible. We make it possible for parents to email the teacher, which can make it easier for busy working parents to quickly and easily sort out any issues."

Rachel has sorted out a problem swiftly by talking to the class teacher informally. She says, "Ben was put next to a new girl who was swearing at him. I wanted to sort this out quickly, so nipped in after school. I had got my concerns clear in my mind and worked out how I wanted them resolving. Ben needs to sit in this particular spot due to his visual problems. I was very smiley and positive and stated my concerns. I asked for the new girl to be moved. The teacher didn't confirm she would do this, but it did happen."

INFORMAL COMPLAINTS

Who should I talk to?

Contact the school and arrange to talk to your child's class teacher, or possibly a senior teacher like the head of year. You probably want to choose someone who has direct contact with your child and is in a position to help with the situation. If your child has special needs you may want to talk to the SENCO. Bear in mind that they may not be aware of the issue. Explain why you are coming, to give the teacher a chance to assess the situation and think about it in advance of your meeting.

Professor Preedy advises, "Don't be too quick to assign blame. Explain the issue to the teacher and see what their take on the matter is. Often the teacher will need to investigate the situation and get back to you. Be prepared that your child may not have told you the whole story. We had a parent complain that their child was coming home saying they never got anything to eat and the food was terrible. A teacher observed the child for a few days, and found that they always ate a decent meal, so we needed to look for other reasons why the child was trying to get attention by complaining."

Helen's daughter was unhappy at school, but Helen found it hard to approach the school in the first place as, she says, "Nothing was being done directly to our daughter, it was the general atmosphere of the school. There was awful language, children threw food over each other at lunchtime, the toilets were difficult to use as people were smoking and hanging about in there."

The family supported daughter Emily as much as possible, and when she started losing weight and becoming anxious, Helen decided she had to take the issue to the school. She explains what she did. "I put a request in writing to meet the head of year. I also sent a statement of issues that I would be raising. When we met, the year head did listen and take on board my strong concerns. He suggested a number of ideas. We tried some of his suggestions, but that brought about further problems as Emily became more noticeable by not eating in the lunch hall, and using the staff loo. It did not solve anything.

"The real problem of the loud unruly behaviour by some was 'beyond the year head's control,' in his own words. He explained at length the great difficulty in removing such students from school, it was almost impossible and, whilst he understood, little more could be offered. At that point we decided to throw our energy into supporting and teaching Emily fully at home, rather than trying to change a system."

When to meet

It may be easiest to have a meeting without your child being there, or you may feel strongly that they need to attend. If you can meet the relevant teacher in school hours it can be easy to do so without your child. If the teacher is only available after school, say, you may want to ask a friend to take your child after school so you can discuss the issue.

Mum Michaela has four children at different stages in their school career, so has had to meet the school on various occasions. She says, "If it is something serious I don't make an appointment. I go in and if they're not available I wait. I always feel it gives me an edge. I don't accept platitudes and always come away with a verbal agreement as to the action that is going to be taken. I make a point of reiterating the points agreed, and give a timescale that is acceptable for the required action. If I have more than one point I write a note and refer to it."

What to say

It can help if you prepare yourself in advance of a meeting. Make rough notes of what you want to talk about. You might want to write down times and dates of specific incidents. If you want to talk about academic work you may want to ask the teacher to have your child's schoolbooks at the meeting.

Mother of three and former school governor Belinda shares her tips for getting the most out of a meeting with the school:

- Write a basic list of the topics you want to cover.
- Take a pen and notebook into the meeting with you and make notes.
- Do not lose your rag, it will help nobody.
- Summarise the meeting clearly using your notes.
- Get the head to agree an action plan.
- Follow it up in writing.
- If necessary copy in the Chair of the Governors and the local authority.

How to say it

Think about how you feel before you go into the meeting. If you are angry and upset, it can help to admit this out loud. Explain how you feel to the teacher, but try to do so calmly so that you can productively work together with the school to address the issue. Be prepared to listen to any responses and to accept that there are always two sides to any story. Professor Preedy says, "Preparation on both sides is important." If you are worried that the teacher won't listen to you or understand, you could practise explaining the problem to a friend. You may want to bring your partner or a friend to the meeting for support. It can help to let the school know who will be attending.

Jane met with her son's school on a number of occasions to try to stop bullying. She says, "It all started after we'd moved. My son, then aged 12, started at a new school and was bullied, physically and mentally, almost from day one." Jane brought the issue to the attention of the school on numerous occasions. She says, "As we didn't know his class teacher that well we first went to the head of year. She tried to sound surprised when we explained the issue. I spoke to her numerous times, and was frustrated that she still tried to express surprise and was unaware that the bullying had continued and worsened.

"I lost count how many times we met. We then met the deputy head and finally the head teacher, although it was a battle to get an appointment with him. I had telephoned on numerous occasions too. They seemed totally unaware of the severity of the damage being done. Steven had stopped learning, his work had deteriorated to such a level that there really was no point in him being at the school."

What action can a school take?

You may be quite clear about how you would like a problem to be addressed. It will help if you can have some ideas of what would improve things for your child. Listen to what the teacher suggests too. In the first place, it may be helpful if the teacher listens to your child and hears what they have to say about the problem. The teacher can then reassure the child that his problem is being taken seriously and talk through possible changes.

Professor Preedy says, "Use the support that the school offers. Talk to other parents, see if the parents' association can help too. Don't be isolated in dealing with your problems."

It might be right for the teacher to talk to another child, or group of children, if they are causing the problem. Alternatively, the teacher may feel it is better to talk to the whole class.

Laura's daughter Aaliyah was unhappy when some girls who were previously good friends starting leaving her out. Laura says, "It wasn't until she lied and said that one of them said that her father would kill her that the teachers finally took it seriously. She sat the whole class down and talked to them about being nice to each other." Laura continues, "The school was understanding, and this helped, but in the end they can't make children be friends with each other. Much as you would like to sort out your child's entire universe, sometimes they have to grow up and learn not to rely too much on particular friends.

"My daughter now has a new, wider set of friends. She values their kindness and moves on if they are being silly."

Other ways to help

The teacher may change their behaviour, giving your child extra praise if they need to build confidence. The teacher may take time to pay more attention to the child's interactions with others if they are being bullied. It can be helpful to ask the teacher to involve the staff who supervise the children at break time and dinner time.

Denise and her son Deacon, five, were reading a story together when Deacon said, "I don't want to go to school tomorrow as some boys have been kicking me." Denise saw the bruises and welts and reassured Deacon that she would sort it out. She says, "The teacher is very approachable. I just went in first thing and spoke to her in the classroom. She got down to Deacon's level and asked who had kicked him. She reassured him too, and told him he could tell a dinner supervisor if it happened again. She then promised to sort things out during the day."

The boys were in reception, the year below Deacon. There was an assembly for the infants that day, and the teacher took action, asking anyone who had been kicking in the playground to own up. She then explained that they shouldn't do this, which seems to have nipped the problem in the bud."

Rearrangements

It may be that your child's problems can be solved by simple rearrangements. Would they find it easier to hear what the teacher is saying if they were moved closer to where she teaches from? Or if your child struggles to get everything done in time, is there a way to allow them extra time for tasks?

At school Matt was constantly frustrated; his greatest difficulty was copying from the board. Mum Liz says, "It takes him much longer than other students as he is dyslexic. We spoke to the class teacher who assured us that the homework was written on the board at the start of the lesson. However, in reality this was not always the case. The result was Matt would be kept behind and arrive flustered at the next lesson, probably reprimanded for being late and in no fit state to learn."

Beating bullying

The school should have an anti-bullying policy. Ask what this involves. How will the teachers assess the situation, how will they talk to the bully?

It can be hard to change other children's behaviour. There are anti-bullying organisations and resources which can help you make suggestions about how the school can act to change things. Check out:

- The Department for Children, Families and Schools website on bullying, **www.dfes.gov.uk/bullying** which includes guidance on cyber-bullying.

- The Anti-bullying Alliance website, **www.anti-bullyingalliance.org.uk** has lots of resources and ideas for schools including:
  - Anti-bullying assemblies
  - Anti-bullying audit toolkit
  - Anti-bullying charter for schools
  - A list of books for children about bullying
  - A briefing on making schools safer

- The NSPCC has a series of guidance booklets called Checkpoints, with versions for Schools, Young People (aimed at Year 6 preparing for secondary school or Year 7) and for parents. You can send off for these or download them from **www.nspcc.org.uk**.

Alongside action at school you can help to build your child's confidence and help them develop friendships by inviting classmates home and encouraging involvement in school activities.

Nell was shocked to find her daughter being bullied in her first year at school. She says, "Dee was four at the time. Her friend Shana had her fifth birthday in January, which seemed to be a catalyst. Shana decided that since she was five, Dee should do what she said. Dee wasn't equipped to deal with this. She was clear that she didn't want to argue with her friend or be rude to her, but neither did she want to be told what to do every playtime. She came home from school every day complaining how Shana had been unpleasant to her.

"I tried to help Dee sort it out for herself, but without success, so I made an appointment with the teacher. We met after school and I explained the problem. The teacher was keen to sort this out, and agreed to pay more attention to how the girls were interacting. She discussed what could be done with the Head of Early Years, and came up with a strategy, which focused on changing Shana's behaviour.

"Dee was told to tell the teacher or assistant if anything happened, and I checked with her after school how her day had been. It all seemed to die down after a while, Shana was told that she couldn't expect other children to do what she told them, the teachers kept an eye on them as far as they could and, of course, Dee had her fifth birthday too."

Carrots and sticks

Some children may need to change their own behaviour. You can use incentives to help encourage children to stick at work they find challenging, to attend school regularly and on time, or to address anti-social behaviour and discipline problems.

Work out a clear target for your child to aim for with the class teacher, and possibly the head or head of year too. Break this down into smaller parts if necessary, so that your child can experience success. Work out what will encourage your child to stick at it. For younger children this can be simply ticks on a chart leading to a sticker at the end of the day. Older children may be motivated by the offer of a much-wanted DVD or trip to the cinema. The school may have incentive and behaviour schemes of their own, which you should be told about.

Kate, a secondary teacher, says, "We try to focus on the good rather than the bad and send postcards and letters home to parents when a child behaves well. We also reward with merits. Those with 50 or more merits at the end of the half term get to go on a free school trip, bowling or whatever. It isn't too hard to get the merits you need for the trip."

Kate has used a similar idea for her own daughter. She says, "My six year old was sulky at school and kept having tantrums. I came up with an idea to encourage good behaviour. Charlie takes a little note pad to school for her teacher to write a note and place a sticker in if she behaves well during the day. If she gets a sticker for every day she chooses a magazine at the weekend.

"Obviously this needs input from home and school, but, in the two weeks we have used the book so far, she has made such a big turnaround that TAs and dinner ladies were stopping her teacher in the corridors to say how they couldn't believe how well she was doing and it was like having a different child. She has been given a 'gold book' award which was a certificate for 'improvement in attitudes towards learning' and has just been so much better generally."

Whatever behaviour change you are trying to achieve, it is important that everyone is clear and consistent. Each teacher needs to be aware of what is expected and what the rewards are. You need to back up the school, and encourage your child too.

MORE HELP

If you're struggling to change your child's behaviour look at this checklist

- What is causing the problem - is there anything that should be changed to help your child?

- Is your child clear how you expect them to behave? Make up achievable targets for them.

- Are all your child's teachers clear about your child's targets for behaviour?

- Is your child praised consistently for good behaviour? Devise a strategy to reward their efforts with something that will motivate them.

Putting things in context

With 30 years of experience as a teacher, and 20-plus years as a parent, Professor Preedy has a few words to help you put your child's problems in context. She says, "Things aren't going to be fine all the time. Life often isn't fair; children will get on better with some teachers than others, but you want to look at the overall package. I wasn't happy at all with one of my daughter's teachers. He didn't seem up to the mark when it came to written work and marking. However, he had a wonderful general and subject knowledge and talked to the students a lot. In retrospect, I think she got a lot from him emotionally and educationally: I hadn't appreciated that at the time."

A FORMAL COMPLAINT

Going to the head

You may decide to talk to the head teacher. You could do this in the first place, if you feel that they have more control over the relevant situation, or you may choose to go to them if you have not got a resolution with the class teacher or head of year. If you're not sure how to arrange to see the head, talk to the school receptionist or secretary. Some heads make a regular time each week to be available to parents too.

Put it in writing

If a meeting with a teacher does not lead to a plan to sort the problem that you are happy with, you may want to become more official and put a complaint in writing. Be as clear as you can. It helps if you can note down significant incidents, and the dates that they happened, as well as who was involved. Think about the outcomes you are seeking. What would you like to see happen? You can write this in the letter so the school is clear about what you want to achieve. You probably want to address the letter to the head at this point. Check out your school's complaints procedure, as they may have appointed someone else as first point of contact for complaints.

Complaints procedure

Ask your school for a copy of their complaints procedure: the advice in this book is general, and your own school's complaints procedure may be slightly different. The complaints procedure should tell you when to expect a letter simply stating they have got your complaint, and when to expect a full written response. There may be information on the school website and there should be some help about how to complain on your local authority website too. The school should respond according to their policy, within a certain period of time. Complaints should be addressed as soon as reasonably possible. Putting a complaint in writing may focus the head's attention on the issue and achieve the change that you want. If not, you can bring in outside help.

Complaining to Governors

If you have had no satisfaction from talking to the class teacher and head teacher, the next stage is to contact the chair of the school Governors, or Parent Council in Scotland. The governing body should have an official complaints procedure. Ask the school for a copy of the procedure so you know what to do. Ask about the timescale for looking into your complaint, so you know what will happen and when. Ideally your complaint should be acknowledged within seven school days. You should get a full response within around 20 school days. This may vary according to an individual school's complaints policy.

What do Governors do?

In England, Northern Ireland and Wales, Governors help run a school by setting its direction. In Scotland, Parent Council members fulfil a similar function to Governors, although as each school can write the constitution for their own parent council, exact responsibilities can vary. A school is run on a day-to-day basis by the head teacher. Governors do not have responsibility as individuals, but the governing body has legal duties and powers.

How can they help me and my child?

Governors can have input to school procedures and policy, including disciplinary matters and target setting. Similarly in Scotland, Parent Council members can have input into school policies discipline, dress, sport, bullying and homework.

Can a Governor back you in a disagreement with the school?

While it can be helpful to get a Governor 'on your side', they do not have the power on their own to make a school change a policy, or a teacher change behaviour. The Governors will discuss this sort of issue and will probably hold a vote to decide a verdict.

By all means tell a Governor about your situation. They may offer a useful perspective or have experience of how the school has solved similar problems for other children.

Can Governors make the school change?

If the Governors feel strongly about a matter of policy they can discuss it at a meeting. They may propose an idea, hold a vote and come up with a way for the school to change. The head teacher is then responsible to the Governors for actually implementing the change.

If the Governors do not deal with your complaint to your satisfaction, you can then write to the clerk of Governors requesting that your complaint be heard by a complaints committee of Governors. This is a meeting of Governors drawn from the governing body, who will meet within around two to four weeks of receiving your letter. You should hear their verdict within five days of their meeting.

If you believe your complaint was not handled fairly according to a school's complaints procedure, you can ask your local authority to investigate, but only after you have been through the school's procedures. Write and explain your complaint. Explain how the school did not follow its complaints procedure, with as much detail as you can. A complaints officer will look at your evidence and decide if it should be investigated. You will get a letter within two weeks telling you what will happen next. The officer only investigates whether the school followed procedure, and does not look at the content of your complaint. If procedure has been followed, they can't make a school change its verdict on a case.

The complaints officer will tell you the outcome of the investigation in writing. If they decide that the school did not follow its procedures, the matter will be referred back to the chair of the governing body. The governing body should then re-investigate the complaint.

EDUCATIONAL EXPERTS

If you feel your child is struggling with work, or their needs are not being met, you may want to get in touch with the local authority education welfare officer or educational psychologist. They can provide an independent opinion, may offer suggestions how to deal with a problem, and may talk to the school on your behalf.

Jane had a number of meetings at her son's school to try to stop bullying. When meeting the head of year and the deputy head had no effect, she went to the local authority. She says, "I spoke to the local authority, but the responses were at best patronising: they seemed put out because I contacted the head person at their department instead of going through all the different levels. I spoke to the Educational Welfare Officer, who agreed to attend a meeting with the head of the school, but she only offered limited support as an observer."

If you are not satisfied with the way your complaint has been handled by the local authority, you can appeal to the Secretary of State for the Department for Education in your country or your Local Government Ombudsman. There are contact details at the end of this chapter. Ask for a copy of their complaints procedure, which in some cases is available on their websites.

Going further

If you believe that your school or local authority has behaved unreasonably or not fulfilled their duties, you have the right to go to the Secretary of State in the Department for Children, Schools and Families in England, the Education Department for Scotland, Wales or Northern Ireland as appropriate. You can only involve the department once the school and the local authority have finished looking into the complaint.

An Ombudsman can investigate problems in the way the local authority looked into your complaint. This covers issues like not giving you the right information, not dealing with your complaint, or taking too long to do so. The Local Government Ombudsman does not look at how schools and colleges are run.

USEFUL RESOURCES AND CONTACTS

If your child has special educational needs you can go to an SEN Tribunal. Read more about this at **www.sentribunal.gov.uk**

England

Local Government Ombudsman
The Commission for Local Administration in England
Millbank Tower
Millbank
London SW1P 4QP
www.lgo.org.uk

Secretary of State for Children, Schools and Families
Sanctuary Buildings
Great Smith Street
London SW1P 3BT

Northern Ireland

Department of Education for Northern Ireland

Rathgael House
Balloo Road
Bangor BT19 7PR
www.deni.gov.uk/

The Ombudsman
Freepost
Belfast BT1 6HN

The Ombudsman's Office
33 Wellington Place
Belfast BT1 6HN

Scotland

The Education Department for Scotland
The Scottish Government
Victoria Quay
Edinburgh EH6 6QQ
0131 556 8400

The Scottish Public Services Ombudsman
4 Melville Street
Edinburgh EH3 7NS
0870 011 5378
www.spso.org.uk/

Wales

The Department for Children, Education, Lifelong Learning and Skills has

offices throughout Wales. Call 0845 010 3300 for your local contact
http://new.wales.gov.uk

Public Services Ombudsman for Wales

1 Ffordd yr Hen Gae

Pencoed CF35 5LJ

01656 641 150

Chapter 4

Changing schools

You may be at the point where your efforts to work things out with the school seem to make no difference. No parent likes to see their child struggling, whether it is because the school can't meet their needs or because of problems like bullying. If you want to find out your options for changing school and other parents' experiences of moving schools, read on.

CHOOSING ANOTHER MAINSTREAM STATE SCHOOL

If you want to move your child to another mainstream state school, you need to start by approaching your local Children's Services or Education Department at the local authority. You may already have a school in mind, and they can tell you if it has a vacancy. The authority will have a list of schools in your area with available places.

FINDING SCHOOLS

There are online databases in the UK you can search to find local schools.

- England: Schoolfinder **http://schoolsfinder.direct.gov.uk/**

- Scotland: Parentzone
  www.parentzonescotland.gov.uk/ChoosingASchool/
  SearchForASchool.asp

- Wales: Schools in Wales
  www.ngfl-cymru.org.uk/6-0-0-0_schools_in_wales.htm

- Northern Ireland: Department for Education **www.deni.gov.uk/**
  http://www.denidata.nics.gov.uk/appinstitutes/instmain.aspx

You may not want to send your child to one of the local state schools with available places, or there may not be a place available. Go on to page 87 to read about independent schools, or Chapter 5 to read about home education, tutors and flexi-schooling.

What does your child want?

Ask your child what they would like in their new school. Friends can be all-important and going to a school where they know someone already may make settling far easier. If your child has a keen interest in music, sport, art or drama, provision of the right facilities or interested staff could be key to their enjoyment. Listen to your child, and note down a few of their priorities to help you sift through possible schools.

Look at your local schools

Before you go further, it is advisable to visit the schools which have places. Contact the school directly. Some may offer regular tours at certain times each week or month, while others will arrange a tour to suit you. It can be a chance to see the head teacher, pick up a prospectus and possibly meet some of the pupils. You can check out the school's specialist subject areas or facilities for music, sports or computer studies.

What to ask when you visit

Make a list of things to check out when you visit. You might want to ask about:

- the dress code and uniforms
- healthy eating
- arrangements for lunch and break times
- playground activities
- after school activities
- support if your child has special needs
- anti-bullying and behaviour policies
- whether classes are mixed ability or in sets
- homework
- whether there is a school council or parent association
- staff turnover
- how the school keeps in touch with parents
- where leavers go – which secondary schools or colleges

Look at school facilities. Are they well maintained? Does the library look as though it is well used? Check out the provision of computers, and whether they are used in class or just in a single computer room. Other indicators of a well-functioning school can be seen on the walls. Read the notices to see what activities are going on. Look out for well-maintained and up-to-date displays of work, or reports back from school trips. Look into as many classrooms as possible to get an idea of how well the children settle to work.

Carole Anne moved both of her children from one primary school to another. She says,

"My younger son was approaching Year 3 and my elder one was approaching Year 5. They had been attending a large primary, and my husband had been the Chair of the PTFA. Our younger son, however, became the target for a child who had been taken into the school on a scheme to re-integrate children who had previously been excluded. After my son's coat had been cut twice in one week, I complained to the headmaster. He explained that this other child was 'worth' three times the funding that my child attracted."

Carole felt that the head's attitude meant that her son could continue to be targeted, so she started to look for other options. She says, "I visited a lovely little Church of England junior school and arranged to transfer the boys in September. Alan grew six centimetres and went from being described as 'average' to being top of his class by the first Christmas, but Phil struggled to adapt a bit more. He, nevertheless, left at the end of Year 6 with a school prize for sporting achievement and with Level 5 SAT results, above the expected performance for his age group."

School performance

Each year, schools get a performance assessment. Sometimes known as league tables, the school receives a score for the achievements of their pupils. As well as the academic successes, you also want to look at the CVA, or Contextual Value Added score: simply, how much the school has helped pupils improve. This takes into account the fact that some schools are in more deprived areas, have a greater number of children with English as a second language or special educational needs, and other factors that can affect the school's outcomes. Ask the school for their results.

School inspection reports

Your local authority should offer information about all their schools. It can tell you facts such as the number of places available, the number of applications, whether a school is selective, and its success rates for exams. As well as visiting the school and reading the local authority information and school prospectus, you may want to read about the results of the most recent independent inspection. The inspectors write a report which outlines what a school does well, areas of improvement since the last inspection, and where it needs to make further improvements. The school may have copies of their report available for you to read. You can also view reports on the website for the inspection organisation for your area:

- In England the inspections are carried out by the Office for Standards in Education, Children's Services and Skills. You can download inspection reports from **www.ofsted.gov.uk**. State schools in England are inspected every three years.

- In Scotland the inspections are carried out by HM Inspectorate of Education. You can download reports from **www.hmie.gov.uk**. Schools in Scotland should be inspected at least once while a child is there, so every six or seven years. This can be an initial inspection or a follow up. Visit **www.scottishschoolsonline.gov.uk** to search for information by school.

- In Wales the inspections are carried out by Estyn. Each school is inspected every six years. You can download reports from **www.estyn.gov.uk**.

- In Northern Ireland the inspections are carried out by the Education and Training Inspectorate, **www.etini.gov.uk**. Each school is inspected every seven years. You can download reports from **www.denidata.nics.gov.uk**.

Does it feel right?

It can be incredibly hard to make a decision about your child's education based on a single visit. Before making a decision, you may want to make an extra appointment to discuss your child's needs with the head, to see if the school can meet them. If you know someone who has kids at the school already, ask them about what they feel the school does well, and where it falls short. The more people you can ask, the better you can see if there are any general problems with the school. Remember that reputations build up over years and may not reflect current practice at a school. Talk to the kids as well as the parents for interesting insights on areas where the school excels.

> Peter was bullied off and on for several years. Parents Denise and Mike had been in to the school on numerous occasions before they decided to move both their sons to another school. Denise says, "It started with some name calling. We had met informally with the teacher, and probably had around 10 more formal meetings over a couple of years. I also asked his class teachers how he was getting on every week – but there were several changes of teacher which didn't help. It was a small school, with only 14 kids in Peter's class, so it was hard for him to make different friends.

"We were unhappy with some of the school's so-called solutions to bullying too. On one occasion, they had sat Peter with a lower year group, another time they had asked him to help with the library so he didn't get picked on at play time. This just made him feel even more left out."

Matters came to a head at the school play. Peter was Joseph, and after the first show was over, the same children started calling him names and stamping on his feet. Denise says, "He came out from the classroom where they were all getting changed crying, in front of all the other parents, which was very out of character, so we knew it was serious."

After that, Denise and Mike felt that the time had come to take things into their own hands. "The school hadn't stopped the bullying, so we moved both boys to a new school after Christmas. It wasn't entirely straightforward. Our younger son had only spent one term at school, and he hated the thought of starting again in a place where he didn't know anyone. However, it has been the right move for Peter. He only had two terms left at primary school, and felt he had an opportunity to make friends without the same bullies spoiling his chances. The new school has rebuilt his lost confidence, and he was able to move on to secondary school in September a far happier boy."

Meeting your child's needs

One element in choosing a new school will be the response they have to the reason why you are moving schools. For example, if your child has been bullied at their old school, you may want to explain this to the new school, and find out about their policies for dealing with bullying. Their attitude will probably play a key part in your final choice of schools.

How to apply

For most schools, there is a common application form provided by the local authority. Some foundation or voluntary aided schools will have their own form. Check with the local authority or school. You will be able to specify a preference for a number of schools, but you are not guaranteed the place of your choice. The local authority must comply with your preference if possible.

Admission criteria

Schools have criteria for admitting children. This may mean that they give priority to children with brothers or sisters at the school, those who live closest, or those with special needs. Faith schools can give priority to children of a particular faith. The criteria for each school will differ, so it is important to check them for the school of your choice. Admissions criteria come into play if there are more children applying for places than places available.

The criteria are most likely to affect your child if you are applying for a place in reception or starting secondary school. If you are applying to enter in any other year, or even mid term, the criteria will only come into play if there is a waiting list or several children applying for a small number of places. For most applications at unusual times it really comes down to whether there is a place available at all. Each school has an agreed number of places available in each year group and there is often little or no scope for the school to take extra pupils.

Under Fair Access Protocols, children may occasionally be admitted over and above the agreed number of admissions if it won't cause problems for the children already at the school. There are specific rules on class size for classes where children will reach the age of five, six or seven by the end of the school year. There may only be 30 pupils with each school teacher.

Think twice

If you have checked whether the school has places available, and found that they do not, you may want to think again. Similarly, if you would like your child to attend a school that you know will be oversubscribed, look seriously at your chances of getting a place. It may be easier on you and your child to apply to schools which you are happy with and which you have a realistic chance of getting into.

A state school is not allowed to take your child's past behaviour, attendance, attitude or achievement into account when allocating a place, and it may not discriminate against or disadvantage children with special educational needs or disabilities.

Appealing

If you apply for a place at a school and are unsuccessful, you must be given reasons and informed in writing of your right to an independent appeal against the decision. The appeal panel will look at whether the admission criteria were properly applied in your case. If the criteria were not applied properly, then the panel must uphold your appeal unless it affects a significant number of children and would cause problems if they were all admitted to the school. This could be the case if, say, there had been a mistake in calculating distances from school. The panel will then look at whether admitting an extra child would adversely affect the school's arrangements for the year group. Next, the panel must assess whether your grounds for suggesting that your child should be admitted outweigh any prejudice to the school. This is a complex area, and this book can only highlight a few examples. You may want to look at the School Admission Appeals Code for information specific to your circumstances.

HELP AND ADVICE

If you feel you need an independent person to help you with finding a school, you can get advice from The Advisory Centre for Education. An independent advice centre for parents and carers, it offers information about state-funded education in England and Wales for five to 16 year olds. Call their advice line on 0808 800 5793 to talk about all education issues, including exclusion from school, bullying, special educational needs and school admission appeals.

Helping your child settle

Hopefully you have now applied for a school and been allocated the place of your choice. There are several things you, and the school, can do to make changing schools easier for your child. Is it possible to arrange a 'welcome visit' so your child can see the school, visit their new classroom and meet their new teacher? Some schools may have a video about the school for new pupils to watch. You may want to book a meeting with the teacher after the first fortnight to see how your child is settling down.

Nell and her family bought a new house in the May of her daughter's first year at school. She says, "Dee was in Reception and we didn't want to disrupt her any more than necessary. We found a new school, and visited it with Dee. We went to the school fair too, which gave her the chance to see the building again. The new school suggested that she come along for the last few weeks of term. This worked well as she got to join in sports day and other end of term events. We invited a little girl over to play after school one day, and I got to know a couple of mums so we could meet over the summer.

"When it came to September, Dee felt less like she was starting a brand new school, and she had friends to sit with from day one. I think it still is a change for her, though. She's gone from a school where she had known some of the children practically since birth, and been to playgroups and nursery together. We're well into her first full term now and she seems to be OK."

Befrienders

Making friends can be hard at a new school, especially for older children. Ask the teacher whether there are any buddy schemes so your child has someone to talk to in the first few days while they find their feet.

DIFFERENT TYPES OF SCHOOL

So far in this chapter we have looked at mainstream state schools. However, there is a range of other options which can suit different children.

Pupil referral units

Local authorities may have a Pupil Referral Unit (PRU). This is a small specialist 'school' which is there to meet the needs of children who because of illness, school phobia or exclusion, for example, cannot attend a mainstream school. There may be a local PRU for school-aged mothers and pregnant schoolgirls.

The hours a child attends a PRU will depend on why they are there. A child who has been excluded may be required to attend full-time, while a child with a long-term illness may only be able to cope with a few hours each week. The PRU may have staff who teach, or may involve external agencies including FE colleges or voluntary organisations. For some children, the aim of time at the PRU may simply be to re-integrate them to mainstream education. Some pupils may attend the PRU on a part-time basis while remaining on the roll of their mainstream school.

Special educational needs

If you are looking for a school which has extra provision for your child's special educational needs, you can go through your local authority as above, or look for independent schools too. There may be a school locally which has special provision for children with particular needs. If there is a suitable local state school, the local authority does not have to support you if you want to send your child to an independent school, a non-maintained special school (run by a charity) or a school in another local authority area.

You can get help from your local Parent Partnership service (in England). In Wales the Special Needs Advisory Project can offer assistance. You can get extra advice and an independent support-er may be able to visit schools with you.

Your options for SEN:

- A unit within a mainstream state school.
- A special school.
- A residential school.
- An independent or non-maintained school. You can pay the

fees for this sort of school yourself, or go through the process to ask the local authority to fund your child at this particular school in order for their needs to be met.

Independent schools

There are many different sorts of independent school. Because of their independence these schools can vary enormously and may be able to offer your child something that is right for them, and outside that offered by state schools. Read on to find out about different theories of education, on which some schools are based, as well as small schools and boarding schools. You can also find out about how to find an independent school, and, of course, how to get any help with fees which may be available.

TEACHING PHILOSOPHIES

In the UK there are two main ways of 'alternative' teaching – Steiner Waldorf and Montessori – that have given rise to a number of educational establishments. Read on for a short introduction to each method, and find out about the new wave of Small Schools which aim to provide for children in a way that larger establishments can not.

Steiner Waldorf schools

This way of teaching is offered in around 35 schools in the UK, for pupils up to the age of 18. There is an emphasis on artistic and practical learning and a focus on the spiritual, physical and moral wellbeing of a child, alongside academic achievement. Formal learning is not forced, with the emphasis on learning in a creative and artistic environment. The school day is focused around the 'main lesson', where a class looks at a subject in depth over three to four weeks, using literacy and numeracy skills as part of their study. In the early years of a child's education, work tends not to be graded, although written evaluations and records may be made.

Steiner Waldorf schools base their teaching on the educational philosophy of Rudolf Steiner.

Christopher Clouder of the Steiner Waldorf Schools Fellowship says, "Steiner Waldorf schools accommodate children from all backgrounds. Our curriculum is artistically structured to respond to the developmental needs of children. This applies to content, art of teaching and timetable. Steiner education respects the essential nature of childhood, enabling children to develop their strengths in a structured and child-sensitive environment." Most Steiner Waldorf schools are fee-paying.

The Steiner approach is not for everyone. Some Steiner schools have been criticised by OFSTED for not placing enough emphasis on basic skills such as reading and writing – although it may be the case that OFSTED inspectors are not sufficiently familiar with Steiner modes of assessment. Victoria Dawson expands on some further issues, "Steiner methods involve story telling rather than reading to the class from a book. Developing a love of books is so important for young children that it seems a terrible shame that Steiner schools aren't using their staff as role models for readers. Staff also only have to attain a Steiner teaching qualification rather than be state-qualified which means that you could be paying to have poorly qualified staff teaching your child. When it comes to secondary education you really do need your child to be taught by specialists in the subject area."

Abigail's daughter, Phoebe, was in middle school when she started to be bullied. Abigail explains, "I think it was because the other girls were starting to get interested in make-up and fashion, swearing and trying to be cool, while Phoebe just wasn't interested. They picked on her verbally, and one day she said she was crouched down in the playground while they all circled round her. We talked to her class teacher and the head, but the school just didn't seem to be able to stop it."

Abigail's husband was initially against the idea of going private, but they decided together to look at the local Steiner school. She says, "We were impressed from the very start. There was a display of woodwork in the front hall of the school: the children had not only made the work, they had made some of the tools too. The school was not academically pushy which was a lovely contrast as Phoebe was in the run-up to SATs and her school seemed to have stopped all the nice activities in favour of preparation for the tests."

Abigail moved Phoebe to the Steiner school at the age of 11 and she immediately settled in. Abigail comments, "It was lovely and inclusive. In the early days they went on a trip: when Phoebe was scared by a horse all the children gathered round to reassure her. The girls didn't mind if she shared interests in fashion – they accepted her for who she was. The classes were smaller and the atmosphere and friendships really helped her build her confidence. There were plenty of trips and activities, so Phoebe got a really broad education. She has gone on to sixth-form college now, but I think would still really prefer to be back at the Steiner school."

Montessori schools

There are around 700 nursery and junior schools in the UK using elements of the Montessori method. Children are allowed to choose their own activities, while observed by the teacher (who may be known as a director). The environment and choice of activities is important in helping the child develop, and should allow children to be independent and discover for themselves. The Good Schools Guide comments that, "The apparent lack of structure can be a problem for some youngsters: others relish the freedom to explore."

Older and younger children share the same classrooms. The Montessori method is based on the child development theories of Maria Montessori, an Italian from the late 19th and early 20th century. She believed that children up to the age of six have limitless motivation to perfect skills, learn and understand things. There is no legal requirement to go through a particular training, so any school can describe themselves as adhering to Montessori methods. Most Montessori schools are fee-paying.

Glen House Montessori is a small school for up to 20 children. The small numbers give the school, "an atmosphere of a 'large family' rather than an institution". As in most Montessori based schools, mixed age groups work together. Unusually, Glen House offers education for children up to the age of 15 who can take two or three GCSEs early before moving on to a sixth-form college to take the rest of their GCSEs in a year.

Children aged two and a half to six attend the Children's House. The Elementary is for children aged six to 11 and the Secondary Group for 11 to 15 year olds. The two older groups often work together. They share the management of the snack shop and have regular school meetings.

Margret Scaife, head of the school, says, "Montessori is the only educational philosophy that gives the children the freedom to learn by following their own interests over the age of six years. Montessori Schools have a unified, internationally developed curriculum, which integrates all areas of development such as physical, intellectual, social, emotional and spiritual. The role of the teacher is to stand back and direct the child when necessary. The child will ask the teacher for help, so the teacher will not interfere with the child's work."

Small schools

In the UK there is a number of parent-led projects to set up small schools for anything from six to 60 pupils. Most of these schools operate outside the state sector, so they do not have to stick to the National Curriculum, and are run on democratic principles. The schools try to keep fees low and may do fundraising activities to help with this. Small schools can be particularly good for children who have had problems at their previous school. Many of the schools aim to be environmentally sustainable, and they may offer mixed age learning. Visit the Human Scale Education website to find out more: **www.hse.org.uk**.

Parents Julie Kelly and Liz Baker founded Great Oaks Small School after their 11 year old children both struggled to cope with the transition to secondary school. Liz explains, "My son joined his secondary school just as it was becoming a technology college. At first we thought this would be great for him: he is dyspraxic and struggles with organisational skills but is quite technically minded. However, it soon became clear that the transition to a tech-based school was far from straightforward for the teachers and assistants, and my son suffered because of this.

The Learning Support Assistants who were supposed to help him deal with his organisation problems had not been trained in the new technology. He was in a laptop-based class. His LSA asked him to bring out his science file, and then shouted at him for trying to access the file on his laptop: she was expecting a folder of papers. There were big issues with homework too.

We counted up to nine different ways that the school had asked for home-work to be handed in. We were never clear whether we should be sending in a disk, a worksheet, or uploading a file onto the school's main system. I looked in my son's cupboard one day and found around 50 pieces of work: he had been too scared to hand them in in case he got the format wrong. In the end, he was afraid to go out at weekends and after school in case he ran into fellow pupils and he was having daily panic attacks. I knew we had to do something different."

Liz and Julie took it in turns to home educate their children, and soon found another couple of kids joining them. Once it got to five pupils, they needed to make things more official and so the idea for Great Oaks Small School came about. The school has grown slowly and organically over nine years. It now offers small classes for around 16 pupils studying subjects up to A level. Around half of the pupils are placed by the local authority.

Liz says, "We offer provision for children for whom there is nothing else suitable, filling the gap between specialist and mainstream provision. Children come to us with a range of concerns. Some have been bullied, or simply struggle to cope with the large numbers of pupils in a school. Others have missed chunks of schooling due to illness, and some have mild learning disabilities, poor concentration, or poor co-ordination. In response to this we offer neurodevelopmental exercises every day."

If parents want to get their child into a school like Great Oaks, Liz advises, "Apply to your local authority as soon as possible. It can take 18 months to go through the process, and parents need to be very determined. I would always suggest starting the process before your child gets into Year 9."

Learning is focused on each child's needs. "We try to teach children the subjects they want to learn about. If a child is interested in, say, classical civilization, one of the teachers will adapt and teach according to that child's interests. We have three students in the current sixth form, which means that a lot of one-to-one teaching takes place. We have nine part-time teachers, which allows us to be this flexible."

The school is democratically run. Liz says, "It takes the kids a long time to get their heads round this and understand what is possible. However, two out of the three former pupils who started at university this year have signed up to be year reps, which shows how they appreciate and believe in democracy."

Small schools are, like all schools, inspected on a regular basis. Liz says, "We registered as a school once we reached five pupils. We are now accredited for Key Stage 3 and 16-plus education. We had our Ofsted inspection this year and the inspectors left no stone unturned. We were very pleased with their report."

Independent schools

Independent schools come in many different forms, and can cover primary or secondary age children, or sometimes both. They all charge fees. An independent school is any establishment that provides full-time education for five or more pupils of compulsory school age, or one or more pupils with a statement of special educational need, or in public care, and which is not a school maintained by a local education authority or a non-maintained special school.

Julie made the decision to move her son from a state school to a private school after his first year. She says, "My son is very bright. The school he was attending was unable to keep him stimulated and he began to get into constant trouble. He was withdrawing and becoming unhappy. I found an independent school by looking through the phone book as they did not advertise. I took him for a visit and the atmosphere was lovely. All of the children were polite and engaging. I had visited another school the week before so I was able to compare the two. I was shown some of the work that the children had done and was impressed with what the head teacher said that she could offer my son. I paid a registration fee and sent off the form and I had to wait to find out if there was a place available."

After a stressful couple of months waiting to hear, Julie found that her son had a place. She took him into the school for an assessment, and then had to get him kitted out. She comments, "The uniform cost a small fortune. Private schools can demand that you buy the uniform from a certain supplier rather than at Tesco. The blazer was £45, shirts £12, and trousers were £13 each. On top of this were the school fees, accident insurance, fee protection insurance, the after school activities, and trips."

Julie's son settled in fairly well. She explains, "Starting school was easy for him but it took about a year for him to get used to doing homework. The levels of discipline are far higher in the private sector so I found that he was getting into trouble for minor things but he was getting more attention than he was at his old school and the work was more appropriate to his academic needs.

"I find that there are big differences between the parents so it can be quite hard for a parent to fit in. There are those who you never see because they are working to pay the fees and those who are active members of the school because their partners work so they have lots of free time. A parent is expected to make an effort for the school. Parents are expected to listen to their children read every night and make sure they complete their homework. It is expected that parents attend meetings with their child's teacher unless they have contacted them and rearranged the time. Parents are encouraged to fundraise for the school and to attend their child's plays and concerts, most of which are not free.

"Most private schools have long holidays and it can be hard to find employment to fit around their terms. Holiday clubs outside the school only run during state school holidays so there is often a week or two where there is no holiday care. Then you have to do all of this again when your child moves to a secondary school, which costs more money. At my son's school they are prepared for the common entrance exam, which takes months of preparation. You have to look for a school, register, which costs £75-£150 depending on the school, then the child sits an exam. Then you wait, again, to see if they have a place."

FINDING OUT MORE

Schools belonging to the Independent Schools Council are inspected by the Independent Schools Inspectorate, **www. isinspect.org.uk**. The Independent Schools Inspectorate is a body approved by the Secretary of State for Children, Schools and Families for the purpose of inspecting independent schools as part of the Education Act 2002. Inspections take place every six years, and around 1280 of the more than 2000 independent schools are part of this body. The majority of other independent schools are inspected every three years by Ofsted, in partnership with Cambridge Education, the National Inspection Services Provider for independent schools, and you can find reports on them at **www.ofsted.gov.uk**. Focus Learning Trust looks after the remaining 64 educational charities which are registered as independent schools: these mainly religious school establishments are inspected by School Inspection Services, which is monitored by Ofsted.

Independent schools aren't always the solution for every child, and can vary enormously. Naomi chose her son Neil's school after viewing numerous prospectuses and visiting several schools on a number of occasions. She made her choice of school after being, she says, "impressed by the discipline and old-fashioned morals. The boys have exceptional manners, their respect towards adults is impeccable: they stand when an adult enters the room and wait to be told to be seated, they hold the door open for you and don't push past.

"The classes are small, no more than 18 to a class. Additionally the school has a good reputation for music and sport achievements and we were assured that every boy is given the chance of being on the school sports teams: participation was encouraged over winning. The lunches were prepared in house by a chef from locally sourced fresh produce. Ultimately we felt a good vibe from the school."

Neil has language difficulties which Naomi discussed with the school before starting. She explains, "We were assured that it wouldn't be an issue, as all children develop at different rates and boys identified with SEN receive additional support from the SENCO. He has had 15 minutes a day with the SENCO since starting. But when I asked whether there would be any additional support costs for the next school year, the school suggested that they don't want him there because they believe he's autistic."

Naomi is now looking at other schools. She says, "I've viewed the local state schools but believe that if he's finding it difficult to cope in a class of 12 he won't cope in a class of 30, even with additional one-to-one support as the distractions are too great. We're holding fire at the moment pending the outcome of his assessment by the local autism team and will see what recommendations they make with a view to perhaps being able to use the information to ensure he gets a proper education in a setting that is conducive to his learning. We'd move house again to get him a place in the right school for his needs."

Finding schools: inspections, databases and directories

If you are looking for a fee-paying school you may want to use one of several directories which are now available as books or online. There is no single definitive directory, and not all schools will be listed in all directories. It is worth checking more than one directory to get different views. In some places schools can pay to advertise, while other guides are based entirely on independent assessments: make sure you are clear which you are reading.

- The Independent Schools Council maintains a searchable online directory of schools at **www.isc.co.uk**. It offers links to the inspection reports from the Independent Schools Inspectorate.

- The Good Schools Guide is available as a book and also has a free directory online at **www.goodschoolsguide.co.uk**. It offers in-depth, independent views on over 1000 state and private schools. There is the option to subscribe to the website to see information for schools in the same detail as in the book. They also offer a guide for Special Educational Needs schools.

- The Independent Schools Guide covers in the region of 2000 schools. Most schools are listed by area, with the number of pupils, contact details and fees. Some schools pay for a profiled entry.

- Which School? is a directory of more than 2000 independent schools in the UK, with accompanying website **www.schoolsearch.co.uk**. It also offers directories of special needs schools, boarding schools and 16-plus education. Some schools pay for a higher profile in the guide.

- The Sunday Times Parent Power section has a range of league tables for independent and state primary and secondary schools:

http://www.timesonline.co.uk/parentpower/league_tables.php

Boarding school

Many parents will not have thought of boarding school as an option. "It costs too much'," or "I couldn't send my child away": there may be many reasons, but boarding school can be exactly right for some children. And nowadays, boarding does not mean that you don't see your child for weeks at a time. Many children now board weekly.

Why board?

There are different reasons to send your child to a boarding school. It may be that you want your child to have some stability if your job, and home, move round the world. As the pupils are in their care 24 hours a day, boarding schools work hard to create a family atmosphere. That can be good for some children who find it hard to fit in. If your child's problems at school actually derive from some kind of problem at home, such as divorce, an alcoholic parent, or a disabled sibling who takes a lot of attention, a boarding school can provide a home-from-home and the chance to get away from the source of the trouble during term time. Hilary Moriarty, National Director of the Boarding Schools' Association, says, "Reasons for going to boarding school include the complete unavailability of a local school which parents think will be suitable or the belief that a child will be better off removed from a particular environment or group of peers."

Hanford School is for girls aged seven to 13 in Dorset. Rated as 'one of the nicest' girls' boarding schools in the country, it has a range of practices and traditions which have built up over time to ensure that girls feel at home. One way that younger girls are looked after is through the system of committees. The school explains: "The committees are formed by groups of sixth forms ... the committees look after the younger girls and the school. They are helpful and are always looking out for the homesick juniors."

The school arranges clubs and activities at the weekends. "Some children may be involved in matches; others may ride, look after the chickens, swim, climb trees, walk in the hills, play music or organise clubs which are entirely voluntary and are for their own diversion and amusement. These include Art Club, Gym Club, Wiggle Club (dancing), Acting Club, computers and other games. All activities, while organised by the children, are supervised by a member of staff." And birthdays are made special too. "If your birthday falls during term time, your friends will take a pillowcase around the dorms so people can put things in them – maybe writing paper and, if you are lucky, some sweets. Your pillowcase is a little bit like a Christmas stocking."

Boarding may be the only way for your child to access specialist facilities for drama, dance or sport. Hilary Moriarty comments that boarding school may be the solution if parents have "a wish for a child to have more facilities and activities available to them in the evenings and at weekends, or a conviction that a particular school offers a particular service – such as expertise with dyslexic pupils, for instance – which the child needs."

Boarding school may offer children with special needs the help that they need round the clock. New College Worcester, for example, is a residential school and college for young people aged 11 to 19 who are blind or partially sighted. Children study while developing independence skills, including mobility, living skills, and ICT. A residential school can also allow your child with special needs to attend the school that is right for them, even if it is located too far from home to travel daily.

Hurtwood House is a sixth form boarding school, famous for its performing and creative arts facilities. The Good Schools Guide recommends it for "... the 'I need a change' fraternity and the performing arts enthusiast".

Around a third of the pupils study art and a similar number focus on theatre studies, with input from over a dozen hands-on theatre practitioners as well as visiting professional companies and guest tutors from film, stage and television. Media studies students learn to write, direct, shoot, mix and edit films, music videos, advertisements and documentaries using digital cameras and digital editing suites; they produce radio shows in the school radio station; they learn print and journalistic skills, layout and design, graphics, photography and editorial management and, in the 'new media' they produce web-work to a professional level using industry-standard software.

Headmaster Cosmo Jackson says, "The point about Hurtwood is that it enables the aspiring actor, singer, artist, fashion designer or film director to follow their dreams at the same time as undertaking a full A level programme. What is often overlooked is that Hurtwood is outstanding academically."

Of course, boarding schools vary like any school. Hilary Moriarty says, "A child who is unhappy in a day school, for whatever reason, may find boarding school is exactly the right answer. On the other hand, school for 24 hours a day may feel like a double dose of something a child already hates and it may not work at all. If a child is deeply unwilling to go, boarding is unlikely to work. There are many instances of a child discovering that boarding is a whole different world which suits the child despite their fears or even convictions that they would hate it. But no school will be successful for a deeply unhappy child who may believe he or she has been got out of the way because they are a nuisance or they are unwanted and unloved."

Sarah was at boarding school from the age of six, nearly seven, due to her father's job in Argentina. She says, "My parents decided that a British education was better than the international school in Buenos Aires. They had both been in boarding schools, so I guess they didn't think it unusual. My sister and brother started a year before me at age 10 and eight. I went to the same school as my sister, although we were in different boarding houses so didn't see much of each other. I was happy to go. I guess I just wanted to be like my siblings, but the reality of being away from home was different and I remember feeling very homesick. I left after my 11-plus and went to another boarding school until my parents moved back to the UK when I was 14.

The best thing for me about school was friends. My life was always full of people to hang out with, and the friends I made at school are still friends today. They shared everything with me. They knew about my first period weeks before my mum: she was thousands of miles away! We also had lots to do after school, mostly sports, but at the weekend we did cooking too and we never watched TV. It makes you very independent. At six I could get myself dressed and ready for school with no help. I changed the sheets on my bed, polished my shoes: there were no parents to nag you.

I remember feeling lonely in the holidays because I was away from friends but didn't feel close to my siblings who I didn't see for weeks on end. My parents didn't really know how to discipline me either, so when I went to day school at 14 they let me run riot. My relationship with my family is fine, but we don't have many shared memories from our youth.

I think boarding school suits the more sociable and sporty child, and it works if a parent has problems or if there is an acrimonious divorce maybe, but I won't be sending my kids away – no way."

Finding the right boarding school

Boarding schools vary enormously, and finding the right school for your child is the key. Hilary Moriarty explains, "They may have boarding in common, but they will feel different, be in town or in the country, have weekly boarding available or not, emphasise music or drama or sport differently, be co-ed or single sex, and expect differing levels of academic excellence, and offer differing levels of support for weaker pupils. All this needs exploring with the child before the decision is made. See at least a couple if you can, so that the child feels he or she is involved in the choice, not being 'dumped'."

State boarding

There are 35 state boarding schools in the country, where a parent pays for the boarding element, but not for the education, because it is a maintained school like every other. This means fees are substantially lower than would be the case in an independent school.

BOARDING SCHOOL INFORMATION

You can find information on boarding schools in the independent school directories listed on page 91. For further information on boarding schools and lists of schools and addresses, contact the Boarding Schools' Association, **www.boarding.org.uk** 020 7798 1580.

Help with fees

Figures indicate that between a fifth and a third of all pupils at independent schools get some form of financial assistance with fees. The most common source of assistance is the school itself. Scholarships may be offered to children who show potential in academic subjects, music, art or even sport. Scholarships usually cover up to half the school fees. Means tested bursaries may be available to cover a proportion of the fees, to help parents who could not afford the full fee.

A number of educational charities offer help towards school fees, in certain circumstances. Some focus on particular groups, such as sons of the clergy, while others may offer help to families living in a particular location. Many will offer help towards fees only if independent education is necessary for the child, or perhaps if they would otherwise have to leave a private school due to a change in circumstances. Some may offer grants for school uniform, books, travel expenses, materials for courses, but not help towards the actual fees.

If you have to work abroad, your company may make a grant towards your child's education in a UK boarding school. Similarly, the Ministry of Defence and other government departments may make a grant towards school fees to parents who are posted overseas. Your local authority may occasionally make a grant if they cannot provide an appropriate education for your child: this may be the case if your child has special needs.

The Government offers means tested funding under the Music and Dance Scheme for boys and girls with outstanding talent in music and dance. The scheme helps parents pay the fees and boarding costs at eight specialist independent schools which are centres of excellence in their field. There are means tested grants for part-time dance and music tuition at a number of Centres for Advanced Training around the country. You can find out about these schemes at **www.dfes.gov.uk/mds**, where participating schools are listed. There is also a Choir Schools Scholarship Scheme (**www.choirschools.org.uk**) to help boys and girls from low income families wishing to train at any of the 36 independent choir schools in England.

Ask your local authority's children's services department for information on grant-making bodies in the area, or ask your local library to order the Directory of Grant Making Trusts (£99), which lists bodies that may help you with fees, or The Educational Grants Directory (£34.95). You can also buy both books from **www.dsc.org.uk**.

Chapter 5

Home education, flexischooling and tutors

For some children, school is not the right option. They may need a break for a term or more, or you may decide that they are better off learning through home education on a long-term basis. In this chapter, read about how to take your child out of school, and find out how some families home educate their children. You can also read about flexischooling and home tutors.

YOUR OPTIONS FOR TAKING A BREAK FROM SCHOOL

You do not have to send your child to school, but you must make sure your child learns at home. Your local authority will check what you are teaching but does not have to help you, and does not offer funding for home education.

Chartered psychologist Dr Paula Rothermel is an expert on home education. She says, "When there are problems with school, when your child is seriously unhappy, home education is a real option. It is not as difficult as it can seem from the outside. To start with, your child can go along with your interests, and they will develop ideas of what they want to find out about. It will help enormously if you are interested in what they are learning. You can then show them how to find things out for themselves. It can take six months to settle into home educating. Rather than feeling you are making a commitment for years, think about trying it for a single school year, then discussing with your child how it is working. This will give you time to develop a routine."

Home education and the law

The legislation which allows you to take your child out of school and home educate differs slightly depending on which part of the United Kingdom you live in. It is also different if your child attends a special school. Read on to find the law that applies to you.

ENGLAND AND WALES

Age four or five or moving area?

In England and Wales, if your child has never been to school, you do not need to notify anyone of your intention to home educate.

Leaving a mainstream school

If you are taking your child out of a mainstream school, you need to write to tell the head teacher what you intend to do. You do not need the school or local authority's permission, and can start to home educate from the date that you notify them. The head teacher will take your child's name off the school register and tell the local authority. See below for an example of a letter you could use: this letter is from the organisation Education Otherwise, which supports families whose children are being educated outside school.

Deregistration letter: from Education Otherwise
[**www.educationotherwise.co.uk**]

Your address

Date

Head teacher [name]
School name
Full address and postcode

Dear [head teacher's name]

Re: [your child's name] (date of birth)

After careful consideration I/we have decided to withdraw my/our son/daughter from school in order to take personal responsibility for his/her education. Please delete his/her name from the register in accordance with Education (Pupil Registration) Regulation 8(1)(d) 2006, as he/she is now receiving education otherwise than at school.

Please will you confirm receipt of this letter and inform us of the date that our son/daughter's name was removed from the register.

Yours sincerely,

SCOTLAND

Mainstream state schools

The law is slightly different in Scotland, where you will need local authority consent if your child is currently at a state school. The law states that as far as possible children should be educated according to the wishes of their parents. The local authority will assess the education you propose to provide and base their decision on that. You are entitled to see a copy of what they report.

Other schools

You do not need local authority consent in Scotland if your child has never been to a mainstream state school, or has not been to a mainstream state school in the area you now live in. You can decide to home educate without consent if your child has finished primary school and has not yet started state school, or if their school closes. You can withdraw your child from an independent school without consent.

If you want to adapt the letter, above, the relevant piece of legislation in Scotland is the Education (Scotland) Act 1980, section 30. You should also remember that you may need to ask for consent from the local authority, and could substitute a phrase like:

> I/we would like consent to withdraw my/our son/daughter from school in order to take personal responsibility for his/her education.

To speed things up, Scottish Home Ed support group Schoolhouse [**www.schoolhouse.org.uk**] recommend including an outline of your 'educational objectives' and the resources you will use when teaching your child. The charity also recommends sending your letter by recorded delivery.

NORTHERN IRELAND

In Northern Ireland there is no legal requirement to inform anyone that you are home educating. Much as in the rest of the UK you simply have a duty to ensure that your child receives "efficient full-time education suitable to his age, ability and aptitude and to any special educational needs he may have, either by regular attendance at school or otherwise".

How to deregister

You must deregister your child by writing to the school head, and can adapt the letter above. The legislation for Northern Ireland is the Education and Libraries (Northern Ireland) Order 1986, Article 45.

Support

The Home Ed support Group in Northern Ireland is called HEdNI. They offer an email group, and a website (**www.hedni.org**) with useful resources, articles, and further details on the legal aspects of home education.

Special needs

In all parts of the UK, you will need to ask permission to de-register a child attending a special school. According to S324 of the Education Act 1996 the Local Authority (England and Wales) is obliged to provide for a child's special educational needs unless you make "suitable arrangements" at home: similar conditions apply in Scotland and Northern Ireland. Solicitor Louise Melia of the Education Law Unit in Govan says, "The local authority might have more reasons to object though. They might need convincing that the education being provided at home is suited to that child's additional support needs. Also, if the child receives additional support by way of speech and language therapy, or another kind of therapy at the school, this might be difficult to supply if the child does not attend school (or so the local authority might argue)."

Deregistration letter for a child at a special school: from Education Otherwise and Issie Brookfield of NAS

Your address
Date

Director of Education [name]
Anytown Council
Education Department
Full address and postcode

Dear [name of Director of Education]

Re [Child's name – date of birth – special school attending]

We are writing as the parents of the above named child, who is a child for whom the local authority currently maintains a statement of special educational needs and who is a registered pupil at [name] Special School, [address].

After careful consideration, and following amicable discussions with staff and teachers from the above named school, we have now decided to take full responsibility for providing for our child's education, 'otherwise than at school' in accordance with section 7 of the 1996 Education Act [for England and Wales] OR section 35 (1), and section 37, of the Education (Scotland) Act 1980

We therefore seek the consent of the local authority to allow [child's name] to be deleted from the admission register of the school, in accordance with

Education (Pupil Registration) Regulation 8(2) 2006. Once consent has been given we will provide our son/daughter with an efficient full-time education suitable to his age, ability, aptitude and to his special educational needs.

We look forward to consent for [child's name] to be deleted from the admission register being given to the proprietor of [name] Special School in the very near future and request that confirmation of such action be forwarded to us within the next 14 days.

Yours sincerely,

HE-Special is an email support group for families home educating a child with special needs. It offers a range of articles on the website, **www.he-special.org.uk**. There is a list of parents with home ed experience on the Education Otherwise website's Local Groups page.

Liz took Matt out of school when the school was unable to adapt to meet his needs. Liz says, "I still find it hard to accept that his needs were not met. If he had been blind he would not have been expected to write quickly from the board, so why with dyslexia is he expected to correct something that he has no power over?"

Liz and Matt followed the National Curriculum loosely, adapting it to suit him. Liz says, "Matt is a visual thinker so we did as many field trips as we could. For example, when doing geography, we tracked our local river to its source and took photos all along its path tracking it to the estuary. He looked at erosion and measured flow rates. We have travelled around the UK looking at various landforms, the Lake District, the Peak District and our local coastline. If we could not see something visually we have used clay to understand the concept." Matt has had plenty of opportunity to socialise and play sport too. He plays, teaches and umpires at his local hockey club.

Possible hurdles

Some local authorities may pay more attention to your plans for home education than others. You may be asked to arrange a meeting or the authority may ask for a home visit. You do not have to meet with representatives of the local authority and could, instead, supply them with written evidence of the work you are doing. Remember that it is your choice to home educate your child, and you do not have to justify this to the local authority.

How to do it?

Many parents are daunted by the idea of planning a whole day, or week, or term of schoolwork, but in reality home education is rarely 'school at home'. Dr Rothermel explains, "Children who are home educated are not necessarily trained to sit and study at a desk for hours. Many home educating families spend an hour a day on formal study, some as little as an hour a week. If you are worried about withdrawing your child, don't focus on keeping up with schoolwork. Your role as a home educating parent is to give them the skills to find things out for themselves.

"Your child will learn through all the things they are exposed to that children miss while they are at school. This could be a visit from a man to fix the washing machine, or you may have them with you when you go to the bank or lawyer. One criticism of home educated children is that their language is too advanced for their age, but this is the natural consequence of what they absorb from all these day to day interactions. Life and learning merge after a while."

Your qualifications

You may worry, when embarking on home education, that perhaps you should be a teacher, or have a degree. In fact, no parental qualifications are necessary, just a willingness to help your child and look for resources that will inspire their interest. Join a support group, either online or in your local area, and you will find a whole range of mums and dads who are involved in home education, from different educational backgrounds. Look for Local Groups on the Education Otherwise website: Education Otherwise is happy to accept members who are not yet home educating.

Dr Rothermel says, "Every home educating parent will have moments of doubt whether they are doing the right thing. This can be reinforced by pressure from relatives, other parents and the local authority. If you are even considering home education, join a local group and sign up to an email group. The national email list 'UK home ed' is found at **www.home-education.org.uk**. That way you can find out about your options. You have the support in place if you need.

"There are more other people home educating than you think. You might want to attend a local home ed group before making a decision about what is right for your child. Some parents go along for a day or even try it for a month before making a final decision."

You will probably find that you learn lots of things alongside your child as you study new subjects together. If you don't know where to start when looking into a new subject, ask your local librarian to point you towards some good books on the subject. You will find the library a great resource, and may regularly order and take out books on subjects that interest your child.

Your time

Educating your child at home is a major commitment of your time. Some parents successfully run a business from home alongside educating their children, but many make it their full-time job. If you would struggle financially to do this, could you share home education with another family? Talk to your local Citizens Advice Bureau or Jobcentre and check whether you are getting all the benefits you are entitled to.

What you don't need to do

If you are starting home education, it is helpful to note that you do not need to follow the national curriculum, nor do your children need to take SATs. Don't ignore the curriculum altogether, as it may be a good place to look if you are lacking ideas and inspiration, but you can pull out parts that appeal to you and your children and treat it as one of many useful resources.

You do not need to stick to a 9am to 3pm timetable, or any timetable at all. Learning can take place at any time of the year, which has many advantages. You can plan trips and visits at times when facilities are at their quietest, or choose good weather for outdoor learning.

Do not feel you have to focus on exams and qualifications either. Dr Rothermel says, "Home educated children don't need to do exams at the same time as they would have at school. They may take one or two GCSEs early, in topics which interest them, or do them later. Many home educated children go on to FE colleges. They are self motivated to study from early on. FE colleges are often open to taking on home educated kids and may ask to see a portfolio of work in place of exam passes.

If your child wants to go to university they may choose to go straight to A levels and skip GCSEs. However, they may not decide this until they're in their 20s, when it can be much easier to take A levels."

See Chapters 6 and 7 for more information on GSCEs and A levels outside school, and how older children can opt into exam systems.

Home ed in practice

It can take both parents and children some time to adapt to home education. Think about whether you want to follow an informal system, based on your child's interests, or whether you will all benefit from a timetable. Many families start off with one approach and change as they find what works for them.

Veronika has educated her daughters at home since they were small. She says, "Life isn't neatly divided into subjects which you drop at the clang of the bell. When we are working on something at home, my daughters might ask if it is science, or art, but the projects we work on cross many areas of learning. We have the freedom to pursue something for as long as the girls are interested, be it three months working on a nature garden, or a question that can be answered in three minutes."

Veronika aims to let her daughters lead the way in choosing what to learn. She says, "At school, learning can be very much controlled by the teacher, and some parents who home educate try to control what their child learns too. But I find many parents fall away from that. Following your child's interests works beautifully. You are always learning something. We talk non -stop if we are walking or shopping. And although we don't go away that often, if I have to give a talk the kids can come with me. We all went to Ireland to tie in with a talk I was giving on home education."

At the age of 11, older daughter Bethany developed an interest in school, so she and Veronika went to have a look. Veronika says, "Initially Eliza, nine, wasn't interested at all, but she changed her mind after Bethany and I paid a visit. Both the girls started school at the start of the summer term. Initially they loved it and were up at six, thrilled to be putting on their uniforms, and experiencing school life like they had read about.

"That soon changed. It wasn't just the morning routine, although we all found it hard to get the girls breakfasted and on the bus. Eliza started to say that she had only had one good lesson that day, and then complained that the following week, because there was a substitute teacher, she didn't even have the lesson she enjoyed. We talked about it, the girls had made friends, but they saw the good things about being educated at home too, and after eight months both girls decided to be home educated again."

Veronika had noticed physical and emotional changes over the time her children were at school. She says, "At the end of the day they just wanted to blob. We had more back chat too. All of that gradually slipped away once they stopped school. I'm no longer the enemy either. While they were at school I enjoyed the time I had to get on with my work, but it feels like we are a family again now. We see each other in all our phases, our ups and downs.

"Now the girls are back to working on home education projects which interest them. They each have a month to find out about a different composer, find a piece of music, and read about his life. At the end of the month each of the girls will present what they have found to the family, and might play some of the music too. I encourage them to look in book-shops and use the library as well as the internet. We don't grade their work, so they don't become emotionally dependent on learning to get good grades or a star. I hope they will learn because they want to learn. My nine year old could tell you anything about the Romans or Jupiter, because she has a passion for finding out. When they grow up I hope this will enable them to spend their life doing something they love."

Deschooling

Many home educated children have gone through a time, varying from a few weeks to a few months or longer, of 'deschooling'. This time without formal lessons can help a child adjust to the more flexible approach of home education, and let them think about what interests them, away from a rigid school timetable.

Unschooling or child-led learning

You may also hear people who know about home education mention unschooling, or child-led learning. This is the process where you allow your child to pursue their interests, knowing that they will acquire skills such as reading and writing while, for example, finding out all they can about anything from aeroplanes to Egyptians. Think about how much time you want to spend letting your children learn in this way. It can increase motivation. Some families spend part of the time on projects, which are initiated by the child, and part of their time on basic skills such as reading and writing.

Helen's daughters were very motivated to work at school, but hard work wasn't seen as cool by their peers. Helen says, "My eldest daughter's problems started in Year 7. She was anxious at lunch times when areas were very crowded, and there was lots of difficult behaviour from other students. It was not directed towards my daughter, but made her feel very uncomfortable with the situation. The staff seemed ineffective, and let the loud mouths be heard, whilst the quieter kids were left behind.

In the end, Helen says, "We decided that school was doing more harm than good for our kids and the way forward was to home ed. The girls were anxious every Sunday evening, and sometimes sick with fear. They couldn't eat breakfast in the morning, were tearful, and even fearful to go out of the house. We took a two-week 'holiday' from school to see how they felt about home ed before informing the schools involved. We sent in a standard deregulation letter, and were slightly surprised that the school didn't even acknowledge receipt of the letter. They simply passed it straight on to the LEA."

Helen has some advice for anyone who is worried about how their child is getting on at school and considering home education: "Get in touch with your school. Don't wait too long for problems to ease – you know your child better than anyone, go with your gut instinct. Get in touch with the LEA and Education Otherwise, go to local home ed groups, speak with as many people as possible to make an informed choice."

Helen's daughters have thrived on home education. She says, "My younger one is relaxed and focused on learning. She enjoys learning music, going to Education Otherwise groups and many other groups. She says she might like to try high school, which we will fully support her with if that remains her choice. Of course, I no longer work as I am at home with the kids so our finances can be difficult. It took the kids a long while to recover, but they have now got a positive outlook on the world and are not fearful of situations."

Staying sane when you home educate

When your child was little, you may have been to mother and baby groups where everyone compared when their children were walking, talking and potty training. It can be the same at the school gate. If you choose to home educate, Dr Rothermel explains, "you have to accept that you are not in the same race as everyone else, and your child doesn't have to jump through hoops at the same time. Some parents will still ask you, 'My son is on level nine, what is yours doing now you are not at school?' You just have to realise that you don't have to compete."

Classes, museums and other trips

You do not have to limit your learning to the home. Open up the home education experience to take advantage of all the resources around you. Can you go to a park or into the countryside to look at plants and animals, or study geology and geography? Are there museums which are full of ideas to help your child find out more about subjects of interest? And are there classes which they might like to join in? Many home educated children play sport in a team or enjoy learning music outside the home. Check out what is available in your local area and see how it can support your home learning.

However many classes you organise, your child will also need to develop some resources of their own. Dr Rothermel explains, "A home educated child needs to be one who is happy with their own company. Even if you organise some shared classes or clubs, there will be times when they need to get on with their own projects while mum or dad works from home, for example."

Groups, camps, conferences and events

You don't have to home educate your child in isolation. There are networks of home educating families across the UK. Look on the Education Otherwise website for a list of local contacts. Local groups will vary in size. There are also occasional camps and conferences which can help inspire and motivate you.

LEARNING ZONE – HOME ED ON THE ISLE OF WIGHT

The Isle of Wight is home to a large home ed group, with up to 65 families as members. In the group, there are around 60 primary age and 60 secondary age children. There are also around eight young adults aged 16 to 19.

Mum of three Bex Smith explains a little about what the group does: "I don't think there is such a thing as a typical month in the Learning Zone (LZ) calendar. Events often follow a seasonal bent and may be organised around what the weather is doing. In the summer we have camps, a cardboard boat regatta, and walks. The winter months have seen a regular weekly club, which offers a variety of activities for all ages of children. It is open to all zone members and we pay subs to cover the hall hire.

There is a LZ choir, made up of parents and children, so we pay for things like our singing teacher to coach us. At the club the kids get to do cooking, music, or drama. A group of older kids are currently working doing a full production of Twelfth Night at a local arts centre, which will count towards two members' GCSE oral exam marks. We have had talks from the local zoo and bat hospital, and a workshop using Fimo which was a great success. LZ members put on an art exhibition in Ryde library which included works of art from all ages. My oldest daughter, Freya, was chuffed to bits that her painting was put up."

Members often use their own talents to teach something to the group. With more than 100 adults taking part there is always someone who has expertise in a particular area. Bex explains, "I took a sewing machine in one week and we did a teddy making session. Another mum took her hand sewing machine, which was great to show the differences between old and new. Some of the kids would have said that they weren't interested in sewing, but with the opportunity in front of them they loved it."

Learning Zone children also get the chance to take part in activities like country dancing, and outdoor games in the playground as the club is held at a large youth centre. Bex says, "In the summer this particular club will quite probably make way for other activities that are much more outdoors based." The group also holds a monthly committee meeting and an annual AGM, in order to meet requirements of being a registered charity.

Parents and children both get a lot out of being part of the Learning Zone. Bex Smith again: "It is not just the social side. The first thing that a non-HE person will ask is, 'How on earth do they get enough social inter-action when not in school?' In reality they get far more, with children and adults from all walks of life, and all ages; currently my children have friends who are aged from two right through to 15 plus, and they get on well with all of them, and they're friends with many adults too. They get to work with other children, and have the opportunity to do group activities and projects.

"As a parent, I get loads from being a part of the Zone too. The community feel is fantastic. I know parents who share similar aims to my own, who I can share experiences with, can look to for advice and sugges-tions if I am unsure which way to do something, or even look to for inspiration if my children want to do something which is beyond my knowledge or experience. As one example, my middle son, Ferdy, has said he wants to learn to play trumpet. We have one, but don't know how to play. I chatted to a dad at our weekly club who plays a few brass instruments and he is happy to help Ferdy get started.

"A group of parents has got together in the last few months and created our own band which will provide music for some ceilidh dances at the Christmas party. If there are other things going on around the Island then families may get involved as a result of the information being spread through the LZ grapevine. LZ is more than just a group of home educators, invariably it becomes a group of friends who are there on many levels."

Bex joined the group within a couple of months of moving to the island, "My youngest, Felix, was just nine days old, and it was our first outing from the house. I was daft enough to put my hand up when they wanted someone to do the newsletter, and I have to say that jumping in at the deep end has definitely been worth it. I am not normally good at putting myself forward: self-confidence has always been a major issue for me. Two years on I feel very much a part of the Zone, my own self-confidence has grown, as well as my confidence in my ability to provide enough interest and variety for my children to learn what they need to at least in these early years of their 'school' life.

"The reports I have had from our local EOTAS [Education Other Than at School] lady have been very positive, and make it sound like we do loads more than I ever give myself credit for doing with the kids. "

Home educating in a family

It is very common to home educate one child while others go to school. A child who is happy at school will not thank you for taking them out, even if you are home educating a sibling. Children who are home educated may ask at some point to opt back in to school, perhaps because they want to try secondary school. Home education is enormously child centred, so children usually get the choice to go to school if they want. It is rare for a child to be exclusively home educated up to 18.

Cost

All this talk of trips and classes may make you worry about the cost of home education. There is no financial support from local authorities towards home education, and the time commitment can leave two-parent families relying on a single income. Single parents can feel stretched trying to juggle looking after a child and earning a living, while any parent may occasionally wish for the respite that school used to offer. With time, you will get to know how to keep the cost of home education manageable.

Make the most of libraries and free museum entry. Friends and family can be a valuable, yet free, source of expertise in different areas and may be delighted to help an interested youngster who wants to hear all about something they share a passion for. You will also get to know which resources you have to pay for, and can stock up on paper and art materials in the sales. The internet offers an enormous range of resources. You may want to subscribe at home, or make use of free internet access at your local library.

Home education can lead you to take a fresh look at how you live. Many parents who home educate are committed to a healthy lifestyle. Growing vegetables and cooking meals from scratch can be part of the learning experience for your child, and help you keep your budget under control too. And finally, of course, you can take holidays at times which suit you, avoiding costly school holidays. House swaps may be a good way to get time away without breaking the budget.

Flexischooling

Before you go all out for full-time home education, you may want to look into flexischooling. This approach allows a child to remain registered at a school while having time out to meet their needs. This can work for a child who has problems with a full-time school day due to health issues or school phobia, or may work well for parents who feel that the school is not meeting their child's needs in some way.

The parent agrees with the head and class teacher that the child will attend school for, say, mornings only, either indefinitely, or for a term or year. This approach relies on the agreement of the head, and will only succeed if the class teacher also is committed. Otherwise, a child can end up feeling that they are missing out on part of school life. You may want to spend the time your child is not at school doing some one-to-one study, or different activities. You will need to talk to the school about a co-operative approach to covering the same curriculum.

If you need help to convince the school, you need to quote Section 444 of the Education Act 1996 which explains how the school can deal with 'irregular attendance' in England and Wales. The Act makes provision for leave to be granted from school by "any person authorised to do so by the governing body or proprietor of the school". There is no such provision in Scottish law, but of course that does not mean that you could not discuss flexischooling with a co-operative teacher.

Tutoring

Many parents do not feel that they know enough to teach their own children. You may feel well equipped to help with some subjects and not others. A home tutor could be just what you need to get some external input. This individualised help comes at a price, of course. The Good Schools Guide quotes prices ranging from £15 to £60 per hour.

Finding a tutor

Tutors do not have to have specialist qualifications – anyone can advertise their services, so you may want to ask about their previous experience and qualifications. There are lots of online directories too: find out whether they simply act as central check point for tutors' qualifications and certificates, or whether they meet and interview each tutor. Get references, or a personal recommendation. You may want to look for someone who has a current CRB check (a check that they have no criminal record). If your child wants to take specific exams or qualifications, make sure the tutor is familiar with the requirements.

Beyond the basics, and perhaps most importantly, you also want someone who can inspire and challenge your child. If you meet the tutor by yourself initially, it can be worth meeting them with your child too, so you can see how they get on. If you go through an agency, do insist on meeting the tutor before committing to anything. Look out for free introductory lessons, and you may want to shop around before signing up to a long series of lessons.

What to ask

Find out what resources the tutor provides, and what they will want you to supply in the way of books or computer facilities. How often do they suggest meeting your child and what work will they set for completion in between? Ask how they will keep you up to date on your child's progress.

Rosie took her son out of school and arranged for him to go to a number of tutors. She explains why: "After Tom's father died, he managed to hold everything together, just, until he took his 11 plus. I think he just let go emotionally after that, and his behaviour at school deteriorated. We'd had intermittent behaviour problems for years because he's very bright and has Asperger's. This time the school handled it badly and Tom was in no state to cope.

"He'd been seen for years by a wonderful clinical psychologist and she came to the school with me and explained that their approach was likely to make things worse, and outlined techniques that could help. His form teacher was hugely supportive, but the head teacher refused to budge and insisted that bad behaviour must always be punished. I just couldn't bear to see him so miserable, and his behaviour at home was dreadful as a result of all the stress. As he had only two terms of Year 6 left to go I decided to get him out of school before he became any more unhappy."

Rosie had a friend who was a maths tutor who put her in touch with other tutors. She says, "I organised a timetable for Tom which involved 15 tutors in all. We met them all to ensure Tom got on with them. He spent three hours each morning split between two tutors. I picked him up at 12.30 and in the afternoon a tutor would come to the house. I looked for people who weren't bound by conventional approaches to teaching as Tom thrives on the stimulation of doing things differently – day visits, field trips and plenty of variety.

"We started with a good range of tutors, with a bias towards Tom's favourite subjects, but over the two terms a couple left and I added one or two. In the end he studied maths, science, biology, English, drama (he took his LAMDA grade exams), history, geography, Chinese, cookery, touch typing, IT (he built his own website), animation, natural history, gardening, music (mostly studying film scores), art, design technology, circus skills, martial arts, tae kwon do and squash.

"The best tutors were the ones who steered clear of the conventional 'sit down with a workbook and pencil' approach and went for more novel ways of teaching. I can certainly say that Tom learned far more about a wide range of topics than he would have done if he'd stayed at school. And he was blissfully happy – countless people commented on what a different child he was, not just from the months leading up to taking him out of school, but different from how he'd been for years.

Rosie found using tutors expensive, but was able to do it for the six months until Tom started at grammar school. She says, "The tutors mostly charged around £23 an hour and he had four and a half to five hours tutoring a day. I reckoned that this worked out at about the same cost as a good public school, and less than some.

"The biggest problem was that tutors would occasionally phone or email and say, 'Sorry, I can't do this week'. I remember one week when five of them pulled out. That was a nightmare to reorganise as Tom got very bored if his day wasn't reasonably full. If I did it again I would have fewer tutors covering more topics each. Another difficulty was that although I work full-time from home, there are times when I need to be out or away. I'd been used to the boys being at school from 8.30 to 4.30, but suddenly I had a child at home in the middle of the day who was too young to be left unsupervised."

Chapter 6

Education 11-16

Entering secondary school can bring up a range of new challenges. Some kids relish the greater freedom, but for many a bigger school can seem overwhelming. The pressure starts to grow to pass exams and make life choices too. Read on to find some different ways to approach these challenges. This chapter also looks at the types of bullying that are more likely to crop up at secondary school and how to deal with it.

THE FIRST YEARS OF SECONDARY SCHOOL

Children in the first few years of secondary school may find themselves learning in a very different way from before. There will be tests, more homework and ongoing assessments. Some children struggle with the increased academic demands. Here are some ideas to help them keep up:

- Make a routine. Find your child a quiet place to study and help them to do their homework at the same time every day. You may need to be available for encouragement.

- Keep younger siblings entertained with a quiet activity at this time to support your older child.

- Some children may not know where to start. Maybe they want to start with something difficult to get it out of the way. Doing an easy piece of work first can help a child get going, but you may need to make sure that the harder stuff is done next.

- Find out which homework has to be in when to help them prioritise.

- Ask the teacher how long they should be studying for each evening. Most children are tired at the end of the day, so keep the time spent on homework to a manageable level.

- Sometimes it is better to take a break from a big piece of work and try again later.

- Know when it is time to stop. A child can make less and less progress as it gets later in the evening. Occasionally it may be best to tell them to stop, even if you have to explain to a teacher why they could not complete the work.

- Allow time for your child to relax and wind down. Have a chat over a piece of toast about how the day has gone, or play some games to make a break between homework and bedtime. A good night's sleep makes it easier for them to do well at school the next day.

- Be interested in their work. Talk about what they are studying. If they are interested in a topic help them find library books or websites, or take the family on a relevant trip. Ask the teacher for ideas to help your child in subjects where they struggle.

- Praise your child whenever you can. This might be for great results, or for sticking at something they find hard.

SECOND STAGES

From Year 9 your child will be making choices about their future. They will need to decide which GSCEs to take. This decision can seem overwhelming at the age of 13, and there can be enormous pressure to get it right. Most schools will require your child to take a core of subjects including maths and English and science, and your child may be left with only a small range of choices.

Career choices

Now is a good time to explore career choices with your child. Many children at this age have little or no idea what they want to do. While it can be useful to look at which subjects will help them in later life, they also need to know that it is worthwhile picking subjects that they enjoy. And it is entirely possible to study for an additional GCSE later in life if needed. It is one of those areas where many people will look back and wonder what all the stress and pressure was about when, a few years down the line, interviewers rarely if ever want to know about GSCE subjects or even results.

There are other options too. You child may prefer a more vocational BTEC or OCR Nationals course in subjects like art and design, business, health and social care, science or sport. Some schools can offer these courses at age 14 to 16 alongside courses in Key Skills such as English and maths.

Doing it differently

If your child is struggling at school or you are considering home education, you may be worrying about GCSEs and A levels. Don't feel that there is only one way to succeed in life, which involves passing several GCSEs in one sitting at school. There are other routes which still allow your child the possibility to go on to further or higher education, or into vocational training to do something they enjoy. In England, a new Diploma for 14 to 19 year olds is being rolled out, and will combine literacy and numeracy with skills for life and the option to focus on a vocational area such as engineering in a practical way.

Matt has dyslexia and studies at home. He decided to take GCSEs in physics, chemistry, biology, geography, English, maths and ICT. His mother, Liz says, "We were lucky enough to find Sheffield College online learning. They have inspired him and turned around his previous failure at Key Stage 1 and 2 to find that although dyslexic he is talented at English.

"From dreading having to do English at GCSE, he has been nurtured to develop a love of writing and carried on to A level. His educational psychologist also suggested that he did a touch typing course at the Helen Arkell Centre which has made life so much better for him when writing for English. I'm delighted that he obtained excellent grades for all his GCSEs and is now taking four AS levels."

Correspondence courses

It is possible for children to study remotely, using the post, email and the internet to enable them to learn, submit work and have it assessed. There are a small number of providers who offer Key Stage 3 courses for 11 to 14 year olds, as well as GCSE and A level courses. This sort of provision can be a boon to any parent who wants help in deciding what to study, and in delivering it.

Key Stage 3

At Key Stage 3 there is a limited range of distance learning subjects available, including maths, English and science and history. There are many more subjects available if you look in a bookshop, and of course at this stage you do not need to be restricted to the Key Stage course. However, if you are thinking of entering your child for GCSEs it can make things easier if they have gone through the Key Stage 3 work first.

Jenny Langmead, head of Little Arthur School, says, "GCSE courses rarely spend much time on elementary principles. The usual outcome of this is that the child gets frustrated and soon gives up. I do think it's important that parents take a longer term view of where they're going with home education. If they and their children want to reject formal exams, fine, but, if they hope to equip their children with GCSEs, it's far less painful to slowly work through Key Stage 3 topics during the 11 to 14 period."

Little Arthur School is an independent school on the Isles of Scilly, geared exclusively to the needs of home educated children. Head teacher Jenny Langmead says, "We offer a service to parents who really want to provide the same sort of education that their kids would get at school. For 11 to 14 year olds we offer English, maths and science. Families who sign up get sent a file of work. You need to work through each part with your child and then send in an assignment. We suggest you aim to complete one assignment each month, but some families complete the whole file in six months while others take three years. It is important to work with your child at this age. They do not yet have the motivation to just get on with it by themselves."

Services like that offered by Little Arthur can help parents who are unsure about educating their child themselves. Jenny explains, "When you send in the assignment you get the feedback to reassure you how your child is getting on. If you're stuck, we can send help sheets, and we can share with you examples of the sort of work your child should be aiming for. Parents can find it very hard when faced by a wall of books in a book shop to know what to choose: our courses make it easier. It can be difficult to assess your child's work too."

Jenny set up the school when home educating her children, in response to the lack of support available for parents. She explains, "We don't offer 24-hour a day support or online provision, because we are aiming to keep the costs down. Our Key Stage 3 courses cost in the region of £105, and IGCSEs cost around £145. If you have more than one child you can photocopy the worksheets and simply pay for extra marking."

Older children can study University of Cambridge International GCSEs through Little Arthur. There is a wider choice of subjects, and by this stage children may be more motivated to study. They are sent text books and 10 to 12 assignments. After that they can complete a mock exam, and further exam practice is available if needed.

GCSEs

A range of distance learning subjects are available for GCSEs. You may need to opt for courses which are assessed by examination rather than coursework if you are studying from home. It is harder to study experimental subjects like physics and chemistry without lab facilities, but some providers have adapted the courses so these subjects can still be taken. If you are thinking of entering your child for GCSE courses, it pays to plan ahead.

Jenny Langmead says, "Many parents are unaware of the actuality of taking IGCSE exams: both the cost and the time involved in locating an exam centre and in registering for exams. Because children in school do not pay for exams, the cost often comes as a shock. Also, a lot of parents fail to appreciate that exams need to be registered for a long way in advance. Many people find it hard to locate an exam centre which will accept them. A lot of correspondence courses offer to mark course work. Unfortunately, they don't point out that exam centres are often unwilling to accept course work set and written by teachers not in the school. Parents really need to be aware of the pitfalls when considering exam options."

Examples of GSCEs available by distance learning include:

- Additional Science
- Biology
- Business Studies
- Chemistry
- Child Development
- Economics
- English Language
- English Literature
- French
- Geography
- History
- Information & Communication Technology
- Law
- Mathematics
- Physics
- Psychology
- Science
- Sociology
- Spanish

Some distance learning providers

Edexcel: Provides IGCSEs which home educated children can take as private candidates – **www.edexcel-international.org** 01204 770696.

Oxford Home Schooling: GCSEs and Key Stage three and A levels – **www.oxfordhomeschooling.co.uk** 0800 0111 024.

The Sheffield College: English at GSCE and A Level by online learning – **www.sheffcol.ac.uk** 0114 260 3603.

National Extension College: GCSEs and A levels – www.nec.ac.uk 0800 389 2839.

Little Arthur Independent School: Key Stage three and IGCSEs – **www.littlearthur.org.uk** 01720 422457.

Checks and accreditation

You should make some checks before paying for a distance learning course. Look for colleges which are accredited by the Open and Distance Learning Quality Council (ODLQC). Check exactly what qualification is being offered and whether there is a refund policy. Make sure you are clear about the level of tutor support and whether this will be enough for you and your child. You may want to ask to see an example of course materials before signing up, or get recommendations from satisfied students.

Local FE colleges

If your child has reached 16 and needs a GCSE in a fundamental subject like maths or English, your local college of further education is likely to have these courses on offer. They are less likely to make the courses available to under-16s, but check with the principal as this decision is up to them.

> Emily is studying GCSE German, English, and maths through a distance learning company. It sends all the materials and marks course work but does not provide exam venues. Mum Helen says, "We have to find an exam venue that is wiling to accept private candidates and of course pay the costs involved."
>
> Emily is also studying at home for IGCSEs in biology, French, history and geography. Helen explains, "These are much more straightforward. We purchase books from any bookshop for approx £16 and then pay a further £99 to a company who provide the exam venue in either Bristol or London. Had we realised this option was available, we probably would have taken this route for the other subjects too. IGCSEs are recognised by colleges here in the UK. Just like GCSEs you need five with a pass mark of C or above to gain a place. We have recently found out that some colleges take students without GCSEs. Instead they offer an interview as selection. It is interesting should you not want to go down the GCSE route. It seems much of a postcode lottery though, as some of ours offer that and others not."

BULLYING FOR BIG KIDS

There are some sorts of bullying that happen mainly to children at secondary school. This section gives you some pointers if your child is being subjected to cyber bullying or racist or homophobic bullying.

Cyber bullying and mobile phone abuse

It can be very frightening to receive a threatening phone call, text or email, and unfortunately children can find themselves being bullied in this way. Some may have rude or abusive posts made about them online. It can seem hard to know what to do to solve the problem, but a lot of the messages or posts will be illegal, and the police, phone company or internet service provider can work with you to get the bullying stopped.

Net names

If your child gets an abusive email, tell them not to delete it. Contact the company providing the sender's email facilities (such as Hotmail) with details of the email. Even if the sender is using an anonymous email address, the company can use information contained in the email to track them down.

Website gossip

If a website is displaying rumours or abuse about your child, get in touch with the internet service provider. The company hosting the site can find the owner and ask them to remove the problem content, or take down the site.

Phone abuse

If your child is on the receiving end of silent calls or gets threatening messages, note down when the calls took place and what was said. If a message is left, keep that too. This provides the police with evidence of harassment. Even if the caller is anonymous, the police can get mobile phone service providers to find which phone a call was made from. The simplest way to protect your child in this situation may be to change their phone number by buying another SIM card

TIPS FOR YOUR TEEN

Help your child to stay safe by chatting about the following tips:

● Don't give out personal details online.

● Only answer phone numbers you recognise.

● Just say 'hello' when you answer your phone and leave the caller to say who they are.

● Share your phone number only with people who need to know it.

● Don't flash your phone in public.

● Show abusive texts or email to your parents.

Homophobic and racist bullying

Make sure your child is clear that no one has the right to call them names. The Equality Act (Sexual Orientation) Regulations 2007 outlaw discrimination against pupils on grounds of their sexual orientation. This means that schools must deal with bullying on grounds of actual (or perceived) sexual orientation as seriously as bullying on grounds of race, gender, disability, religion or belief, and age.

It is easy for the usual cliques and friendships that form in school to turn into bullying, sometimes on the grounds of race. Equal opportunities consultant Kamaljeet Jandu says, "The heads and leaders of any school need to clearly state their zero tolerance of bullying, in particular racist bullying. They need to employ a programme of awareness raising with teachers, Governors pupils and the parents. The awareness raising should include:

- What is racist bullying
- Acceptable and unacceptable behaviour
- Clear system of redress
- Possible penalties if proven guilty

"All new pupils and parents should be made aware of racist bullying and potential disciplinary measures."

Bexhill High School has been working to improve the way students treat each other and members of the local community in and out of school. Student support co-ordinator Trudy Hillman says, "Two students approached us, concerned about racist comments which were from fellow students, mainly outside school. In school there were clear ways to report and deal with racist bullying, but it was less clear to the students what they could do outside school."

Bexhill High has relatively few students from ethnic minorities, which could have left them feeling isolated. Instead, the school decided to use Anti Bullying Week to tackle the issue head on.

Hillman explains, "Students ran an experiment where some kids were given a red card and others a green one. With the assistance of senior staff they explained that those with green cards could come in later, go home earlier and go first in the dinner queue. This led to a discussion in assembly about how students felt being discriminated against based on a colour. This was backed up by activities in form time to carry on the message. Students looked at what had happened in Rwanda, for example.

We also ran a Football Against Racism tournament, which got the message to a different group of students. The student leadership body, about 100 students, were out and about with flyers to engage younger students in discussion about racism and its impact."

Since that week in October, Hillman says, "the school has been looking together at how we want people to treat each other. Students have been working together in form time to come up with ideas which will become a charter. We are asking questions like, 'If your mum came into school, how would you like people to treat her?' Pupils have been sharing experiences of racism in class. Every student has been given small tasks to do on a daily basis over a period of two weeks. One day we asked them all to hold a door open for someone, on another to smile at a stranger. We then talk about the response they got."

Some children may be bullied and called 'gay' or subjected to other homophobic attacks. Nigel Tart of Schools Out says, "Unfounded fear of Section 28 led most schools to censor LGBT [Lesbian, Gay, Bisexual or Transgender] issues from the curriculum. Many teachers even believed it prevented them from challenging homophobic bullying. Even now, most teachers are unaware of their legal responsibilities to create a safe and supportive learning environment."

Tart continues, "The period between self-identifying as LGBT and coming out to other people (on average two or three years) makes LGBT young people particularly vulnerable. Homophobic and transphobic bullying usually goes unreported – partly because the target knows little will be done about it, but mainly because of the stigma attached to LGBT identities. Parents shouldn't assume their children will confide in them. Kids are bombarded with cultural homophobia every single day, so even a throwaway comment about a gay TV character can jeopardise their confidence in you.

Also, don't forget: many straight kids experience homophobic bullying too and are just as likely not to confide."

The Schools Out website [**www.schools-out.org.uk**] contains model anti-bullying and equal opportunities policies with guidelines for their implementation, as well as a Student Toolkit for dealing with homophobia and transphobia. Tart concludes, "Anti-bullying measures are essential, but schools really need to proactively challenge the stigma by reintroducing LGBT issues into the curriculum. LGBT History Month (every February) is an excellent starting place, and **www.lgbthistorymonth.org.uk** has some excellent education resources."

Both racist and homophobic bullying should be included in a school's anti-bullying strategy. School staff need to be committed to develop, implement and monitor the policy. Citizenship lessons can help children look at how to beat prejudice and discrimination. There is a history of reticence when it comes to addressing lesbian, bisexual, gay and transgender issues in schools. Children may only come across the subject in a negative way when discussing sexually transmitted diseases in PSHE classes.

As well as Schools Out, Stonewall has a range of materials to help students and schools at **www.stonewall.org.uk**. There is advice on dealing with bullying on the Equality and Human Right Commission website at **www.equalityhumanrights.com**.

MORE HELP

Get more help and advice about stopping bullying from BullyingUK [**www.bullying.co.uk**]. Your child can also call Connexions Direct for free confidential advice on almost any issue relevant to 13 to 19 year olds, from health to studying – 08080 013 219 **www.connexions-direct.com**.

Chapter 7

Education post 16

In some ways, it becomes easier to deal with school problems after the age of 16. School is no longer compulsory. But what do you do if your nearly adult child is keen to continue their education, but experiences problems while they are learning?

PARENTING PRINCIPLES

Parentline Plus has some great principles for dealing with teenagers, based on freedom, love, listening, privacy and setting boundaries. It is difficult to negotiate the fine line between letting teens have the freedom to make their own decisions, and setting enough boundaries for them to feel cared for. Teenagers will often want to make decisions alone, even if they then need your help to deal with the consequences. Setting careful boundaries can help them make choices safely. Show them that you feel that their thoughts matter. Listen to their views, and practise negotiating outcomes that work for both of you. Bear these ideas in mind and they will help when you and your 16 or 17 year old are negotiating your way through further education. Visit **www. parentlineplus.org.uk** for more help.

Your teen's options

Most 16 year olds will have looked at their options while in Year 11 and already have ideas about whether they want to continue to study, and where. The usual options include:

- continuing at their current school
- moving to a different school
- moving to a local sixth form college or further education college

Teenagers can also opt for A levels or choose work-related qualifications such as BTECs, City & Guilds and OCR Nationals. Different schools and colleges offer different balances between vocational and academic courses.

Starting college

If your teenager has made the choice to study full-time and passed the GSCEs they need to get into the college they want, you hope that everything will be straightforward. There can be teething problems in the first few weeks. College work can be very different. It can take even the quickest student a while to adapt to the requirements of an A Level course. There are social challenges too. At a new college it can take time to find friends, and even at the same college different subject choices can mean that old friends don't often meet. If your teen is still struggling to make friends, encourage them to join clubs either at college or outside. Most colleges offer a range of different activities one afternoon a week where students get a chance to mix with new people and meet others who might share similar interests.

Study troubles

Whatever the teething problems, encourage your teenager to try things out for a few weeks, Find out if there is a parents' evening or other opportunity to discuss things with staff to sort out academic issues.

Changing course

Sometimes it won't be apparent until term starts and students are discussing their courses that there may be new and different subjects to study. It may be possible to change courses, especially if this is flagged up as early as possible, and this can make all the difference to how your child feels about studying.

Many colleges get students to take four AS levels, with the idea of dropping one subject at the end of the first year. If your child is struggling academically, they may want to drop one subject sooner to focus on doing well at the others. Check that the remaining subjects leave their options open for future career choices. Go back to Chapter 3 for more tips on working through issues with the school.

Stephanie says, "I was studying geography, photography and art. I didn't enjoy the first year. I'd found there was a lot of work and not enough time to do it. At secondary school with one lesson after another you were consistently busy, but there were lots more gaps between lessons, so I found it hard to get back into concentrating when I needed to. By the end of the year I was ready to leave."

Her mother, Sarah, continues the story, "We decided we needed to speak to the tutor before Stephanie decided to leave. We wanted to check they thought it was worth her going back, and to make sure that she was capable of doing the exams. The tutor was helpful and said it would be a shame to give up now."

Stephanie says, "I didn't want mum to phone my tutor at the time, but it did help, because the tutor hadn't been aware that I was so unhappy. He talked to me about planning my work, and giving myself time for study and time for fun. He suggested I didn't work on Sunday, say, and took one evening off, while setting free periods aside to do my work."

Sarah says, "That was great advice which came better from the tutors than from us as Stephanie's parents."

Stephanie also changed from studying photography to geology, which she preferred. She comments, "It was hard going, and I still felt like leaving at times. It was difficult at Christmas because the exams were coming up, and even after I got my results I didn't feel very motivated as I felt lots of my friends had done better."

Mum Sarah says, "We tried to break it down for Stephanie, and said, 'Go back in September and try it for six weeks until half term.' Then, we persuaded her it wasn't that long if she stayed and completed the term. Once we'd made it through Christmas it was really only one more term, and then it wasn't so hard to persuade her that it was worth doing the exams. I was a bit worried what would happen if we persuaded her to go back and she failed in the end, but that didn't happen."

Stephanie and her mum both agree that they are really pleased she hung in there and got grades that she was happy with. "I carried on and in the end I passed all my subjects. I'm pleased I have some qualifications and can go to uni if I want."

A levels are not the only option

Education in a school or college setting is not right for everyone. If your teenager is continually complaining about college, take a step back. Ask them why they chose to go, and what they would like to do in the future. It may be that college is necessary in order to achieve a career, or simply somewhere to go while they are working out what they want to do. Are they there because they want to be, or are they there because you expected them to go on to further education, regardless of their interests? Look again at their choice of course too.

> Eleanor is now 22 . At 16 she was quite clear about the career she wanted. She says, "I've been riding since I was eight or nine, and I knew I wanted to work with horses. I didn't see the point of doing A levels, but Mum and Dad were really keen. We came up with a compromise. I was down for one A level at my old school, one at an evening class, and my parents had agreed that I could spend the rest of the week training to become a riding instructor.
>
> "Going back to school part-time was awful, and I really wasn't interested in the evening class either. It was easy to skip classes and after the first term I just didn't go back at all. I'm now a qualified instructor. I run my own business and am fully booked for riding lessons every week, but I never completed the A levels."

Further ed, further away

There is scope to go away to study at this age, with financial assistance available if the course is not on offer within 15 miles of home. You can find out about applying for help with accommodation and travel costs under the Residential Support Scheme funded by the Learning and Skills Council. The grants of a few thousand pounds a year are based on household income and are available for up to three years.

Tom chose not to go on to study A levels but made the most of the options on offer to him to get started in a career in sport and leisure. He says, "I have dyslexia and swapped schools before GCSEs so I could take more practical subjects. After GCSEs I stayed on in the sixth form. My school offered a diploma of vocational education (DVE) so I took that alongside three more GSCEs at evening class.

"I'd really got into canoeing and wanted to do an outdoors course, but you have to be 17 or 18 to do many of the instructors' courses, so I felt a bit like I was filling in time doing the DVE. It was the first year the school had run the course and there were lots of people who were doing it because there was nothing else they wanted to do. Students kept missing deadlines for work, and the staff kept extending the deadlines. It all became a bit demotivating.

"There were some really good things at the school. The youth worker did an awful lot to help me organise things that I was interested in like going caving, canoeing or taking part in the Duke of Edinburgh's Award scheme. The careers office was a good resource too. They helped me find out about outdoor pursuits courses.

"I ended up working three or four days week to save up so I could go away to Bicton College of Agriculture in Budleigh Salterton to do a BTEC national diploma in outdoor leisure. That was brilliant. It gave me lots of insights into different areas. There was a bit of finance and accounting, marketing, and we learnt about websites. There was a good work placement too where I worked in a sports centre as a canoe instructor.

"The tuition fees were paid by the council, and I got some help from a grant and my parents towards my accommodation. I'd saved up enough to get through the first year, and the college accommodation was cheap. By the end of the second year I was £1000 overdrawn but that wasn't bad."

Other ways to get qualifications

At 16 it is possible to get qualifications without attending school or college five days a week. If your teenager's study arrangements aren't working out, here are some alternatives:

Further education colleges

FE colleges have many courses on offer which can be studied on a part-time or evening basis. Courses are generally free for 16 to 18 year olds. Your teen may prefer to have a part-time job and study part-time at a FE college.

Day release

If your teenager is interested in a vocational career there are advantages to looking into studying on a day release basis. They get practical experience plus training, and the chance to try out new skills in the workplace.

Helen says, "I didn't want to stay on after school, but fancied trying hairdressing. I got a job and spent one long day a week at college. I enjoyed the training, but the salon I worked in was awful. I didn't feel I was earning anything, rarely got the chance to practise what I was learning at college and usually got left just to clean up.

"I talked to the college. They were fairly helpful and suggested I looked round for other jobs. However, they were quite clear that it was essential that I had a job as it was part of the course requirements, and suggested I should stay at the salon until I found something else. It wasn't easy to find another job, especially as most of my time was spent working and studying. Mum and I looked around and eventually I found somewhere else to work where they would also let me do my training. It was much better as, although I still needed to sweep up and make the coffee, the owner made the time to ensure I got to practise too."

Evening classes

Taking a range of evening courses can give independent teens the freedom they want. Being part of a class of adult learners will bring them into contact with people with a wider range of experiences and different attitudes to studying, which can be helpful. Your teen should be able to get their course fees paid for if they are studying A levels, OCR Nationals or an equivalent.

Correspondence courses

It is possible to do A levels and many other qualifications by correspondence course, although you may need to pay for this. Most funding for 16 to 18 year olds is linked to attendance at a state funded school or college. Remember to add up all the costs. In addition to the course fee you may have to pay for books, equipment, and taking the examination. Also factor in travel and accommodation if there are residential elements to the course.

Think carefully before your teen embarks on a course like this and ask about the sort of support they receive. Correspondence courses will suit those who are motivated enough to study by themselves. Check the Open and Distance Learning Quality Council website [**www.odlqc.org.uk**] for a list of accredited colleges and courses. Look at the different providers and compare what they offer.

> Matt is taking four AS levels. He is studying maths and English by distance learning, and attends college to study the more practically based physics and chemistry. As Matt is dyslexic, he has a scribe to support him in his college courses: he knows someone is there if he has not finished, which lowers his anxiety levels enabling him to perform well.

> Matt's mum Liz says, "Matt has studied at home, taken correspondence and online courses, and is now enjoying college life part-time too. Our approach to his education means he has had time to develop as a whole person, enjoy his childhood and become part of his local community, and the community of home educated families. I think he will stand out on his UCAS form as he has learnt how to learn and take a certain amount of responsibility for his learning from a young age."

In it for the long term

There are highs and lows in every sixth former's college career. It can help if you are forewarned about the low points. Everyone struggles when there are assessments and coursework to complete, mid-year exams, mocks and of course the end of year exams.

Study struggles

In the run-up to exams, parents get the chance to repeat the advice that it does help to study in advance, and sometimes a teen's active social life has to suffer. This can be particularly hard if exams come straight after Christmas when the rest of the family is relaxing.

If you can encourage your child through each set of challenges, they will work out what method of study works for them. Some people always leave everything to the last minute. If you think this description fits your teen, you may need to acknowledge that all your exhortations may not be able to change this.

> Louisa says, "When I had exams coming up, I didn't like people thinking I was trying too hard. Some nights I'd watch TV, even if mum and dad were reminding me to work, and then start studying once everyone else had gone to bed. I did a lot of my revision this way. It just suited me better."

For some teenagers it may be necessary to let them muck about and even fail mid-term examinations in order for them to realise how much work they need to put in. This can be a time when you need to bite your tongue and acknowledge the pressure your child is under. Provide chocolate biscuits, cups of tea and a listening ear if needed.

Money problems

There may be financial pressure on all the family if a 16 or 17 year old is still studying. The Education Maintenance Allowance (EMA) is available to teens in full-time study from families with income under a certain threshold and offers £10, £20 or £30 a week to help out with the costs like books, travel or equipment. There may also be bonuses for meeting targets set by school or college. It is still available even if your teen has a part-time job, and doesn't affect parents' benefits.

Most sixth forms and colleges also have Learner Support Funds, for students facing financial hardship, to help with emergencies, childcare costs, and accommodation costs if your teenager has to live away from home, travel costs and essential course-related equipment, materials and field trips. The student support or welfare officer at the college can help you and your child find out more about this fund.

Young parents and studying

There is also help available for young parents who want to study, under the Care to Learn scheme. If your daughter becomes pregnant during her course, both of you should talk to her college about her options. Depending on the timing and the college, she may need to take some time out, or choose to carry on studying part or full-time. The education department at the local education authority should also be able to help, and possibly arrange home tuition if necessary.

Care to Learn can help pay for childcare and travel costs while young parents are studying. It is available for full and part-time courses as well as learning through work. If you are looking for independent advice for teen parents-to-be, look up your local Brook Centre or similar young people's service where counsellors can help explore feelings and give impartial information.

Teen choices

In summary, the most important thing to remember is that most teenagers have reached the stage where they want to make their own choices. Try to look at your own expectations for your children and separate them from their desires. It can be painful and fruitless to try to force your teen into a career path, however worthy or in their best interests. Instead, help them to work out their interests, give them plenty of information, and draw on your reserves of patience while they spend a few years working out their future.

Conclusion

I hope if you have got this far you have some ideas, and can start helping your child who hates school. This book is not going to solve your child's problems on its own, but I hope it has shown you that you don't have to solve things by yourself either.

Almost every parent worries that they are doing a bad job at one time or another, especially if their child is unhappy. You are doing the best you can, with the resources you have. Make time to look after yourself, and share your worries with a friend or your partner. If you have internet access, take advantage of some of the many parenting forums to find another mum or dad who is going through the same thing, or who perhaps has found a solution.

Whatever the cause of your child's problems, it can help if you listen to them. Whatever their age, they will feel better for having talked about the issue. They may have some ideas of how to improve things too. If your child is at a stage where they won't talk to you, think about who else they respect: a family friend, relative, or older teen may be the outlet they need.

If your child has a problem at school, ask yourself, "Who can help?", and talk to a teacher, your GP, or someone at the local authority. You will find that there are many people with access to resources that you didn't even know about. A referral for extra help at school, or to a group for kids with similar issues, may make a real difference to your child.

Few children get through growing up without some problems, and school life can seem like a battle. There are ways through it, and I hope that you and your child can successfully navigate the current hurdle, and go on to enjoy life again.

Useful contacts

We've put together a list of useful organisations to contact which are referred to in this book. As contact details often change we've put the list on our website where we can update it regularly, rather than printed it here. You can find the list at **www.whiteladderpress.com**; click on 'useful contacts' next to the information about this book.

If you don't have access to the Internet you can contact White Ladder Press by any of the means listed on the next page and we'll print off a hard copy and post it to you free of charge.

Contact us

You're welcome to contact White Ladder Press if you have any questions or comments for either us or the authors. Please use whichever of the following routes suits you.

Phone: **0208 334 1600**

Email: **enquiries@whiteladderpress.com**

Fax: **0208 334 1601**

Address: **2nd Floor, Westminster House, Kew Road, Richmond, Surrey TW9 2ND**

Website: **www.whiteladderpress.com**

What can our website do for you?

If you want more information about any of our books, you'll find it at **www.whiteladderpress.com**. In particular you'll find extracts from each of our books, and reviews of those that are already published. We also run special offers on future titles if you order online before publication. And you can request a copy of our free catalogue.

Many of our books have links pages, useful addresses and so on relevant to the subject of the book. You'll also find out a bit more about us and, if you're a writer yourself, you'll find our submission guidelines for authors. So please check us out and let us know if you have any comments, questions or suggestions.

Tidy Your Room

Getting your kids to do the things they hate

Are you sick of yelling at the kids to hang up their clothes? Tired of telling them to do their homework? Fed up nagging them to put their plate in the dishwasher? You're not the only one. Here, at last, is a practical guide to help you motivate them and get them on your side.

Parenting journalist Jane Bidder draws on the advice of many other parents as well as her own experience as a mother of three, to bring you this invaluable guide to getting your kids to do the things they hate.

The book includes:
- what chores are suitable at what age, and how to get them to co-operate
- getting homework done without stress
- where pocket money fits into the equation

Tidy Your Room is the book for any parent with a child from toddlerhood through to leaving home, and anyone who has ever had trouble getting their kids to do chores or homework. That's just about all of us, then.

Jane Bidder is a professional author and journalist who writes extensively for parents. She also writes fiction as Sophie King. She has three children, the eldest two of whom are now at university, so she has extensive personal as well as professional experience of getting kids to do the things they hate. She is the author of *What Every Parent Should Know Before Their Child Goes to University*.

£9.99

the art
of Hiding
Vegetables

sneaky ways to feed your children healthy food

How are you supposed to get your kids to eat the recommended five portions of fruit and vegetables a day? How do you get them to eat even one or two?

The answer is simple: you trick them into it. All you need to do is disguise or conceal healthy food and your children won't notice – or even know – they're eating it.

This is the real world, so you need practical ideas that will work in a busy household with a realistic budget. Well here, at last, you'll find the answers:

- how much is a portion of fruit or vegetables
- what to hide and how to hide it
- how to save time and effort
- how to feed the family a healthier diet than before (even if it isn't always perfect)
- ideas for breakfast, snacks, main meals, lunchboxes, parties, eating out and holidays

If you've already tried being honest with your kids and it hasn't worked, maybe it's time to start hiding the vegetables.

Karen Bali is a working mother of two who hates cooking and wanted to write a book to help other parents offer a healthier diet for the family. She has teamed up with Sally Child, an ex-health visitor turned nutritional therapist who has three grown-up children. Together they have written this guide to getting healthy food inside your kids with or without their co-operation.

No child should miss out on their future success because they lack fuel for learning at the start of the school day. Magic Breakfast (charity number: 1102510) provides nutritious breakfast food to primary schools in most need. Free of charge.

£9.99

THE PRINCE SCOWLED. HE FACED A pair of heavy gilded doors that were shut to him. From beyond, he could hear music and laughter. The party, *his party*, had already begun. Crystal clinked as guests toasted the night and wandered about the ornate ballroom, their eyes no doubt widening as they took in the hundreds of priceless objects that lined the walls. Beautiful vases, detailed portraits of faraway places, rich tapestries, and solid-gold serving plates were just a few of the many items. And they all paled in comparison to the beauty of the guests themselves. For the Prince did not invite just anyone to his parties. He invited only those he deemed beautiful enough to be in his presence. So they came from all over the world, each one as much on display as the inanimate objects in the room.

Standing in front of the closed doors, the Prince barely noticed the servants as they bustled about him, nervously putting the finishing touches on his costume. His majordomo hovered nearby, pocket watch in hand. The stuffy older man hated the Prince's utter lack of respect for time. In turn, the Prince took great pleasure in wasting the majordomo's. A maid stood next to the Prince, a feather brush in her hand. Gingerly, she painted a white line on the young man's face. The paint glided onto his smooth, flawless skin with ease. Finished, the maid pulled back her hand and cocked her head to the side as she took in her work.

The mask had taken hours to paint, and it showed. It was exquisite. The Prince's face had been transformed by the pale veil of paint. No detail had been spared, down to the faintest tracings of gold feathering and blue accents around his eyes and the dusting of rouge that sharpened his already striking cheekbones. Matching the latest fashion, two beauty marks had been perfectly placed – one beneath his right eye and one above his crimson lips. Underneath the masquerade make-up, the Prince's blue eyes shone coolly.

Stepping back, the maid waited as the head valet draped a long jewelled coat over the Prince's shoulders and then carefully inspected it to make sure not one jewel was out of place. Satisfied, he nodded at the maid, who then dusted the Prince's wig with powder. Then both bowed and waited with bated breath for the Prince to act.

Lifting one gloved hand, the Prince gave a single haughty wave. Instantly, a footman appeared. "More light," the Prince ordered.

"Yes, Your Highness," the footman said, turning and reaching for the candelabrum placed nearby. He lifted it so it illuminated the Prince's face.

The Prince held a small mirror. It was silver, with flourishes along the back and a delicate handle. In his large hands, the mirror looked tiny and incredibly fragile. Holding it up so he could see his face, the Prince preened. He turned left, then right, then left again before looking straight on at his reflection. He nodded once, and then, as though it were only a dishcloth, the Prince dropped the mirror.

The maid, who had nearly fainted in relief at the Prince's nod of approval, gasped as the mirror began to

fall. Not even bothering to turn at the noise, the Prince had the majordomo open the doors to the ballroom. As he entered, the footman lunged forward, catching the mirror just before it hit the floor. The servants let out a collective sigh as the doors swung shut behind the Prince. For the next few hours they would be able to relax, out of sight of their cruel, spoiled and unkind master.

Unaware of his servants' thoughts, or perhaps aware but unconcerned, the Prince made his way across the ballroom. It was a sea of white – per his invitation. Many of the guests were hard to distinguish, save their masks. The result was enchanting. His mouth remained pulled down, however, and his solemn expression did not indicate any pleasure at seeing such beauty in his castle. He never allowed others to see if he felt joy or pain. It afforded him a sense of mystery, which he enjoyed immensely. As he walked, he heard the whispers of young women wondering excitedly if this would be the night he singled them out for a dance. A smug smile tugged at his lips, but he tamped it down and continued on his way.

Pushing through a circle of eligible maidens and their chaperones, the Prince arrived at his throne. It was raised above the ballroom floor, allowing him the best spot from which to view the party. Like everything else in the room, the throne was decadent in its design. A huge majestic coat of arms dominated the seat, making it clear, if it weren't already, whose throne it was. Standing beside it, the Prince turned and stared out at the ballroom. He watched a small animated man sit at the grand harpsichord across the room. The Prince locked eyes with the man, who smiled kindly in return, flashing teeth that had seen better days. The Prince grimaced but nodded. This was, after all, the premier Italian maestro. He and his wife, the elegant operatic diva who stood beside him, were known the world over for their sound. They were, simply put, the best. Because of that, the Prince had needed to have them at his ball.

With the Prince's nod, the maestro began to play and the diva began to sing, her voice filling the ballroom. The Prince strode out onto the floor and started to dance. His moves were smooth and practised, honed from years of training. Around him, ladies moved in reverse to the Prince, their dancing equally well practised and smooth. Yet somehow they paled in comparison to him. His presence was bigger than the ballroom, his looks more beautiful, his coldness more chilling than the wind and rain that howled outside.

The diva's voice had just swelled to an almost painful note when, suddenly, above the music and over the wind, the Prince heard the unmistakable sound of someone knocking at the door that led out to the gardens. He lifted his hand, and the music came to an abrupt stop.

The knock came again. For a moment, no one moved. And then all the windows blew open, followed by the door. Rain billowed into the ballroom, and a strong wind caused the candles in the sconces along the walls to flicker and go out. The ballroom was plunged into darkness, and the Prince heard his guests begin to mutter nervously. In the remaining light from the candelabra on the tables, the Prince watched with a mixture of anger and curiosity as a hooded figure entered through the open door. The stranger was hunched over, clutching a gnarled cane with a shaking hand. The visitor moved out of the cold and into the warmth of the ballroom. As the door shut, the hooded figure sighed audibly, clearly happy to be somewhere he – or she – seemed to think was safe and inviting.

That couldn't have been more wrong.

His initial shock fading, the Prince felt rage well up inside him. Grabbing a candelabrum from a nearby table, he stormed through the crowd, pushing people out of his path. By the time he arrived at the door, his face was red, despite the layers of face paint. He noticed that the uninvited guest was an old beggar woman. Hunched as she was, the Prince towered over her.

"What is the meaning of this?" he demanded with a snarl.

The old woman looked up at him with hope in her eyes. Holding out a single red rose, she said in no more than a whisper, "I'm seeking shelter from the bitter storm outside." As if on cue, the wind rose to a fever pitch, howling like a mad beast.

The Prince remained unmoved.

He did not care if the woman was cold and wet. She was haggard, old, and a vagrant. And worse still, she was ruining his ball. Another wave of red-hot anger

washed over him as he saw the ugliness amid all the beauty he had so carefully and painstakingly created. "Get out!" he sneered, waving her away with his hand. "Get out now. You do not belong here." He gestured around the room at the elegantly dressed guests.

"Please," the old woman begged. "I am only asking for shelter for one night. I will not even stay in the ballroom."

The Prince's frown deepened. "Don't you see, old woman? This is a place of beauty," he said, his voice cold. "You are too ugly for my castle. For my world. For me." The woman seemed to shrink as the Prince's words tore into her, but the Prince did not appear to have any remorse. Signalling to his majordomo and the head footman, he ordered the woman escorted out.

"You should not be deceived by appearances," the woman said as the two servants approached. "Beauty is found within...."

The Prince threw back his head and laughed cruelly. "Say what you will, hag. But we all know what beautiful looks like – and it is not you. Now go!"

Turning, the Prince moved to leave. But a gasp from his guests gave him pause. As he looked over his shoulder, his eyes grew wide. Something was happening to the old woman. Her dirty cape and hood seemed to engulf her in a cocoon of sorts until she all but disappeared. Then a flash of light erupted, blinding him.

When his vision cleared, the old beggar was gone. In her place was the most beautiful woman the Prince had ever seen. She was floating above him, emitting a dazzling golden light not unlike the sun's. Instantly, the Prince knew exactly what she was, for he had read about such things. She was an enchantress – a woman of magic who had put him to a test.

And he had failed.

Falling to his knees, the Prince held up his hands. "Please," he said, now the one to beg. "I'm sorry, Enchantress. You are welcome in my castle for as long as you like."

The Enchantress shook her head. She had seen enough to know that it was a hollow apology. The Prince had no kindness or love in his heart. Magic coursed through her and then washed over the Prince.

The transformation began instantly. The Prince's body was racked with pain. His back arched and he groaned as his body began to grow. His jewellery popped off. His clothes ripped. The surrounding guests screamed at the sight of their host and fled. The Prince reached up, trying to grasp a nearby man's hand, but to his horror, he discovered his own hand resembled that of a monster. The man jumped away and made his escape, along with the others.

Amid it all, the Enchantress calmly watched her punishment take effect. Soon the ballroom was empty save for the staff, the entertainers, and a lone dog that belonged to the diva. As they looked on in shock, the Prince's transformation became complete. Where once there had towered a handsome man now, cowered a hideous beast. But he was not the only one to have transformed. The rest of the castle and its inhabitants no longer looked the same. They, too, had changed....

The days bled into years, and the Prince and his servants were forgotten by the world until, finally, the enchanted castle stood isolated and locked in perpetual winter. The Enchantress erased all memory of the castle and

those who were in it, even from the minds of the people who loved them.

But there did remain one last bit of hope: the rose she had offered the Prince was truly an enchanted rose. If the Prince could learn to love another and earn that person's love in return by the time the last petal fell, the spell would be broken. If not, he would be doomed to remain a beast forever.

CHAPTER I

BELLE OPENED THE FRONT DOOR of her cottage. Taking in the picture-perfect pastoral scene in front of her, she sighed. Morning in the small village of Villeneuve began the same way each day. At least it had for as long as Belle had lived there.

The sun would rise slowly over the horizon, its rays turning the fields that surrounded the village more green or gold or white, depending on the season. Then the rays would move along until they touched the whitewashed sides of Belle's cottage, which stood right on the outskirts of the village, before finally illuminating the thatched roofs of the homes and shops that made up the village itself. By the time that happened, the villagers themselves would be stirring, preparing for the day. Inside their homes, men would sit down for their morning meals while the women readied the children or finished stirring the porridge. The village would be hushed, as though still shaking off sleep.

Then the clock on the church would strike eight.

And just like that, the village would come alive.

Belle had watched it happen hundreds of times. Yet this morning, like every morning, it still amazed her as she stared down at the little town, full of the same people going about their daily routines. Narrowing her warm brown eyes, she sighed at the mundanity of it all. She often wondered what it would be like to wake up differently.

Belle shook her head. It did her no good to wonder or wish. This was life as she'd always known it, the life she had shared with her papa ever since they had moved from Paris many years earlier. It was a waste of time to dwell on the past or the what-ifs. She had things to do, errands to run, and – she looked down at the book clutched in her hand – a new adventure to find. Straightening her shoulders, Belle pulled the door closed behind her and set off into town.

Within minutes, Belle was making her way down the cobblestoned main street. As she passed other villagers, she nodded distantly. While she had lived in the village most of her life, she still felt like a stranger there. It, like so many in the French countryside, was isolated and insular. Most of the people Belle passed on her way had been born there and most would spend the rest of their lives there. To them, the village was the world. And outsiders were viewed with caution.

Belle wasn't entirely sure that even if she had been born in the village she wouldn't still have been treated as an outsider. She really didn't have much in common with most of the others. And if she was being honest, she tended to enjoy reading more than idle small talk – travelling to distant lands and having wondrous adventures, even if only in the pages of her favourite books.

Weaving her way through the street, she listened as the rest of the villagers greeted each other. She felt a pang of loneliness watching them talk to one another. They all seemed perfectly content with the monotony of their morning routines. No one seemed to share her desire for something new and exciting, for something *more*.

Belle reached the baker's stand, the sweet smell of freshly baked bread wafting through the air. As always,

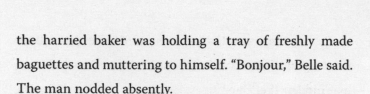

the harried baker was holding a tray of freshly made baguettes and muttering to himself. "Bonjour," Belle said. The man nodded absently.

"One baguette ..." Belle peered at the row of jars filled with rich red jam. "And this, too, *s'il vous plaît*," she said, picking one up and sliding it into her apron pocket. After she'd paid and collected her goods, she moved on to complete her next errand.

She was just about to turn a corner when she paused. Jean, the old potter, was standing next to his mule looking confused. The cart attached to the mule was loaded with freshly made pottery. Looking up, Jean caught Belle watching him and smiled.

"Good morning, Belle," he said, his voice scratchy with age. He was peering into his cart, a puzzled expression on his face.

"Good morning, Monsieur Jean," Belle said in return. "Have you lost something again?"

The older man nodded. "I believe I have. Problem is, I can't remember what," he said sadly. Then he shrugged. "Well, I'm sure it will come to me." He turned and pulled on the mule's reins, trying to lead the stubborn animal away. The mule was having none of it. He tried to stick his nose in Belle's pocket, searching for the apple she had hidden there just in case she ran into Jean. Giving the creature a hard yank, Jean succeeded in drawing the mule's attention away from Belle. But he *also* succeeded in knocking the cart off balance.

Gasping, Belle reached out and grabbed one of the beautiful clay pots just before it fell. Then, satisfied nothing else would fall, she gave the mule the apple and turned to leave.

"Where are you off to?" Jean asked.

She looked back over her shoulder. "To return this book to Pére Robert," she said, smiling and holding up the well-worn book. "It's about two lovers in fair Verona –"

"Are either of them potters?" Jean interrupted.

Belle shook her head. "No."

"Sounds boring," he said.

Belle sighed. She wasn't surprised by Jean's reaction. It was the same reaction she got anytime she mentioned books. Or art. Or travel. Or Paris. Anything other than talk of the village or the villagers was met with indifference – or, worse, disdain.

Just once, Belle thought as she patted Jean's mule on the nose and gave the potter a wave good-bye, *I'd like to meet someone who* wanted *to hear the story of Romeo and Juliet. Or any story, for that matter.* She started to walk more quickly, more eager than ever to get to Pére Robert's, get a new book, and return home. At least in her own cottage, she had no one to bother her or judge her. She could just get lost in her stories and imagine the world beyond the provincial town.

Absorbed in thoughts of what new bookish delights might be awaiting her at Pére Robert's, Belle didn't even notice the attention she was getting. Nor did she pay any mind to the barely concealed comments her presence sparked. She had heard them all before. It was not the first time she had passed by the school and heard the young boys call her strange. The washerwomen, their hands pruned and covered in suds, also loved to whisper among themselves whenever they saw Belle. "Funny girl," they would say. "Doesn't fit in" was another favourite. To the gossipy women, this was the worst offence of all. It never occurred to them that Belle *chose* not to be part of the crowd.

Finally, Belle arrived at her destination – the vestry of the church. Pushing open the doors, she breathed a sigh of relief as the quiet and serenity of the building enveloped her. The hubbub and noise of outside faded away, and for the first time that morning, Belle felt at peace. Hearing her enter, a kind man in a long black robe looked up from his book. The man was tall and slender, with warm eyes that crinkled as he smiled at Belle.

"Good morning, Belle," Pére Robert greeted her. "So where did you run off to this week?"

Belle smiled in return. The well-read priest was one of two people in the entire village Belle felt she could talk to. The other person was her father. "Two cities in Northern Italy," she answered, her tone growing animated. She held out the book, as if showing Pére Robert would somehow help bring the story fully to life. "You should have seen it. The castles. The art. There was even a masquerade ball."

Reaching out, Pére Robert took the book gingerly from Belle. He nodded as she continued to tell him the story of Romeo and Juliet as though he had never heard it before, even though they both knew he had read the story

at least a dozen times himself. It was just part of their ritual. When she was done, Belle took a deep satisfied breath. "Have you got any new places to go?" she asked hopefully. She turned and her eyes lingered on the town's library.

Calling it a library was an exaggeration, to say the least. A few dozen books lined two small dusty bookshelves. Scanning the shelves now, Belle saw the same well-worn spines and faded titles. It was rare for anything to be added to the inventory.

"I'm afraid not," he replied. Despite the fact that she had anticipated this, Belle's eyes showed her disappointment. "But you may re-read any of the old ones that you'd like," he added kindly.

Belle nodded and moved in front of the shelves. Her fingers brushed the familiar books, most of which she had read at least two times. Still, she knew better than to complain. Picking one up, she smiled back at the older man. "Thank you," she said softly. "Your library makes our small corner of the world almost feel big."

Book in hand, Belle left the vestry and made her way back out onto the village's main street. Opening to the first page, she planted her nose firmly in the book and blocked out everything else. She ducked under the cheese vendor carrying his tray of goods and swooped out of the way of the two florists, their arms loaded with huge bouquets, all the while never losing her spot on the page.

While she had been disappointed not to find anything new, this book *was* one of her favourites. It had everything a good story should have − far-off places, a charming prince, a strong heroine who discovered love ... but not right away, of course.

CLANG! CLANG!

Startled by the loud noise, Belle finally tore herself from the book. Looking up, she saw that the noise was coming from Agathe. If the town thought Belle was odd, they considered the older woman an outcast. She had no home or family and spent her days begging for spare change and food. Looking past the dirt that covered her cheeks and the rags she wore, Belle had always had a soft spot for Agathe. She felt Agathe deserved as much care and respect as anyone else, and hated to see other villagers ignore Agathe, or − worse − mock her among

themselves. Whenever she saw Agathe, Belle tried to give her a little something.

"Good morning, Agathe," she said now, smiling gently. "I have no money. But here...." She reached into her bag, pulled out the baguette she had picked up especially for the older woman, and handed it over.

Agathe smiled gratefully. Then her smile turned playful. "No jam?" Anticipating the response, Belle already had her hand in her pocket and produced the jar of jam. "Bless you," Agathe said. Lowering her head, she ripped a chunk off the baguette, Belle's presence instantly forgotten.

Belle smiled. She felt, in some strange way, a kinship with the woman. Agathe simply wanted to have food and be left alone. Belle was the same way with her books. As lonely as she could be at times, she couldn't stand unwanted attention – hated it, in fact.

CHAPTER II

GASTON LOVED ATTENTION. HE lived for it, in fact. Ever since he had been a small boy, he had sought out ways to make himself the centre of attention. He walked before anyone else his age. He talked first, and as he got older, he grew taller and more handsome than anyone else. With his dark hair, piercing eyes, and broad shoulders, he was indeed good-looking. The girls loved him; the boys worshipped him. And Gaston? He soaked up the attention and revelled in it.

But there was a limit to just how much attention Gaston could get growing up in a small village. And it had irked him. Then, to his great delight, France had become involved in the war. Gaston had seen the war not as an opportunity to defend his country but as a chance to wear a dashing uniform and woo the ladies, which he had done, with gusto, when he became a certified war hero – twelve years ago.

Gaston still wore his uniform.

And he *still* believed himself the most handsome and manliest man in the entire village.

Now he sat astride his large black stallion, staring down at his village from the promontory that overlooked it. His chest bulged beneath a dazzling gold breastplate. The muscles on his arms rippled as he pulled back on the horse's reins, making the animal dance nervously. Strapped to his saddle were his trusty musket and the spoils of his hunt. As usual, he'd had a successful afternoon in the woods.

"You didn't miss a shot, Gaston," said the man beside him.

If Gaston was a lion of a man, which many a person had called him over the years, the man beside him was a house cat. LeFou was everything Gaston was not. Where Gaston was tall and muscled, LeFou was short and soft. Where Gaston was all smooth, practised moves and well-rehearsed lines, LeFou was stumbling incoherent babble. And where Gaston was known and worshipped by all,

LeFou was barely a footnote in the eyes of the villagers. Still, Gaston had a soft spot for the little guy – mostly because LeFou was his biggest fan.

"You're the greatest hunter in the village," LeFou went on. Gaston shot him a look and he quickly corrected himself. "I mean ... the *world*."

Gaston puffed out his already puffed-out chest even more and raised his chin in the air, as though posing for an unseen artist. "Thank you, LeFou," he said. He looked down at what LeFou had 'caught' – a handful of vegetables – and raised an eyebrow. "You didn't do too badly yourself," he added insincerely.

"One of these days I'm going to learn to shoot like you," LeFou said, oblivious to Gaston's mockery. "And talk like you. And be tall and handsome like you."

"Come now, old friend," Gaston said, pretending not to love every compliment. "Reflected glory is just as good as the real thing."

LeFou cocked his head, confused. He opened his mouth to speak but stopped when he saw Gaston sit up straighter in his saddle. The dark-haired man's eyes narrowed, as if he were a wolf spotting his prey.

Following Gaston's gaze, LeFou saw what had caught his friend's attention. Below, Belle was making her way through the village square. Her bright-blue dress was flattering against her rich auburn hair. Even from such a distance, LeFou could see that her cheeks were flushed becomingly.

"Look at her, LeFou," Gaston went on. "My future wife. Belle is the most beautiful girl in the village. That makes *her* the best."

"But she's so well read, and you're so ..." LeFou caught himself. He had almost just done the one thing he prided himself on *never* doing – offending Gaston. Quickly, before Gaston could wonder about the hesitation, he finished his sentence. "Athletically inclined."

Gaston nodded. "I know," he agreed. "Belle can be as argumentative as she is beautiful."

"Exactly!" LeFou said, happy to see his friend talking with some sense. "Who needs her? You've got us! *Le Duo!*" He threw out the nickname almost hopefully. When they had first returned home from the war – because of course LeFou had gone with his pal to fight – the little man had tried in vain to get the village to call the pair *Le Duo*.

But it had never stuck. It was usually Gaston and "the other one". Or more often than not, just Gaston.

Absorbed in himself, Gaston barely registered the neediness in his friend's voice. "Ever since the war, I've been missing something," he said, still looking at Belle. "And she's the only girl I've met who gives that sense of...." Gaston stumbled, trying to find the right words.

"*Je ne sais quoi?*" LeFou finished for him.

Gaston turned and looked at him, confusion on his face. "I don't know what that means," he said. "I just know that from the moment I saw her, I knew I would marry Belle. And I don't want to stand here any longer, wasting time." Kicking his horse into a gallop, he headed towards the village, the picture of a hero returning from war. Behind him, LeFou spurred his pony's sides. The furry animal pinned back its ears and broke right into ... a slow trot.

Belle heard the sound of hoofbeats moments before the horses burst through the village gates. In truth, one burst through; the other sort of meandered. Instantly, Belle recognized the large black stallion and the man astride its back. It was Gaston. Behind him, his ever-present sidekick, LeFou, was struggling to keep up on his shaggy pony. She stifled a groan and quickly ducked behind the cheese seller, hoping Gaston would not notice her.

She'd had one too many run-ins with the war hero. Every time, it went the same way. Gaston would preen like a peacock while he boasted of his latest hunt or told her a tale from his glory days in the war. Belle would try not to roll her eyes. The villagers – especially the female ones – would swoon and whisper how lucky Belle was, and ultimately, Belle would walk away feeling the need to bathe. She knew that Gaston was considered by many – well, *all* if she was being honest – to be quite the catch. But she just couldn't stand the man. There was something *beastly* about him.

Like now, she thought as she peeked out from behind the *fromagerie*. Gaston was clutching flowers in his hand and scanning the crowd like a wild animal. Belle groaned as his eyes locked on hers and he began to push through the villagers to get to her. She turned and hurried off in the opposite direction, hoping the other villagers would distract him.

Unbeknownst to Belle, just as Gaston was about to reach her, Agathe stepped in front of him, her cup raised. Gaston looked down at the homeless woman and his lips curled. Then he saw the shiny metal cup. "Thank you, hag," he said, grabbing it out of her hands and turning it upside down. Coins spilled to the ground as Gaston checked out his reflection in the bottom of the mug. Satisfied with what he saw, he shoved the cup back at Agathe and moved past her.

"Good morning, Belle," he said, running to come to a stop in front of her. She took a step backwards. "Wonderful book you have there."

Belle raised an eyebrow. "You've read it?"

"I did a lot of things in the army," he answered vaguely.

Belle swallowed a laugh. It had taken him less than a minute to bring up the army. *Must be a record,* she thought.

With a flourish, Gaston presented the flowers. "For your dinner table," he explained. "Shall I join you tonight?"

"Sorry," Belle said hastily, shaking her head. She inched around him, looking for the quickest escape route. "Not tonight."

"Busy?" Gaston asked.

"No," Belle said, and then before Gaston could reply or process her refusal, she was ducking back out into the street. Behind her, she heard Gaston twisting her words for the audience of villagers who had stopped to watch the pair. It was clear that the hunter had interpreted her "no" as part of a game of hard-to-get.

She didn't care what Gaston said or how he made himself feel better. She knew the truth: Gaston, despite his massive physical size, was no bigger than the small provincial town. And there was no way she would ever share her dinner table with him. Not now, not ever.

Quickening her pace, Belle made her way out of the village centre. Moments later she arrived back at her cottage. It was a cosy little house, with a small staircase leading up to the front door and large picture windows. There was also a nice garden out front and a detached basement workshop for her father.

The soft tinkling melody of a music box drifted up from the closed hatch doors. Her father was already working, despite the early hour.

Careful not to disturb him, Belle opened the hatch

and tiptoed down the stairs. Sunlight streamed through a small window, illuminating Maurice as he sat hunched over his workbench. Bits and pieces of his projects were scattered about. Small knobs, tiny screws, half-painted boxes, and delicate figurines sat on various shelves and tables. Some were newer, their surfaces bright and shiny, while others had accumulated a fine layer of dust waiting for Maurice's attention to turn to them once again. But for the moment, he was focused exclusively on the music box in front of him. As Belle watched, he tinkered with one of the gears. The inside was beautifully painted, depicting an artist in a small Parisian apartment. The artist was painting his wife's portrait. She was cradling a small baby and holding a rattle resembling a red rose in her other hand.

Belle took a step farther into the room. Maurice looked up distractedly at the sound. Seeing his daughter, he smiled. His eyes, the same warm colour as Belle's, were bright and focused. When he straightened his shoulders, he grew taller and leaner, still handsome in his older age. "Oh, good, Belle, you're back," he said, turning again to the music box. "Where were you?"

"Well, first I went to Saint Petersburg to see the tsar, then I went fishing in the bottom of the well," she began, smiling as he nodded absently. When he was working, he didn't see or hear anything else. Belle understood. She was the same way when she was entranced by a book.

"Hmmm, yes," Maurice said. "Can you please hand me the –"

Before he could finish, Belle was handing him the screwdriver.

"And the –"

This time she held out a small hammer.

"No, I don't need...." His voice trailed off as a spring popped off. "Well, yes, I guess I do."

As he went back to tinkering, Belle walked over to a shelf full of completed music boxes. Her long thin fingers trailed over them as she moved down the row. Each one was a piece of art, depicting famous landmarks from around the world. She knew her father made them for her, as a way to give her a glimpse beyond the village. Maurice never said as much, but Belle knew he was aware of her longing to explore, to get out of the small world where he felt she was safe. She thought of the small village and the gossiping people who lived there. Softly, so as not to startle him, Belle asked, "Papa, do you think I'm odd?"

Hearing her tone, Maurice looked up from his work. He frowned. "Do I think you're odd?" he repeated. "Where did you get an idea like that?"

Belle shrugged. "Oh, I don't know ... People talk."

"There are worse things than being talked about," Maurice said, his tone growing sad. "This village may be small-minded, Belle, but it's also safe."

Belle opened her mouth to protest. That was the line her father used all the time. She knew it came from a good place, but she just didn't understand why he wanted to *stay* in their small town.

Seeing his typical explanation wasn't going to work on Belle today, Maurice quickly changed course. "Back in Paris," he said, "I knew a girl who was so different, so daring, so ahead of her time that people mocked her until the day they found themselves imitating her. Do you know what she used to say?"

Belle shook her head.

"She used to say, 'The people who talk behind your back are destined to stay there.'" Maurice paused for a moment, letting the words sink in. Then he added. *"Behind your back. Never to catch up."*

Slowly, Belle nodded. She enjoyed Maurice's little stories that served as life lessons. She had, in fact, thought she'd already heard them all. But this was a new one. Her father was trying to tell her it was all right to stand out, be apart from the crowd. She nodded once more. "I understand," she said softly.

"That woman was your mother," Maurice added, smiling and reaching out to take his daughter's hand. He gave it a squeeze.

Belle smiled back, warmth and sadness filling her heart. She didn't remember her mother. All she had were the stories her father told her. But remembering was hard on Maurice, so he gave her only snippets – like this one – from time to time. "Tell me more about her," Belle prompted as Maurice tried to return to his work. "Please. One more thing."

The older man's hand hovered over the music box. Slowly, his fingers closed and he looked back at his daughter. "Your mother was ... fearless," he said. "To know anything more, you just have to look in the mirror."

He picked up a pair of tweezers and placed the last gear in the music box. With a click, it snapped into place.

"It's beautiful," Belle said as music tinkled forth. As she looked up, her eyes landed on the portrait hanging above her father's workshop. It showed the same image that was depicted on the inside of the newest music box. Her mother was the woman holding the infant and the rose rattle. And Belle was the baby. It was the only image of her mother Belle knew. "I think she would have loved it," Belle added softly.

But her father didn't hear her. He was once again lost in the world of his music boxes. Belle knew that talking more about her mother would only sadden him. She turned and headed back upstairs. She loved her father so much, and she didn't want to cause him any more pain or heartache than he'd already experienced in his life. But sometimes she wondered if there was a chance anything would ever happen to set her life on a different path from the one she and her father were so firmly planted on now.

CHAPTER III

BELLE WAVED TO HER FATHER AS HE drove his cart away from their cottage. Philippe, their gentle giant of a draught horse, tossed his head in the air and whickered happily, ready for the adventure.

As he did every year, Maurice was heading to the large market a few towns over to sell his music boxes. The cart was loaded with every piece he had worked on for the past year, carefully packed and stored to protect them during the long journey. And as he did every year, Maurice was leaving Belle behind. It was for her own safety, he always told her. Or because he couldn't leave the cottage unattended, he would sometimes add. Either way, every time it was the same. He packed up the cart, Belle made sure Philippe was ready for the journey, and then they went through their ritual of saying good-bye. Belle would tuck Maurice's cravat into his shirt, and Maurice would ask Belle: "What would you like from the market?"

"A rose like the one in the painting," was always Belle's reply.

Then, after a quick hug and a pat for Philippe, Maurice would head out.

This year had been no different. When her father and Philippe were finally out of view, Belle sighed. *Well*, she thought as she walked back into the cottage, *now what?* She knew she could read or clean or work in the garden. But for some reason none of those things appealed to her at the moment. She needed to do something more. Something that would get her out of her own head – which was beginning to fill with worry about her father's trip, as it did every year. Catching sight of the large pile of laundry, she raised an eyebrow. Normally, she hated doing the laundry. The washerwomen were always by the fountain, gossiping and jabbering away. When she arrived, they would inevitably get louder, their laughter colder – lasting the excruciating length of time it took to get the clothes clean. If only it didn't take so long....

She looked around the room, noticing one of Philippe's leather harnesses and the basket of apples. Suddenly, she had a thought. Smiling, she ran into the barn, grabbed what she needed, and headed into the village. To her delight, when she arrived, the only person at the fountain was a young girl with sad eyes. Belle had seen the girl around the village before. She was always by herself, and judging by the way she hunched her shoulders and avoided eye contact, Belle was pretty sure she didn't have a lot of friends. As Belle watched, the girl plunged a shirt into the fountain and then pulled it out and began scrubbing at it.

Taking her pile to the fountain's edge, Belle began to pull her other supplies from her apron pockets. She walked over to Jean the potter's mule, which was standing by the door to the tavern with its head down, lips twitching, and one hind foot cocked. After attaching one end of Philippe's harness to the mule's halter, Belle secured the other end to a small wooden barrel. Then she dumped all the clothes and a few soap chips into the barrel before lifting it and dropping it right into the fountain. The barrel bobbed on its side, filling slowly with water. Belle walked in front

43

of the mule. Holding up one of the apples enticingly, she walked backward. The mule followed. She set it on a path walking around the fountain.

"What are you doing?"

Belle saw that the girl was watching her, a perplexed look on her face.

"The laundry," Belle answered matter-of-factly. She pointed to the barrel. The mule was dragging it through the water, churning up the liquid and covering the clothes in a nice layer of suds. Satisfied with her work, Belle took her book out of one of her apron pockets and sat down to read. Glancing at the girl, who was eyeing the book with something close to hunger, Belle smiled. "Well, what are you waiting for?"

Belle wasn't sure how long she had been sitting by the fountain. Jean's mule was still doing laps, the water was less sudsy, and the clothes were much cleaner. But Belle barely registered any of that. She was too focused on the girl sitting beside her. She had spent the morning and some of the afternoon trying to teach her to read. She knew that the village elders frowned upon girls reading – hence the local school was open only to boys – but Belle had never agreed with that narrow-minded way of thinking. So when the girl had sat down on the fountain wall and asked in a voice barely above a whisper if Belle would tell her a story, Belle had been excited to be able to share the thrill of reading with her. The idea of living in this village and not being able to escape through books was alarming. And the girl lived that life every day. Belle was determined to change that.

They had come a long way. The girl was much further along than Belle would have thought possible. She just needed practice.

"T ... th ... the blue bi-ir-ird flies ..." the girl stammered.

"Over the dark wood," Belle prompted. She opened her mouth to read the next line but was interrupted by a shout from nearby. Looking up, Belle saw the thin cruel face of the headmaster in the school's doorway. She sighed. Their moment of peace and quiet seemed to be over.

"What on earth are you doing?" he shouted, storming over to her. A line of boys followed him, their matching uniforms making them look like a small army. "Girls don't read."

His shouts quickly garnered the attention of more

villagers. Jean the potter appeared, followed by the fishmonger and even Pére Robert and Agathe. They waited to see what Belle would say or do.

Raising one perfectly arched eyebrow, Belle met the headmaster's angry gaze. For a moment, they remained that way, eyes locked. Then Belle turned back to the girl and smiled. "Try again," she said.

As if she had ignited a powder keg of explosives, the villagers who had gathered went off. Some, like the fishmonger and the headmaster, expressed outrage at Belle's audacious behaviour. Others, like Pére Robert, cheered her on. Amid it all, Belle sat unbothered. *Let the headmaster scream and shout and throw a fit,* she thought. *He* should *be concerned with his students' education.*

Suddenly, over the increasingly loud shouts of the villagers, a shot rang out.

Startled, Belle looked up. Then she rolled her eyes.

Gaston stood, or rather posed, with one hand on his hip and the other holding his hunting rifle to the sky. Smoke still wafted from the tip of the recently fired weapon. LeFou, ever the aide, was pushing his way through the villagers. "Make a lane, people," he shouted. "Come on, don't make me say it twice."

Walking behind him, Gaston lowered the rifle and handed it to LeFou. Then he looked over the crowd. "This is not how good people behave," he said, shaking his head. "Everyone ... go home. *Now!*" If the gun hadn't been enough to get their attention, the man's deep bellow did the trick. The villagers, mumbling to each other, began to disperse. Within moments, the area around the fountain was almost empty. The only ones left were Belle, Gaston and LeFou. Even the young girl had taken off, frightened by the war hero's shout.

Belle didn't know whether to laugh or cry. Gaston surely thought he had just come to her rescue, but all he had done was given the other villagers what they'd wanted and ended her reading lesson. Not to mention frustrate her.

Belle got to her feet and walked away from the fountain. Gaston fell in step beside her. For a few glorious moments, the large man was silent as they walked towards Belle's cottage, and Belle wondered if perhaps she had been wrong.

Maybe Gaston wouldn't make this all about him. And then he spoke.

"I was pretty great back there, wasn't I?" he said. "Like being back in command during the war...."

"That was twelve years ago, Gaston," Belle pointed out.

"Sad, I know," Gaston said, clearly missing Belle's tone. He slowed his steps, and his expression grew serious. "Belle, I'm sure you think I have it all. But there *is* something I'm missing."

Hoping to get away, Belle quickened her own pace. "I can't imagine...."

"A wife," Gaston went on, his tone earnest but the line too well practised to sound genuine. "You're not really living until you see yourself reflected in someone else's eyes."

Oh, no, Belle thought. This was just what she had feared might happen. And she needed to nip any further talk of wives right in the bud. "And you can see yourself in mine?" she asked, trying to make her tone as disinterested and removed as possible.

Gaston nodded. "We're both fighters," he said, clearly referring to the incident at the fountain.

"All I wanted was to teach a child to read," Belle protested. *Not be a fighter,* she added silently.

"The only children you should concern yourself with are ... your own."

Gaston's words hit Belle like a runaway cart. *As if he knows me, or what I want, at all,* she thought. *How dare he make assumptions?* She clenched her fists at her sides and tried to keep her voice steady as she said, "I'm not ready to have children."

"Maybe you haven't met the right man," Gaston responded.

"It's a small village," Belle shot back. "I've met them all."

"Maybe you should take a second look...."

Belle shook her head. "I have."

"Maybe you should take a third look," Gaston went on, not picking up on the hint. "Some of us have changed."

Enough! Belle wanted to shout. Gaston could change into Mark Antony and she into Cleopatra and she *still* wouldn't want to be with him. Ever. Never, ever, *ever.* "Look," she finally said. "We could never make each other happy. No one can change *that* much." Picking up her pace still more, she tried to get away from Gaston. This conversation had gone on long enough. Up ahead, she could see the front door of her cottage, like a beacon of safety.

But Gaston wasn't having it. His long legs quickly closed the gap between them, his boots crushing the vegetables in the little garden. "Belle, do you know what happens to spinsters in our village after their fathers die?" he asked, the earlier softness of his voice gone. When Belle didn't answer, he went on. "They beg for change in the street." He waved at Agathe, who was wandering past. "This is our world, Belle. For simple folk like us, it doesn't get any better."

"I may be a farm girl," Belle said, climbing the steps with Gaston close on her heels. She came to a stop and turned to look straight at him. "But I'm *not* simple. I'm sorry, but I will never marry you, Gaston."

Without another word, she pushed her way inside and firmly shut the door, preventing the hunter from following. She knew he couldn't have liked having a door slammed in his face, but he'd left her with no choice. Hopefully this would be the end of Gaston's unwanted advances.

Someday, she thought as she slumped against the door, *someday I'll find someone who will understand me, someone who will let me be me. Someday I'll show them all. I want so much more than the people in this town could ever understand.*

CHAPTER IV

LIGHTNING FLASHED, ILLUMINATING the woods with a menacing white light. A moment later, the wind picked up. Leaves whipped across the ground at Philippe's feet as he trotted nervously forward. The horse's eyes bulged as a moment later a loud crack of thunder roared in the sky above. Jigging his head, he rattled his bit.

In his spot on the carriage's front seat, Maurice knew what the big animal was trying to say: *Let's turn around now, before it's too late.* But he also knew it already *was* too late. They had somehow got stuck in the middle of what locals called the dark forest. Rumours swirled around that thick patch of woods. Some said witches lived there. Others claimed it was full of packs of wolves smarter than most men. There were even those who said the trees had been known to speak. It was the type of

place where one saw dark and hostile eyes wherever one looked.

It was *not* the type of place to get lost in at night – especially in the middle of a storm.

"Perhaps we should have turned *right* at those crossroads, old friend," Maurice said, his hands shaking on the reins as more lightning streaked the sky. "Or perhaps I should stop pretending my horse understands me."

Just then, another bolt of lightning flashed down. Only this time, it nearly hit Maurice and Philippe. It missed them, barely, but a gnarled and withered tree did not fare so well. The lightning tore it in two. As it split, one half fell onto the road right in front of Philippe. The other half fell sideways. When Maurice looked closer, he saw that the second half of the tree had fallen right next to a previously hidden narrow path.

Glancing back and forth, Maurice pondered what to do. A rational, reasonable part of him knew that he should find a way to keep going on the road. But a smaller part of him realized that was never going to happen. At least not that night. He couldn't get the cart, himself and Philippe around the fallen tree. With a sigh, he tugged on the reins, steering his horse towards the path.

"It will be all right, Philippe," he said as the horse whinnied nervously. *I hope,* he added silently.

As they moved farther and farther down the path, Maurice became less and less confident that things would turn out well. The weather, which had already been stormy, grew worse – and stranger. Even though it was summer, a light whirling snow began to fall, dusting his jacket and turning Philippe's coat from dappled grey to white. It also grew eerily quiet. The rumbling of thunder vanished, and soon the only sound echoing through the seemingly empty woods was the clip-clop of Philippe's hooves.

And then there was a piercing howl.

An instant later a huge white wolf burst out of the bushes, barely missing the cart. Looking over, Maurice saw an entire pack of the beasts running parallel to them. "Go, Philippe!" he cried, slapping the reins against the horse's neck, as if the creature needed any encouragement. "Hurry!"

The horse wasted no time. He broke into a gallop.

But the sudden movement combined terribly with the cart's age and general disrepair. Just as the horse started to pull away from the wolves, the cart began to buckle and the harness loosened. Within seconds, the cart tipped.

Maurice cried out as the cart fell to the ground and he was thrown into the air. He heard the sound of his beloved music boxes breaking as they fell and the slavering howls of the wolves, and he knew it was only a matter of time before he, too, fell and was destroyed. But just then, his plummeting body came to a jerking stop. Looking up, he saw that his descent had been stopped by a low-hanging limb. He dangled from it helplessly.

Shaking off the last bits of his leather harness, Philippe kicked out a hind leg, toppling one of the wolves. Seeing his owner hanging from the tree, he raced underneath it. Maurice didn't waste a minute. Reaching over his shoulder, he freed himself from the limb and fell onto the horse's back. Then, with a loud *h'yah*, he kicked the large animal forward.

As they raced through the woods, Maurice clung to Philippe's mane. The wolves followed, their eyes mad with hunger, their jaws open to reveal sharp teeth.

Just then, Maurice thought he saw something glimmer from the corner of his eye. Could there be some sort of structure ... a safe haven in this godforsaken place? A moment later, he knew he hadn't imagined it. A huge ornate gate, frozen over with ice, had suddenly appeared in front of them. As they raced up to it, the gate swung open slightly. Philippe plunged through. The tip of his tail had only just made it inside the gate when it closed. Behind them, the wolves' howls turned to yelps of fear and then faded altogether as the creatures ran away.

If Maurice had not just barely escaped a pack of wolves with his life, he might have taken pause at their sudden disappearance – or the odd gate that opened and closed by itself. He might even have wondered *how* a castle as large and ornate as the one that rose in front of him could seem to appear out of nowhere. But as it was, he didn't stop to think about it. Instead, he kicked Philippe forward, towards the large castle and whoever lived inside.

Maurice had seen great buildings before. After all, he had lived the majority of his life in Paris, where beautiful buildings dominated the skyline. He had seen the artistry that went into creating such architectural wonders and, as an artist himself, was in awe of those who crafted their visions into reality. But nothing he had ever seen in Paris could have prepared him for the castle he saw now.

It seemed to defy gravity, with large turrets that reached high into the stormy sky. Its sides were made of grey stone cut so that it seemed the castle had grown out of the ground. The path Philippe now trotted on was actually a long bridge that spanned a frozen moat and ended in front of the castle's massive entryway. To the right of the huge front doors was a large colonnade. To Maurice's surprise, growing behind the colonnade, despite the strange cold weather, were beautiful rosebushes. White roses blossomed on all of them, so pure that they even stood out against the snow.

A small shiver of fear flashed over Maurice. Roses growing in the snow? It was most unnatural. But as quickly as the feeling came, it went when Maurice noticed

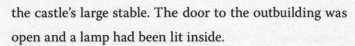

the castle's large stable. The door to the outbuilding was open and a lamp had been lit inside.

Maurice steered Philippe over, then quickly dismounted and led him inside the stable. He paused on the threshold and looked around. It seemed like an ordinary enough stable. "Water, fresh hay," Maurice observed, giving the large animal a pat. "Looks like you're set, old friend. Rest here" – he looked back outside to the castle beyond – "while I pay my respects to our host."

Turning, he headed across the courtyard and cautiously walked up the steps to what he assumed was the castle's front door. The tingle of fear returned as he gazed up at a row of torches held by hands sculpted from iron. The hands were so lifelike Maurice couldn't help reaching out and tapping one, just to be sure. The hand remained still. But the door did not. It swung open in front of him.

"Hello?" Maurice called, peering in. "Anyone home?"

His voice echoed through the large empty hall. Maurice could just make out the faint sound of a harpsichord coming from somewhere deep within the castle. Someone, it seemed, *was* home.

Letting out a nervous breath, Maurice walked inside. "Forgive me," he said as he went. "I don't mean to intrude. I need shelter from the storm. Hello?" Tall windows let in the faint light from outside, barely illuminating the castle's interior. Noticing a coatrack, Maurice took off his hat and coat and hung them to dry. With the cold layers gone, Maurice felt a bit better. He continued inside. Focused on what was in front of him, he didn't notice that as soon as his back was turned, the coatrack came to life, shaking the snow off Maurice's coat and hat like a dog shaking off the rain.

Maurice also failed to notice a large candelabrum and ornate mantel clock sitting on a nearby table. As he passed them, the candelabrum slowly turned, watching the man.

"What are you doing?" the clock whispered as the candelabrum craned its neck. "Stop that!"

Instantly, the candelabrum stopped. But it was not because the mantel clock had told it to. It stopped because Maurice had heard the clock's barely hushed whisper and spun around.

For a tense moment, Maurice eyed the candelabrum and the clock. He approached the table on which they were placed and picked up the candelabrum. He held it up to the dim light and inspected it. He turned it upside down, then right side up. He shifted it to the left and then the right. Finally, he flicked it with his finger. *Ping, ping, ping.* Seemingly satisfied by the candelabrum's "candelabrum-ness", he put it back down on the table and moved on.

Behind him, the candelabrum rubbed its head, ignoring the "I told you so" look the clock was shooting at it.

Maurice continued his exploration of the castle. A grand staircase rose from the middle of the massive foyer. Almost tiptoeing – the huge empty space made Maurice feel even more like an intruder than he already had – he made his way behind the staircase. His heart beat faster when he noticed an entire wall covered in weapons of all sorts, shapes and sizes. Whoever lived there, or had lived there, knew his armoury.

Suddenly, Maurice again heard the faint sound of music being played. He followed the soft, slow melody,

passing several closed doors before coming to a pair
of large gilded doors that hung open. Inside, through
the thick shadows, Maurice saw a ballroom of massive
proportions. The music seemed to be coming from a
dusty harpsichord in the corner. But as soon as Maurice
took a step forward, the sound abruptly stopped.

"Hello?" Maurice called, peering into the now silent
room. Remnants of decorations, long since decayed,
were strewn about, and when he squinted hard enough,
Maurice could make out a hastily repaired window.
But there was no sign of anyone, no musician seated
on the harpsichord's bench. Maurice shook his head,
wondering if he'd imagined the music.

Shivering, Maurice turned his back on the ballroom.
In addition to the phantom music, there was something
infinitely sad about the space. It was a room meant
for joy and was now a room of disrepair and sadness.
As he made his way back into the foyer, he couldn't help
wondering what had happened there to give the ballroom
such a feeling. Perhaps he had been hearing remnants
of the past. Maurice had only just shrugged off the
melancholy that had descended on him when, out of the

corner of his eye, he saw someone lunging towards him.

Maurice recoiled in fear, his breath catching in his throat. But a moment later, he let out that breath as he realized what he had seen was simply his own reflection. A broken mirror hung on the wall. In the centre was a large hole, with long shards of glass radiating from it, as though the mirror had been struck by a fist. The hole had distorted Maurice's reflection. He stared at his face, the lines around his eyes made deeper, his nose moved from the centre to the left. He raised a hand to his cheek, as if to check that it was in fact just the reflection, not an actual change in his appearance.

As he did so, Maurice heard the sound of a fire crackling from somewhere close by. Turning, he saw an open door, through which he could make out a welcoming light. He looked down at his hands. They were shaking with a chill that had returned upon his seeing the eerie mirror. Without a second thought, he made his way into the room. To his delight, the fire he had heard was huge. It roared inside a large ornate hearth.

"Aaah, that's better," Maurice said, moving in front of the flames and holding out his hands. "So much better...."

When his front felt sufficiently warmed, he turned to heat his backside. His eyes widened. Off the room he was in, was yet another room. And in *that* room was a long dining table covered in an elaborate – and decidedly delicious-smelling – feast. Maurice's stomach growled.

Looking to see if he had missed other guests and finding none, Maurice left the warmth of the fire to stand in front of the table. His stomach growled again. He knew he probably shouldn't ... but he couldn't stop himself. He tore a hunk of bread off a massive loaf and then cut a healthy chunk of cheese from an even healthier wheel. "Do you mind ... I'm just going to help myself...?" he called out to the unseen host of the dinner. His mouth was full, so the words came out a bit garbled. He looked down at the table, hoping to see something refreshing. His eyes landed on a delicate china teacup full of an amber liquid. He was lifting it to his mouth when....

"Mum said I wasn't supposed to move because it might be scary."

Maurice nearly dropped the cup. Had it just spoken to him?

"Sorry."

Maurice yelped. Apparently, the cup – the cup made of china ... the cup full of tea ... the cup that was supposed to be just a cup – *had* spoken to him. Twice.

In the next instant, Maurice did what any man in his position would do when confronted with a talking teacup. He turned and ran towards the front door. Grabbing his hat and coat from the coatrack, he bowed, his manners taking over despite the fear coursing through him. "Thank you," he called out to the shadows. "Really, I cannot thank you enough for your hospitality ... and kindness." Then, his duty as a gentleman done, he slipped out of the door and raced into the darkness towards the stable.

Inside one of the stalls, Philippe stood chewing a mouthful of hay. Seeing his owner tearing inside, he shifted nervously on his big feet. Throwing the reins over Philippe's head, Maurice led him out of the stall, eager to get away from the strange castle once and for all. But as he made his way back towards the gate, Maurice's attention was caught once more by the rose-filled colonnade. He *had* promised Belle a rose. For some reason, he felt it was especially important to return with the gift this time.

Stopping, Maurice gave Philippe a reassuring pat on the neck and slipped inside the garden. Neither man nor horse noticed the dark shape that darted across the top of the colonnade as Maurice entered below. Nor did either of them notice the shape's distinct tail or sharp claws.

"You're not red," Maurice said, spotting a single perfect white rose among the hundreds of others, "but you'll do." Reaching into his pocket, he pulled out a small penknife. He placed the blade against the stem of the rose.

At that exact moment, Philippe whinnied and reared. Maurice whipped his head around. Seeing nothing, he shot Philippe a questioning glance and then turned back to the rose. The blade bit into the fragile stem. With a snip, the rose fell into Maurice's waiting hands.

"Those are *MINE!*"

The roar drowned out any other sound, including Maurice's thudding heart and Philippe's frantic neighs. Shaking, Maurice looked up just as a dark shape leaped down from the top of the colonnade. Maurice stumbled backwards. The rose fell from his hand. His feet scrabbled for purchase on the slippery ground.

In front of him, the shadow took shape. It was vaguely

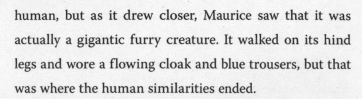

human, but as it drew closer, Maurice saw that it was actually a gigantic furry creature. It walked on its hind legs and wore a flowing cloak and blue trousers, but that was where the human similarities ended.

"You entered my home, ate my food," the creature said, dropping to all fours and circling Maurice. Raising one clawed paw, it pointed at the fallen rose. "And *this* is how I am repaid."

Maurice once again tried to move away, but he couldn't find his footing. Before he could even shout, the creature had grabbed him with two strong arms and lifted him high off the ground. "I know how to deal with thieves," he snarled. Then, with a growl, he turned and headed back into the castle.

Behind him, Philippe whinnied again in terror and bolted, charging through the castle gates and out into the woods beyond.

CHAPTER V

THE SUN HAD JUST RISEN OVER the horizon as Belle made her way outside to give the chickens their morning meal. The birds chirped and a gentle breeze blew across the hillside. Combined with the beautiful, cloudless blue sky, it made for a picture-perfect morning.

And then Belle heard a familiar snort.

Turning her head, she was surprised to see Philippe standing by the gate to his paddock. His sides were heaving and soaked with sweat. The whites of his eyes showed as he shifted nervously on his feet.

"Philippe," Belle said, rushing over and letting the big horse into his paddock so he could drink. She patted him gently. "What are you doing here? Where is...?" Her hand stilled. Then it began to shake as she saw the torn straps where the harness had once been attached. Her eyes grew

even wider as she noticed the tattered reins. Something had happened to her father – something bad.

Not pausing to give her actions thought, Belle threw a saddle onto Philippe's back, tightened the girth, and put a new bridle over his head. She knew she was asking a lot of the horse, but he was the only one who knew where her father was. Mounting, she kicked the horse forward.

Belle knew that her father had gone into the woods. That much she was sure of; it was the route he always took. But as Philippe left the familiar countryside of the village and cantered through the thickening forest, her hopes grew dimmer. This part of the forest was huge. Finding one man among all of it seemed almost impossible. "Hurry, Philippe," she said as the horse veered around a tree that had been split in half. "Lead me to him."

The woods grew still thicker, the sky still darker, but Philippe plunged bravely ahead. Belle scanned the ground and sides of the small path. Suddenly, she spotted her father's cart. It was on the ground, tipped on its side. Her father's beautiful music boxes were strewn about, some broken beyond repair, others less damaged. But there was no sign of her father.

Nudging Philippe with her heels, she urged him on again. The horse cantered forward, seemingly familiar with the thin and winding path. Belle could only hope that was because it was the way he and her father had gone.

To her relief, a gate came into view a moment later. Beyond the thick iron bars, she saw a giant stone castle. Philippe whinnied. Her father had to be in there, somewhere. Belle just knew it. Quickly, she dismounted and patted Philippe. She whispered words of encouragement, leading him inside the gate, and then asked him to wait. She moved to go up the stone steps, then paused. Belle was not about to go running into the strange castle with no way to protect herself. Looking around, she spotted a thick branch that had fallen to the ground. Picking it up, she held it over her head, brandishing it like a club. *Then* she made her way up to the front doors.

Belle didn't even bother to knock. If her father was indeed inside somewhere, she didn't want to waste any time in finding him. Pushing open the doors, she found herself inside a massive foyer. A few candles hung on the walls, barely casting enough light to illuminate the space.

Squaring her shoulders, Belle took a deep breath and walked farther into the castle.

As Belle made her way towards the grand staircase, her eyes adjusted to the dark. She heard muffled whispers, but she couldn't see anyone. Two voices rose and fell, and then she heard one phrase uttered clear as day: "But what if she's the one? The one who will break the spell?"

"Who said that?" Belle asked, whipping around and peering in the direction she thought the voices had come from.

Nothing.

"Who's there?"

Still nothing.

And then, from somewhere deep within the castle, Belle heard the unmistakable sound of someone coughing. *Papa.* It didn't matter who was whispering. She just needed to find her father. Grabbing a candelabrum from a nearby table, Belle began to climb the long staircase, following it up to its very top. When she reached the end of the labyrinthine stairs, she found herself in a tower, which, she noticed with increasing dread, was used as a prison. A grated iron door stood opposite the stairs.

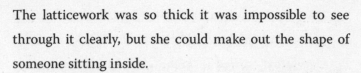

The latticework was so thick it was impossible to see through it clearly, but she could make out the shape of someone sitting inside.

"Papa?" Belle called out. "Is that you?"

"Belle?" Maurice answered in a muffled voice. "How did you find me?"

Belle raced across the dim tower and dropped to her knees in front of the door. A narrow opening allowed her just enough space to see her father. He was hunched over, his shoulders trembling. When their eyes met, she knew instantly he was not well. Setting the candelabrum down on the floor beside her, she reached through the opening. Her fingers closed around her father's. "Oh, Papa," she said, sadness tearing through her. "Your hands are ice. We need to get you home."

To her surprise, Maurice did not agree. "Belle, you must leave this place!" he said. When she ignored him and started to use the branch to hit the iron lock, he grew more and more agitated. "Stop! They'll hear you!"

Belle paused. "Who's 'they'?" she asked, cocking her head. She thought about the phantom voices she'd heard earlier. "Who did this to you?"

"No time to explain!" her father said. "You *must* go!"

Belle shook her head stubbornly. "I won't leave you!"

Her father stifled a groan. He had always loved his daughter's tenacity and spirit, but for once he just wanted her to do what he said. He couldn't stomach the idea of his sweet girl meeting the creature who had put him in that cell. "Belle, this castle is alive!" he said, trying to make her understand. "You must get away before he finds you!"

"'He'?" Belle repeated.

Before Maurice could open his mouth to respond, a roar filled the tower. Belle spun around, raising her branch high in the air. But it was no use. She couldn't see anything in the thick shadows. She could, however, hear a voice – a deep, rumbling voice that seemed to surround her, making her heart pound faster.

"Who are *you*?" the voice said. "How did you get in here?"

"I've come for my father," Belle said, trying to sound braver than she felt. "Release him."

The voice sounded closer as it hissed the next words: "Your father is a thief."

Belle recoiled as if she had been struck, fear turning into outrage. How dare the voice accuse her father like that? "Liar!" she shouted. Her father was a loving and kind man. He was a gentle man. He would never do anything like –

"He stole a rose!" the voice roared.

As Belle's head whipped back towards her father, her brown eyes locked with his. Guilt suddenly flooded through her as the reality of what must have happened hit her. "I asked for the rose," she said in barely a whisper.

"Belle...." Maurice said sadly, confirming what she knew to be true. Her father had taken the rose only because it was the one thing she had asked him to bring her. It was *her* fault he was in that cell – her fault entirely.

"Punish me, not him," Belle said, tearing her eyes away from her father and speaking to the invisible source of the voice.

"No!" Maurice shouted in anguish. "He means to keep me forever. Apparently, that's what happens around here when you pick a flower."

Belle frowned. "A life sentence for a rose?" she said to the shadows, hoping her father might be wrong.

"I received eternal damnation for one," came the voice out of the dark. "I'm merely locking him away." There was a pause, as though whoever the voice belonged to was distracted, thinking of some distant memory. And then the voice came again, colder than ever. "Now ... do you still wish to take your father's place?"

Belle had had enough of talking to air. She wanted to see with whom she was bargaining for her life. "Come into the light," she demanded.

Behind her, her father murmured, "No," and shuffled back in his cell. But the voice did not answer. Belle reached down and grabbed the candelabrum that had been sitting by her father's cell. She lifted it. For one brief moment, the light blinded her. But when her eyes adjusted, Belle gasped.

Standing in front of her was a huge creature unlike any Belle had ever seen. Large horns rose out of his head, and his lower jaw jutted forward. His entire body was covered in golden-brown hair and thick muscles. It was hard for Belle to tell just how big the creature's front paws were, clenched in fists as they were, but his back paws were large and long, with sharp claws that flashed when the light hit them. The word *beast* flashed in her mind as she gazed at the creature. He was a thing of nightmares – the monster lurking in the fairy tales she had read as a child.

But when Belle lifted her eyes to meet the Beast's, she was surprised by how human they looked – and how full of pain they seemed. Blue as the morning sky, they stared back at her, haunted. She felt a strange pang of what was almost sympathy for the giant creature. And then....

"Choose!" The Beast's lips curled back over sharp fangs as he snarled his demand.

All feelings but those of dread and disgust vanished. Belle looked back at her father, who pleaded with her not to do anything rash.

"But you'll die here," she said, knowing all too well it was true.

"I SAID CHOOSE!" the Beast snarled once again.

"No, Belle," Maurice said, trying to reason with his headstrong daughter. "I couldn't save your mother, but

I can save you. Now go!" But his words lost their power as a coughing fit overtook him. The coughs racked his already weakened body and broke Belle's heart.

"All right, Papa. I'll leave," Belle said, trying to reassure Maurice and make him stop coughing. Then she turned to the Beast. "Open the door. I need a minute alone with him." She waited for the large creature to do something. He didn't. "Please?" Still he ignored her request. Anger flared in her chest once more, hot and fierce. "Are you so coldhearted that you won't allow a daughter to kiss her father good-bye? Forever can spare a minute!"

Belle's chest heaved as she waited for the Beast to respond. For one long tense moment, he just stared at her with cold, cruel eyes and she wondered if she had gone too far. He took a step towards her, his massive paw reaching out. She closed her eyes and braced herself for his retaliation.

She heard a clang. Opening her eyes, she saw that the Beast had opened the cell door. He gestured for her to enter. "When this door closes," he warned as she passed, "it will not open again."

Belle didn't hesitate, she rushed inside and embraced her father. "I'm so sorry, Papa," she sobbed. "I should have gone with you!"

Maurice put his hands on Belle's shoulders and gently pushed her back until they were eye to eye. "No, this was my fault," he said, shaking his head. He reached out and pinched her cheek the way he had done when she was a little girl. It had always reassured her then. Now it just made her sad. He went on, his voice choked with emotion. "Listen, Belle. Forget about me. I've had my life...."

"Forget you?" Belle said in disbelief. "How could I ever? Everything I am is because of you."

Belle's words seemed to hit Maurice like a punch to the stomach. He looked at her as though seeing her for the first time – not the smart, sweet little girl he had raised on his own, but the brave, strong woman she had become. It all seemed too much for the older man. Tears flooded his eyes.

"Enough of this," the Beast said, his harsh voice stabbing into both father and daughter. "She must go."

Belle and Maurice clung to each other.

"Now!" The Beast's voice tore them apart.

"I love you, Belle," Maurice said. "Don't be afraid."

"I love you, Papa. I'm not afraid," Belle said, leaning forward and gently kissing him on the cheek. As she did so, she manoeuvred her body so her back was to the cell door, her hands on her father's shoulders. And then, in barely a whisper, she added, "And I will escape. I promise...."

Before Maurice could stop her, Belle pivoted her body. The force swung her father through the door just as the Beast slammed it shut. Falling to the ground, Maurice cried out as the reality of what his daughter had just sacrificed became clear.

It seemed to hit the Beast at the same moment. And while it obviously devastated Maurice, the Beast appeared confused. "You took his place?" he asked Belle. "Why?"

"He is my father," she answered without hesitation.

"He's a fool," the Beast retorted. "And so are you." Without another word, he grabbed Maurice by the shirt and began to drag him away.

Belle stifled the sob that threatened to escape her throat. She watched silently through the gate as her father and the Beast disappeared down the stairs. She waited until she was sure she was alone, and only when silence had descended on the tower did she finally slump to the ground. As the tears fell, colder and harsher than the snow that had once again begun to fall outside, one thought echoed through her mind: what was to become of her?

CHAPTER VI

THE BEAST WAS TIRED – TIRED AND perplexed. He was still not sure how it happened that he now held a beautiful young woman prisoner while her father, the real thief, was making his way back towards the comfort of his home. He shook his head. No, it did not make sense.

But then again, he thought as he pushed open the castle's front door, nothing had made sense in his life in a long, long time.

Storming inside the foyer, the Beast nearly collided with Lumiere and Cogsworth. The candelabrum and clock had been waiting anxiously for him to return. "Master," Lumiere began, "since the girl is going to be with us for quite some time –"

"And I hope 'forever' was an exaggeration," Cogsworth said, his tone every bit as flat and polished as expected of a majordomo. "We don't have the staff for that kind of extended stay...." His voice trailed off as the Beast turned and glared at him.

Not intimidated, Lumiere forged on. "Whether it's for a day or a lifetime," he said smoothly, "you might want to offer her a more comfortable room."

"This whole castle is a prison," the Beast said harshly. As he spoke, Chapeau, the coatrack, tried to take the Beast's cloak. The Beast brushed him off and continued walking towards the grand staircase. Over his shoulder, he added, "What difference does a bed make?" Not waiting for an answer, he disappeared into the shadows.

Cogsworth waited to speak until he was sure his master couldn't hear him, and even then, he did so under his breath. "Yes. It's a prison thanks to you, Sire. I just love being a clock." He sighed bitterly. As head of the Beast's household, Cogsworth knew he was supposed to be the picture of respect at all times. But sometimes that was difficult. Sometimes it was hard to forget that he and every other member of the staff were in the state they were in because of the master they still had to serve. "I knew he wouldn't say yes."

"But technically ... he didn't say no," Lumiere pointed out. Flashing Cogsworth a sly smile, the candelabrum headed towards the stairs that led to the prison tower.

Behind him, Cogsworth remained still. He knew what Lumiere had in mind. The romantic footman was as easy to read as a book. The candelabrum wanted to free the girl and put her somewhere more noticeable – in the hopes that she might be the one who could break the curse they were all under, the curse that had remained unbroken for those long years because of one obvious fact: the Beast was a beast, both literally and figuratively. And the curse the Enchantress had placed on them required someone to love him despite that.

Cogsworth sighed. He knew his friend was well intentioned. But Cogsworth was a realist. No matter where the girl laid her head, she would not love the Beast. And if Lumiere got his way and brought her out of the prison, it would only make the master furious. Cogsworth began waddling towards the stairs. He was going to have to stop Lumiere before the candelabrum did something they would all regret.

But Lumiere had already opened the cell door. "Forgive my intrusion, mademoiselle," he said into the darkness, "but the master has sent me to escort you to your room."

Belle was sitting on the floor, her cheeks stained with tears. Hearing Lumiere's voice, she stood. "My room?" she said, sounding confused. "But I thought –"

"You thought wrong," Lumiere replied. "He is a beast. Not a monster."

A moment later, Belle appeared in the cell doorway, brandishing a stool over her head. She looked around for the source of the voice she had heard.

"*Allô*," Lumiere said.

Looking down, Belle saw Lumiere waving at her with one of his candlesticks. She screamed. Then, as if he were a mouse that had surprised her in the pantry, Belle swung the stool at Lumiere, knocking him to the ground. His candles went out, plunging the tower into darkness.

One by one, the three candles that made up the candelabrum relit. As Belle watched, the flickers of light illuminated two eyes and a mouth in the elaborate design of the metal. "What *are* you?" she finally asked.

"I am Lumiere," the candelabrum replied, flashing Belle what could only be called a rakish smile.

"And you can talk," Belle observed.

Suddenly, Cogsworth waddled into the tower. He was out of breath from the long climb, and for a moment he just stood there, his little clock chest heaving. "Of course he can talk," he finally said. "How else is he supposed to communicate?" Turning, he put his hands on his hips and glared at Lumiere. "As head of the household, I demand to know what you are doing."

"It is better to ask for forgiveness than permission," Lumiere replied cryptically.

As the duo bickered, Belle inched her way back into the cell. She reappeared a moment later with a pitcher of water in her hands. Seeing the potentially harmful weapon, Lumiere held up a golden arm. "*Un moment,* mademoiselle...." he said. Then he pulled Cogsworth aside. He lowered his voice to a whisper. "If we don't break the curse before the last petal falls, we will never be human again. What do you want to be for the rest of your life, Cogsworth – a man or a mantel clock?"

Cogsworth frowned. Lumiere was right. Still ... "If he catches us...."

"We will be quiet," Lumiere promised. He looked at Cogsworth with an expression bordering on desperate. Finally, the clock gave the slightest of nods. Lumiere didn't wait. Turning, he looked back at Belle. "Ready, miss?" he asked, bowing and pointing one of his candles towards the tower's exit.

Belle looked back and forth between the candelabrum and the clock. Then she looked at the cell. While neither option was exactly comforting, following the talking household objects at least meant getting out of a cell. Taking a deep breath, she leaned down, picked up Lumiere, and followed Cogsworth out of the tower.

As the trio made their way across a long stone walkway, Belle's eyes darted back and forth. But no matter where she looked, she could not make out an escape route of any kind. The woods that stretched out behind the castle were vast – and a bit intimidating.

Although, she thought as she looked down at her companions, the castle wasn't exactly making her feel warm or fuzzy. She eyed Lumiere and Cogsworth and, for the umpteenth time, resisted the urge to turn Lumiere upside down and look for the strings that had to be making him move. And once again, she stopped herself from peering over her shoulder to try to spot the ventriloquist she knew must be lurking somewhere nearby, giving voice to two objects that, in her experience, were usually inanimate. Both times, she stopped herself because she knew it would do no good. Somehow, the candelabrum and clock were *alive*.

"You must forgive first impressions," Lumiere said, as if sensing her thoughts. "I hope you are not too startled."

"Startled?" Belle repeated with a sarcastic laugh. "Why would I be startled? I'm talking to a candle."

Lumiere looked aghast. "Candel-a-brum," he corrected, enunciating each syllable. "Enormous difference. But we do hope you enjoy your stay here. The castle is your home now, so feel free to go anywhere you like –"

"Except the West Wing."

In unison, Belle and Lumiere turned to look at the clock. But while Lumiere was shooting him a barely veiled "Would you please shut your mouth?" look, Belle stared at him with evident curiosity. She opened her mouth to ask where the forbidden West Wing might be but was stopped by Cogsworth trying to cover his tracks.

"Which we do not have," he added.

It was too late. Belle wanted to know more. "Why?" she asked. "What's in the West Wing?"

"Uh ..." Lumiere stammered, the flames on his candles flickering nervously. "Nothing. Storage space."

Belle raised an eyebrow, clearly not buying the candelabrum's explanation. She raised her arm so that Lumiere's light illuminated a nearby curved stone window, displaying a tower that rose out of the western portion of the castle. As she did so, the moon appeared over the horizon, casting an eerie light on the tower. Belle could have sworn she saw the Beast's shadow in the white light and heard an anguished cry. Shivering, she lowered Lumiere.

"This way, please," the candelabrum said, eager to move them along.

With one last glance over her shoulder, Belle sighed

and once again followed Cogsworth as he waddled down one hallway and along another. Finally, he came to a stop in front of a large door.

"Welcome to your new home," Lumiere said in a grandiose tone.

Belle's hand hovered over the doorknob. A part of her wanted to turn the knob. Another part of her was terrified to do so. She had no idea what to expect. If the room was anything like the rest of the castle, with its layers of dust and oppressive sad portraits and decaying furniture, she was going to have to insist they bring her back to the tower.

Taking a deep breath, she turned the knob and pushed open the door. The light from Lumiere's three candles filled the space. Belle gasped. She was looking into what appeared to be a gorgeous bedroom – far more elegant than any she had ever seen in real life or imagined in her stories.

As if in a dream, she slowly walked inside, her eyes feasting on every perfect detail of the room. There was a large white-and-gold-painted armoire along one wall, and along another wall a beautiful writing desk had been placed. A chair, covered in rich velvet, was tucked underneath it, and a stack of crisp white paper was placed on one side. Opposite a set of huge picture windows covered by thick satin curtains was an enormous canopy bed that took up nearly a third of the room. And tucked in a corner, delicate and sweet, was a dressing table with a mirror framed in gold. Even the ceiling of the room was breathtaking. White clouds had been painted in a perfect blue sky, the detail so real Belle could have sworn she saw the clouds move.

"It's ... beautiful," she finally said when she realized Lumiere and Cogsworth were staring at her, waiting for a response.

Lumiere smiled broadly while Cogsworth nodded, his pleasure more contained. "Of course. Master wanted you to have the finest room in the castle," Lumiere said, making his way to the bed and leaping onto it. A cloud of dust rose into the air. "Oh, dear! We weren't expecting guests."

As if on cue, a feather duster swooped into the room. Belle's eyes widened as the feather duster quickly moved from surface to surface, sweeping until everything shone.

Stopping, she bowed in Belle's direction. "*Enchantée*, mademoiselle! Don't worry, I'll have this room spotless in no time," she said before turning and jumping into the arms of Lumiere. "This plan of yours is ... dangerous," she said, giggling.

Belle stifled her own giggle as Lumiere waggled his eyebrows and replied, "I would risk anything to kiss you again, Plumette...." He leaned closer and puckered his lips.

Plumette stopped him. "No, my love," she said, her voice serious. "I've been burned by you before. We must be strong."

"How can I be strong when you make me so weak?" Lumiere replied.

Belle averted her eyes from the romantic pair and turned her attention towards other items in the room. "Is everything here alive?" she asked, picking up a brush. "Hello, what's *your* name?"

Cogsworth looked at Belle and shook his head. "Um ... that's a hairbrush," he said as though pointing out the obvious.

Belle opened her mouth to ask just what the rules were for enchanted objects when, suddenly, a loud snore sounded behind her. Turning, she yelped as the large armoire's drawers opened and shut by themselves in time with the snoring.

"Do not be alarmed, mademoiselle," Lumiere said calmly. "This is just your wardrobe. Meet Madame de Garderobe, a great singer."

The armoire let out a long, loud yawn.

"A better sleeper," Cogsworth added as he walked over and nudged the wardrobe.

With a grunt, Garderobe awoke. Blinking the sleep out of her eyes, she gave a surprised little shout when she noticed her audience. "Cogsworth!" she exclaimed in an overly dramatic manner. "You officious alarm clock. A diva needs her beauty rest!"

Cogsworth's springs tightened at the insult and his mouth opened, ready with a sharp rebuke. But Lumiere didn't give him the chance. He jumped in before the clock could say a word. "Of course you do, madame," he said in his most soothing voice. "Forgive us, but we have someone for you to dress."

Spotting Belle for the first time, Garderobe emitted a happy cry. "Finally!" she said. "A woman!" Then, as though she were doing an inventory, Garderobe took stock of Belle. "Pretty eyes. Proud face. A perfect canvas. Yes! I will find you something worthy of a princess." The wardrobe's front drawers flapped open and closed in what Belle could only assume was the wardrobe's version of a happy clap.

"But I'm not a princess," Belle said.

"Nonsense!" Garderobe said, brushing off Belle's protest. "Now, let's see what I've got in my drawers." Opening up the top one, she shouted as a few moths flew out. "How embarrassing!" she said.

To Belle's surprise, both sides of the armoire went from white to a soft shade of pink. The armoire was blushing!

Before Belle could ask how such a thing was possible – how *any* of it was possible, for that matter – Garderobe began to pull things helter-skelter out of her drawers and off hangers. A large hoopskirt went over Belle's head, followed by at least four different dresses cut right then and there by the wardrobe to be used as fabric. Belle was turned and twisted as Garderobe assembled an outfit.

When the wardrobe paused to take a breath, Belle

sneaked a peek at her reflection in the mirror across the room. To her horror, she saw the wardrobe had indeed created something from what she had in her drawers. But the result was the most garish ensemble Belle had ever seen. It seemed to swallow her up in shades of blue, pink and yellow. Catching Lumiere's eye, Belle saw that the candelabrum was equally mortified. But both he and Cogsworth backed towards the door. They knew not to mess with Garderobe when she was in the middle of a creation.

"Anyway," Lumiere said, "if you have further needs, the staff will attend to them. We are at your service. *Au revoir!*" Then, with a deep bow, he grabbed Cogsworth and slipped out of the room. Plumette followed close behind. A moment later, the door closed, leaving Belle alone with Garderobe.

Belle didn't hesitate. She had a feeling that if she was ever going to get answers, the diva armoire was going to be the one to give them to her. Turning to Garderobe, she asked the question she had wanted to ask ever since Lumiere had revealed himself to her. "How did you get here?"

As she suspected, Garderobe's eyes lit up at the

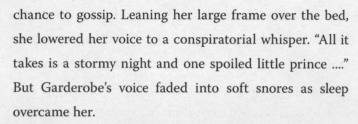

chance to gossip. Leaning her large frame over the bed, she lowered her voice to a conspiratorial whisper. "All it takes is a stormy night and one spoiled little prince ...." But Garderobe's voice faded into soft snores as sleep overcame her.

Belle sighed. It looked as if she wasn't going to be getting answers after all. At least not anytime soon. Belle quickly slipped out of the disaster of a dress. Then she turned and looked around the room. She was alone, her only guardian fast asleep. Now was the time for her to try to make her escape. The only question was, how?

CHAPTER VII

GASTON STILL COULDN'T BELIEVE IT. He had been rejected. Coldly, flatly, completely rejected. As he sat in *his* favourite chair in *his* favourite spot in the town tavern – right below the wall featuring all the antlers and trophies *he* had won – Gaston could not shake the bad feeling in the pit of his stomach. Even LeFou, sitting by his side, telling him how fantastic he was, could not break through the sorrow he felt.

"Picture it, LeFou," Gaston said, taking a big swallow from his drink. He waved his hand in front of him. "A rustic cabin. My latest kill roasting on the fire. Adorable children running around us while my love rubs my tired feet."

"Ooh! What's roasting on the fire?" LeFou said, ever the captive and willing audience. "It's the minor details that really paint the picture."

Gaston shot the smaller man a look for interrupting his monologue. "But what does Belle say?" he asked, the picture painted clearly enough in his own mind. "'I will *never* marry you, Gaston.'" He slammed down his drink in anger.

"There *are* other girls," LeFou pointed out. He nodded over his shoulder at a group of such girls. Gaston barely gave them a glance, but it was enough to send them into fits of giggles.

LeFou was right. Gaston could have the pick of any of the girls in the village – or the next village. Or any village, for that matter. But that wasn't the point. He didn't want any of those girls. "A great hunter doesn't waste his time on rabbits," he finally said. His words echoed through the tavern, causing the girls' flirtatious smiles to fade on their faces.

Slumping down in his chair, Gaston absently played with a piece of string hanging from the fraying cushion. Vaguely, he heard LeFou trying to cheer him up, but he barely paid attention. LeFou's arguments – that he was the bravest, strongest, most admired man in the village – were tired. Gaston had heard them all before. And, of course, he knew they were all true. He was exceptional. He was the town hero, the best hunter there was; he was even good at decoration – antlers made a room, in his opinion – and there was no doubt in anyone's mind he was the largest and most handsome of men.

But what does it matter whether all those things are true, Gaston thought, *if Belle doesn't believe it?*

Just then, the door to the tavern flew open. Maurice stood in the doorway. His eyes were wild and his clothing was torn. He grabbed on to the doorjamb as a cough racked his body. "Help!" he said when the coughing had subsided. "Somebody help me! We have to go ... not a minute to lose...."

As he spoke, Maurice moved into the tavern, seeking out the warmth of the fire that roared in the hearth. Seeing how dishevelled the man was, the tavern keeper tried to calm him. "Whoa, whoa, whoa," he said. "Slow down, Maurice."

Maurice shook his head. "He's got Belle ... locked in a dungeon!"

Gaston sat up straighter, his interest piqued.

"Who's got her?" the tavern keeper asked.

"A beast!" Maurice answered. "A horrible, monstrous beast!"

Shocked by the man's words, the whole inn went silent – for a moment. And then Jean the potter held up his mug and smiled. "What are you putting in this stuff?" he asked, breaking the silence.

The tavern keeper shook his head. "Don't look at me," he retorted. "He just got here."

Down at the other end of the counter, a vagrant who *hadn't* just got there looked up. The man was even more dishevelled than Maurice and his eyes were cloudy, his cheeks weathered. He glanced at Maurice and nodded, as though he and Maurice were in on it together. "What they don't tell you is there used to be a castle and we don't remember any of it!" he said.

Instantly, the tavern filled with laughter.

"No!" Maurice protested. "He could be right! My daughter's life is in danger, why do you laugh? This isn't a joke! His castle is hidden in the woods. It's already winter there!"

"Winter in June?" Jean said, laughing. "Crazy old Maurice."

"Please listen!" Maurice begged, looking around the room at the dispassionate faces. "The Beast is real. Will no one help me?"

Sitting in his chair, Gaston stayed silent. Belle's father was an odd man. He always had been. But as the man continued to beg, an idea began to form in the back of Gaston's mind. An idea that could get him exactly what he wanted and make him look like the hero – again.

Quickly, Gaston got to his feet. "I'll help you, Maurice," he said grandly.

"You will?" LeFou asked, confused by his friend's sudden generosity.

Gaston turned and winked at LeFou and mouthed, *Just watch.* Then he addressed the room. "Everyone! Stop making fun of this man at once!" Instantly, the laughter died. He nodded. He really *was* the most respected man in town.

Maurice rushed over and fell to his knees. "Thank you, Captain," he said gratefully. "Thank you."

"Don't thank me, Maurice," Gaston said, pulling the old man to his feet. "Lead us to the Beast."

Still mumbling his thanks, Maurice headed out of the tavern. Gaston and LeFou exchanged looks as they followed him. The other patrons, seeing their beloved Gaston on a mission, followed, as well. Soon there was a parade making its way through the village. The commotion woke still others, who eagerly joined in, despite not knowing what was going on.

"I see what you're doing," LeFou said in a whisper as they walked.

Gaston nodded. He had known LeFou would work out his plan. He always did. Now Gaston just had to make sure Maurice didn't work it out before it could all unfold. If Gaston was right – and he usually was – he had just found a way to make Belle marry him after all....

Inside the Beast's castle, things were a bit calmer than they were back in the village ... but not by much. Ever since Belle's arrival, the staff had been in a full-blown tizzy. It wasn't very often they had a guest in the castle. In fact, they hadn't had a guest in the castle since that fateful night. Determined to make Belle feel at home – in the hopes that perhaps one day the castle could *be* her home

— every member of the household was doing some part to make everything perfect, starting with dinner.

The kitchen staff hurried about excitedly. Headed by Mrs Potts — a no-nonsense teapot with a heart of gold — they were putting together an elaborate meal for Belle and their master.

Sitting on top of her tea service trolley, Mrs Potts watched with pleasure as plates and serving ware that had long since gone unused came out of their drawers and cupboards. Beside her, her son, Chip, hopped up and down with excitement. "Mama," the little teacup said, "there's a girl in the castle!"

"Yes, Chip," Mrs Potts said gently. "We know."

"Is she pretty? Is she nice?" Chip asked, jumping on his saucer and using it to zip around his mother. "What kind of tea does she like? Herbal? Oolong? Chamomile?"

"We'll find out soon enough," Mrs Potts said. "Now slow down before you break your handle!"

At that moment, Lumiere and Cogsworth entered. The candelabrum quickly made his way over to Cuisinier, the large stove — complete with cooktop, range, vent hood, and ovens — in the middle of the kitchen. "This is your night," Lumiere said seriously. "We are counting on you, Monsieur Cuisinier."

The stove puffed up proudly. "Finally!" he said. His voice sounded rusty, as though it had not been used in quite some time. "A chance to cook again. Do you know what it's been like pleasing a beast's palate? 'Stag tartare with the antlers on' every single day! Who eats chicken for dessert, I ask you? Who?" As he stopped to take a breath, Cuisinier's sides heaved with indignation.

Knowing it was best to appease the rather temperamental stove, Lumiere nodded sympathetically. "Tonight, you make a soufflé!"

"LUMIERE!"

The Beast's roar echoed in the kitchen – it seemed the master was on his way. Instantly, Lumiere's flames dimmed. Cogsworth shook. They both knew the Beast was not pleased.

"Just ... let me do the talking," Lumiere said to the majordomo. While Cogsworth was very good at running a household – and telling time – he was terrible at knowing the right thing to say. He had been known, on more than one occasion, to try to escape blame at any cost. It would be best for all those involved if Lumiere was the one to deal with the Beast. At least, he hoped it would be.

A moment later, the doors to the kitchen burst open and the Beast appeared. His chest was heaving and his blue eyes were stormy as he took in the assembled staff. He sniffed the air, which was filled with the delicious smells of cooking, and his eyes grew even stormier. "You are making her dinner?" he growled.

"We thought you might appreciate the company," Lumiere replied in his most politic voice. He opened his mouth to explain the benefits of dining with another when Cogsworth jumped in. Lumiere shot him a look, begging him to stay silent, but the clock would not be stopped.

"Master," Cogsworth said, trying to cover his own wheels and pins, "I can assure you that I had no part in this hopeless plan. Preparing a dinner, designing a gown for her, giving her a suite in the East Wing –"

"You gave her a bedroom?" The Beast's shout had enough force to blow out Lumiere's candles.

Cogsworth backpedalled. "I ... I ... well," he stammered. "You said ... um ... that the whole castle was a prison, so what difference would a bed make...."

Seeing his friend struggle, Lumiere jumped in. "That is true, master," he pointed out. "And if the girl is the one who can break the spell, maybe you can start by using dinner to charm her." He turned and threw his friend a bone. "Good plan, Cogsworth."

The Beast narrowed his eyes. Then he began to pace back and forth. Finally, he looked at Lumiere and Cogsworth. "The idea is ridiculous," he said. "*Charm* the prisoner?"

"You must *try*, master," Lumiere said. He took a deep breath. He knew that what he was about to say was not something the master wanted to hear. But nevertheless, it needed to be said. "With every passing day, we become less human."

Behind him, the staff piped up, adding their own encouragement. He heard someone say "You can do it," and another member of the staff added, "Please." In their voices, Lumiere heard the same desperation he felt. Their master's fate was their fate – yet only the Beast could change it.

"She's the daughter of a common thief," the Beast pointed out, his staff's pleas falling on deaf ears. "What kind of person do you think that makes her?"

Mrs Potts, who had been silent up until that point, finally spoke up. "Oh, you can't judge people by who their father is, now can you?"

She didn't need to say more; her loaded statement was clear enough. All around her, the staff cringed, prepared for the master to retaliate. But to their surprise, he didn't. He paused for a moment, his eyes locked on Mrs Potts. She knew, more than many, just how deep a wound the master's father had left on him.

Finally, with a resigned grunt, the Beast turned and left the kitchen. Lumiere, Cogsworth and Mrs Potts exchanged glances. And then they rushed after him, knowing he couldn't be left to his own devices to ask the girl to dinner.

CHAPTER VIII

THE BEAST STOOD IN FRONT OF the door to the bedroom that now, against his wishes, belonged to Belle. Beside him, his key staff waited, ready to help if necessary. He glared at them, and then, raising one big paw, he knocked. Twice.

"You will join me for dinner!" he said, not waiting for a response from Belle. "That's not a request!"

On her serving trolley, Mrs Potts gave a small cough. "Gently, master," she advised. "Remember, the girl lost her father and her freedom in one day."

"Yes," Lumiere agreed. "The poor thing is probably in there scared to death."

The Beast sighed. He was getting rather tired of the sudden onslaught of advice. Still, he knocked again.

This time, there came an answer. "Just a minute." Belle's voice was muffled through the thick door.

"You see!" Lumiere said happily. "There she is! Now, master, remember, be gentle ..."

"Kind ..." added Mrs Potts.

"Charming!" Plumette chirped.

"And when she opens the door," Lumiere finished, "give her a dashing, debonair smile. Come, come – show me the smile."

Show him the smile? the Beast repeated to himself. Had Lumiere lost his mind? He hadn't smiled in years. There had been no reason to. He started to point that out, but a look from Mrs Potts stopped him. Reluctantly, he tensed the muscles in his face, pulling his lips back over his teeth.

In unison, his staff took a horrified step back.

"Eh, less teeth," Lumiere suggested.

The Beast didn't need a mirror to know that his first attempt at a smile had resulted in the most hideous grin anyone had ever seen. He tried again.

"More teeth?" Plumette said.

The Beast sighed. Still hideous, he supposed. Once more, he adjusted his smile.

"*Different* teeth?" Cogsworth advised.

"How about no teeth?" Mrs Potts added.

The Beast flashed a warning look. He had had enough. The staff wanted him to ask Belle to dinner. He would ask her to dinner. He would *not*, however, spend any more time trying to smile. Knocking once more, he tried again: "Will you join me for dinner?"

This time, Belle's response was much swifter. "You've taken me prisoner and now you're asking me to dine with you?" Her voice sounded closer now, as though she were right on the other side of the door. "Are you mad?"

As Belle's words registered with the Beast, his expression grew dark. His paws clenched at his sides and his lips pulled up in a snarl.

"Calm yourself, master," Mrs Potts said in her most reassuring tone. She knew the Beast was only moments away from losing his temper.

"But she is infuriating," the Beast replied through clenched teeth. "Difficult."

Mrs Potts tried not to smile at the irony of her master's calling Belle difficult. She attempted to reason with him instead. "So, you be *easy*," she said.

Taking a deep breath, the Beast prepared to try once more. His body shook with the effort and his jaw clenched fiercely, but he managed to speak in a tone that was mostly nice. "It would give me great pleasure if you would join me for dinner."

Belle's response was immediate. "It would give *me* great pleasure," she said through the door, "if you would go away."

That was the final straw. The Beast's eyebrows twitched. His tail thrashed. His claws flashed, and then, as the staff backed away, he lifted his paw and banged on the door with all his strength. The hallway shook.

"I told you to come to dinner!" he snarled, all nicety gone.

Belle did not back down. She banged on the other side of the door. "And I told you *no*! I'd starve before I ever ate a meal with you!"

"Be my guest," the Beast shouted back. "Go ahead and *starve*!" Turning, he glared at his staff. They were the ones who had got him into this mess in the first place. "If she doesn't eat with me, then she doesn't eat at all!"

"Master, no!" Lumiere protested. "Show her the real you."

"This *is* the real me," the Beast said. Without another word, he whipped around and headed towards his rooms. Behind him, he could hear the staff muttering to themselves, their voices disappointed. But he didn't care. What had they expected to happen? For Belle to swoon at the idea of eating dinner with *him*? A *beast*? They were fools if they thought that would happen. And he had been a fool to try.

Pushing open the door to the West Wing, he stalked over to a small table by the window. On top of it were a hand mirror and a glass jar, which held a single red rose that hung, enchanted, in its centre. Picking up the mirror, the Beast gave a single command. "Show me the girl!"

Magic whirled and the mirror's glass slowly shifted and swirled until it revealed Belle. She sat, her back against the door of her room and a look of dread on her face.

Slowly, he put the mirror down. Belle was scared because of him, because of the beast he was – the beast he might very well always be. His eyes locked on the enchanted rose and he sighed, watching as another petal fell to the table. It was only a matter of time now before the last petal fell, and when that happened ....

The Beast shuddered and lowered his head. When that happened, all hope would be lost. And if Belle's reaction was any indication, he had just blown one of his few chances to put an end to the curse.

I have to get out of here, Belle thought as she pushed herself to her feet. The Beast was a monster. His behaviour just then had proved that beyond a doubt. If she didn't get away now, she would most likely be stuck with him forever. She shuddered at the horrifying thought.

Walking over to the window, she looked out. After she had been left alone with a narcoleptic wardrobe as her only guardian, she had wasted no time in putting an escape plan into action. Ripping apart the hideous dress Garderobe had made her, she had used the fabric to create a makeshift rope. It now hung out of the window, the end dangling about five metres from the ground. It wasn't perfect, but it would do.

She had just taken a deep breath and picked up the rope when ... *Knock! Knock! Knock!*

"I told you to go away!" she shouted over her shoulder.

To her surprise, it was not the Beast's deep and grumbling voice that answered. Instead, the voice that replied was gentle, kind and polished. "Don't worry, dear," it said. "It's not the master. It's Mrs Potts." A moment later, the door swung open and a serving trolley rolled inside. Placed on top were a beautifully painted teapot and a teacup with the same design on its side. The pot, Belle had to assume, was Mrs Potts.

Quickly, Belle tried to block the rope that hung behind her. But Mrs Potts had spotted the escape route the moment she had entered the room. It hadn't surprised her. Belle seemed like a clever girl, and the master had given her no reason to feel welcome. Still, Mrs Potts wasn't going to let the girl just leave – not if she could help it. And having lived with a stubborn individual for quite some time, she knew that sometimes the best way to make people do what they didn't want to do was to give them the chance to do it on their own terms.

"It's a very long journey, my lamb," Mrs Potts said sweetly. "Let me fix you up before you go. I have found in my experience that most troubles seem less troubling after a bracing cup o' tea. Isn't that right, Madame de

Garderobe?" Mrs Potts turned and addressed the armoire, who was still fast asleep. "Madame! Wake up!"

With a jolt, Garderobe awoke. "What?" she asked, sounding sleepy and confused. "I fell asleep again?"

"Madame used to sleep eight hours a day," the small teacup piped up. "Now she sleeps twenty-three."

"That'll do, Chip," Mrs Potts warned. "It's not polite to discuss a lady's habits."

But Chip, as Belle now knew him, had given her pause. And since she had got no answers from Garderobe earlier, she decided to try again. "What happened here?" she asked. "Is this an enchantment? A curse?" That could be the only logical explanation for the castle's oddities, in Belle's opinion. She had read many a story about such things, but she had never thought they could be *real*.

"She guessed it, Mama," Chip said, lisping in his little voice through the chip in the front of his cup. "She's clever."

As he spoke, his mother hopped over and filled him with tea. Then she nudged him towards Belle. "Slowly now, Chip," she warned. "Don't spill tea. Or secrets."

Belle smiled despite herself as she picked up Chip. He was so obviously a little boy, yet somehow he was trapped in the shape of a cup. *How sad it must be,* Belle thought, *to not have the ability to do little-boy things.*

As if sensing what she was thinking, Chip asked, "Want to see me do a trick?" Belle nodded, and Chip took a deep breath. Then he started to blow bubbles. The tea splish-splashed inside his cup, making Belle laugh. The sound echoed nicely through the room, and Mrs Potts smiled.

"That was a very brave thing you did for your father, dear," she remarked.

"We all think so," Garderobe said, nodding in agreement.

Belle's smile faded at the mention of her father. "I'm so worried about him," she said softly. "He's never been alone."

"Cheer up, my poppet," Mrs Potts said, trying to get back some of the earlier levity. "Things will turn out right in the end. You'll see. You'll feel a lot better after dinner."

Belle looked at the teapot and cocked her head. "But he said, 'If she doesn't eat with me, she doesn't eat at all.'" She had dropped her voice and tried to make it sound as scary and mean as possible. Mrs Potts held in a sigh. The master really had made a bad impression on the poor girl.

"People say a lot of things in anger," she said. "It is our choice whether or not to listen." As she spoke, she turned the serving trolley towards the door and began to leave. Turning to look back at Belle, Mrs Potts smiled. "Coming, poppety?"

Belle watched as the teapot disappeared out of the door. Her stomach rumbled. *Fine,* she thought, *I'll go and have dinner. But just this one meal. Then I am leaving ... once and for all.*

The kitchen staff was ready. Lumiere had seen to it as soon as Mrs Potts had told him she was going to speak with Belle. He knew it was only a matter of time before the kind teapot convinced Belle to come down for a quick bite.

But Lumiere had no intention of this being any small, quick bite. *This* meal was going to be one Belle would remember forever. It was going to involve the tastiest of hors d'oeuvres, the most delicious of entrees, the most delightful of drinks and, of course, the most decadent of desserts. By the time Belle put her fork down, she would never want to leave. At least, that was what Lumiere *hoped*.

Bursting into the kitchen, he clasped two of his candles together. "They're coming!" he said excitedly. "Final checks, everyone, *tout de suite!*" With pleasure, he watched as every member of the kitchen staff sprang into action. They all knew as well as he how important this dinner was.

All of them, that is, except apparently Cogsworth.

"No, you don't!" the clock said, shuffling into the middle of the fray. He folded his two little arms across his gears. "If the master finds out you violated his orders and fed her, he will blame me."

Lumiere turned and stared at his friend. Then he sighed. How could Cogsworth be thinking of himself at a time like this? Making his way over, he nodded. "Yes," he said, his tone teasing but his intent serious. "I will make sure of it. But did you see her stand up to him? I am telling you, this girl is the one! They *must* fall in love if we are to be human again, and they can't fall in love if she stays in her room."

"You know she will never love him," Cogsworth said softly.

"A broken clock is right two times a day, my friend," Lumiere replied, refusing to let the stodgy majordomo get him down, "and this is not one of those times. We *must* try."

Turning away from Cogsworth, he moved over to Cuisinier. Pots and pans bubbled and steamed on the stove, filling the air with a tantalizing smell. Behind him, Lumiere could feel Cogsworth's eyes on him, and he knew that the majordomo was struggling. Lumiere didn't blame him. He was right. The master would think this was all Cogsworth's doing if he found out. But they had no other choice. It wasn't every day a girl happened upon the enchanted castle – and a girl with the strength to stand up to the master, at that. *No,* Lumiere thought, shaking his head and straightening his candles with resolve. This dinner was going to happen – with or without Cogsworth's blessing.

Finally, the clock sighed. Lumiere waited.

"At least keep it down," Cogsworth said, his voice soft.

A smile spread across Lumiere's face. But he wiped it away before turning to his friend and nodding. "Of course, of course," he said. "But what is dinner without a little ... music?"

"Music?" Cogsworth cried, his voice no longer quiet.

He began shaking his head.

But it was too late. Lumiere was already guiding a harpsichord into the dining room. "Maestro Cadenza," he said as he set him up in a corner of the room, "your wife is upstairs sleeping more and more each day. She is counting on you to help the master and this girl fall in love."

With a flourish, the harpsichord played a scale, grimacing when one of the notes fell flat. "Then I shall play through the pain," he said bravely.

At that moment, Mrs Potts led Belle into the dining room. The girl looked around, awed by the elaborate spread set out on the table, but clearly still hesitant to be there. Lumiere saw the uneasiness in her eyes, and his resolve to make her comfortable grew stronger. He gave the staff one last knowing look, and then, with a flourish, he leaped onto the table.

"*Ma chère*, mademoiselle," he began as a beam of moonlight streamed through the window, making it appear as though the candelabrum were in the spotlight. He bowed. "It is with deepest pride and greatest pleasure that we welcome you tonight. We invite you to relax" – he nodded and the chair behind Belle moved in so that she sat, with a little squeak of surprise, and was pushed in to the table – "while we proudly present ... your dinner."

At first Belle sat with her hands on her lap as Lumiere guided her, course by course, through her meal. But as she listened to him describe the food and watched as the enchanted silverware and dishware made a show and dance, she began to relax. Her hands unclenched the napkin she was holding and her foot tapped to the rhythm of the harpsichord. By the time Lumiere referred to the "grey stuff" as delicious, Belle was smiling. She looked around at the plates and plates of food that seemed to multiply before her very eyes, her stomach growling nearly as loudly as the harpsichord was playing.

While Lumiere and the other staff continued to entertain her, Belle proceeded to eat to her heart's content. She tasted beef ragout and cheese soufflé. She dipped a freshly baked baguette in foie gras and sighed with pleasure as the food melted on her tongue. Each dish presented was better than the last, and every time Belle thought she wouldn't be able to eat a bite more, a platter presented itself and she found room.

Throughout it all, the music played, as wonderful as the food itself. By the time the meal was over, Belle was enchanted. It was hard not to be when all the servants seemed so happy to have her there, so pleased to be working. It occurred to her that with a master like the Beast, they might have been lonely and perhaps even a bit bored. She doubted very much that he had elaborate meals or required much assistance. While at the beginning of the meal she might have thought it silly to feel bad for a talking candelabrum, clock, or teapot, by the end of the meal she had ceased to see any of them as mere objects.

Pushing herself away from the table, Belle thanked everyone and said her good nights. Then she followed Mrs Potts out of the room. After the warmth and frivolity of the meal, the rest of the castle now seemed colder and darker.

"I don't understand why you're all being so kind to me," Belle said, giving voice to a thought that had been in the back of her mind since she had met Lumiere, Cogsworth and Mrs Potts.

Riding on top of her serving trolley, Mrs Potts smiled

gently. "You deserve nothing less, my love," she said in a sweet, motherly tone.

"But you're as trapped here as I am," Belle pointed out. "Don't you ever want to escape?"

Mrs Potts didn't respond right away. "The master's not as terrible as he appears," she finally said. "Somewhere deep in his soul there's a prince of a fellow, just waiting to be set free."

Belle cocked her head; the words *prince* and *free* sounded like pieces to the puzzle she was trying hard to put together. "Lumiere mentioned something about the West Wing ..." she went on, hoping to get a bit more information out of the kind teapot.

But Mrs Potts wasn't falling for it. "Oh, never you mind about that," she said as they reached the bottom of the stairs that led up to Belle's room. "Now off to bed, before the sun starts peeking through the trees. Can I get you anything else, dearie?"

"No, you've already done so much," Belle said sincerely. "Thank you. Good night."

"Nighty-night," Mrs Potts replied as her serving trolley turned and headed back towards the kitchen.

Belle watched, her hand on the railing, until the trolley and Mrs Potts had disappeared from view. Then she glanced up at the stairs in front of her. She began to climb, her mind whirling. She knew that was her chance to get back to her room and make her escape, yet something was stopping her. She paused on the stairs' landing. If she went to the left, she would get back to her room and, perhaps, freedom. But if she went right.... She gazed up the set of stairs that must lead to the West Wing.

Her mind made up, Belle took a deep breath. Then she turned right. She still had a little time before sunrise. She would just take a quick peek in the West Wing. After all, what harm could come from a quick look?

CHAPTER IX

BELLE WAS BEGINNING TO THINK she had made a very big mistake. While her wing of the castle wasn't exactly bright and colourful, it was a breath of fresh air in comparison with the West Wing. As she walked down the long corridor, her eyes widened. The place *felt* lonely. And it looked downright depressing. The walls were scratched and bare, though it was clear from the empty picture hooks that still hung there that hadn't always been the case. The rug beneath her feet was faded and worn, torn in spots by the Beast's long claws. Even the air was heavier somehow.

Belle was on the verge of turning around when she saw light at the end of the hall. A door had been left slightly ajar and through it, Belle could just make out what looked to be a huge suite. Curiosity overtaking her fear, Belle walked forward and slowly pushed open the door.

Instantly, she wished she hadn't. If the hallway had been unnerving, this room was ten times more so. Everywhere she looked she could see evidence of the Beast's temper. Curtains hung in shreds from their rails. Vases that must once have been beautiful lay shattered on the ground. On the huge four-poster bed, a grey coverlet lay, faded and covered in dust, clearly long since used. As her eyes drifted over the room, she saw the reason why. Tucked in a corner was a sort of giant nest made from torn bits of fabric, feathers and antlers that had been shoved together. Belle felt a rush of foreboding at the sight of such a wild and animalistic area in the castle.

She turned and shouted as she found herself staring at a pair of bright blue eyes. For one long, tense moment she thought someone was staring right back at her – until she realized that the eyes belonged to a boy captured in what was clearly a royal portrait. Her heart thudding, Belle leaned forward. The boy's face had been slashed beyond recognition, that part of the canvas in pieces. But the eyes had been left untouched. Belle leaned still closer. They looked so familiar....

Her breath caught in her throat as Belle realized that

they reminded her of the Beast's eyes. Mrs Potts's words came back to her. *A prince of a fellow*, she had said. This must have been the prince she was referring to. She glanced again at the portrait, looking for clues to the past. There were two other people in the portrait – a handsome king and beautiful queen. And though the woman's image – which included kind eyes full of laughter and love – was still pristine, the king's cold, distant stare had been slashed, as well. Belle wondered what the boy in the portrait must have been like, what *anyone* would have been like, growing up with parents such as those, inside these castle walls.

As Belle dragged her eyes from the portrait and tamped down the odd feeling of melancholy that once again formed in the pit of her stomach, her attention was drawn to the far end of the room. Huge doors had been left open, revealing a large stone balcony on the other side. But it was what was in front of the doors that caught her interest. Amid the chaos and destruction of the room, the table would have stood out just based on the fact it was still upright. But it especially caught her eye because of the glass jar that sat on its surface.

The jar was made of delicate glass, blown so thin

it seemed as though it could break with the slightest of touches. Intricate patterns had been etched into the jar's side, looking like frost on a windowpane. And inside, floating as if by magic, was a beautiful red rose. It glowed, the colour rivalling that of the most beautiful sunset Belle had ever seen.

As if in a trance, Belle made her way to the table. Slowly, she reached her hand towards the jar. Belle's fingers tingled as she moved them closer to the smooth glass, unable to resist the sudden rush of desire to lift the bell jar and touch the rose's silky petals. Her fingers inched closer ... closer still ... and closer....

"*What are you doing here?*" The Beast's voice roared over Belle, shocking her out of her trancelike state. He appeared from the shadows, his blue eyes blazing, his paws clenched with barely controlled rage. He looked at the glowing rose and the fire in his eyes grew wilder. "*What did you do to it?*"

She quickly backed away from the table. "No – not – nothing," Belle stuttered, her heart thudding in her chest.

The Beast kept coming towards her. "Do you realize what you could have done?" he snarled. "You could have damned us all!" Lashing out, the Beast's claws tore into one of the thin columns that accented the balcony doors. There was a terrible ripping sound and the column began to crumble, pieces shattering and falling close to the glass bell jar holding the rose.

Panic filled the Beast's eyes. Not looking back at Belle, he threw his body over the rose, desperate to protect it. "*Get out!*" he roared over his shoulder.

Belle didn't need to be told twice. Turning, she fled back the way she had come. She ran through the room and out of the open door. Then she raced down the long hallway and the even longer stairs. She barely registered the shocked looks of Lumiere and Cogsworth as she passed them on the landing, and when they asked where she was going, she didn't stop to speak to them. "Getting out of here!" she cried over her shoulder and kept running.

Because that was exactly what she was going to do – get out. It was what she *should* have done already. But she had been distracted by Lumiere and his dinner entertainment, and then the castle mystery had lured her in further. But she was done with all that. She was going to get out of this place, with its talking dishware and enchanted candles and clocks, and get back to her father. No matter what.

Unfortunately, the castle didn't want to see Belle leave just yet. Hitting the bottom of the grand staircase, she ran straight towards the front door. To her dismay, the door seemed to see her coming, and before she could reach it, the bolt slid shut. Chapeau, the tall coatrack, slid in front of the door a moment later, blocking Belle's exit.

Belle's pace slowed. What was she going to do now? She didn't know the castle well enough to go running through it blindly trying to find another exit. Then, just as she was about to give up hope, she heard the sound of a dog barking. Turning, she saw Froufrou, the dog turned piano stool, who had the run of the castle. He barked wildly as he gave chase and for a brief moment, Belle was worried he was going to pounce on her.

But to her surprise, he ran right past her and scooted through a smaller door that was built into the much larger main door. Belle nearly cried out. Her way out hadn't been blocked. Once again picking up her pace, she shimmied through the smaller door, but not before grabbing her cloak from a befuddled Chapeau. Behind her, Belle heard Mrs Potts's tea tray rolling across the floor and Lumiere shouting. Still, she kept running.

It didn't take Belle long to find Philippe. The big animal had made himself quite comfortable in one of the stable's roomy stalls. Hearing Belle's footsteps on the cobblestones, he looked up mid-mouthful of hay and cocked his head as if to ask, *What are you doing here?*

Throwing the saddle over his back, Belle didn't answer his questioning look. She pulled him out of the stall instead and quickly mounted. Then she gave his sides a kick. Philippe didn't hesitate. He broke into a canter and headed towards the castle's gate.

Moments later, they were safely through the gate and back in the woods that surrounded the castle.

But it didn't take long for Belle to realize she had traded one terrifying situation for another. As Philippe cantered along, she caught glimpses of shadows out of the corners of her eyes. They gradually grew larger and more clear, and by the time Belle heard the first howl, she already knew that she and Philippe were being followed by a pack of wolves.

Urging Philippe on, Belle tried not to panic. Philippe was a big horse with heavy hooves and he was fast when he needed to be. If they could just get close enough to the village, she was sure the wolves would be frightened by the signs of civilization. As long as they didn't run into any obstacles before then, they should be okay.

And then Philippe ran right out onto a frozen pond.

Beneath his hooves, the ice groaned. Belle leaned over and saw cracks begin to appear. Small at first, they grew larger as the horse slipped and slid across the frozen surface. Shouting encouragement, Belle tried to calm Philippe, who was growing more and more panicked as the ice began to give out beneath him and the wolves closed in from behind. Belle felt the horse's powerful haunches bunch beneath him and she grabbed a fistful of his mane. Then ... he leaped.

Belle's breath caught in her throat as they hung, suspended in the air for a moment, before Philippe's front hooves landed on the pond's edge. A moment later, his back hooves followed. But the cry of relief Belle wanted to let out caught in her throat as the first of the wolves, seeing a chance, attacked.

One wolf's large jaws snapped as it went after Philippe's back leg. A moment later, another wolf joined in. Philippe kicked out and bucked wildly, trying to defend himself. On his back, Belle clung to his mane desperately.

But Philippe was just too strong and powerful. As his hind legs once again flew into the air, she was knocked out of the saddle and went flying into a nearby snowbank.

Getting to her feet, Belle looked around wildly for something she could use to defend herself. Spotting a thick branch, she grabbed it and waved it in the air in front of her.

The wolves, seeing a new and potentially easier target, closed in. Belle's arm shot out and she managed to hit one on the nose. Another came at her and she swung the branch, slamming it into that wolf's side. Despite her efforts, the wolves kept coming. Belle backed up, her heart pounding and fear flooding over her. Hearing a howl from above, she saw the biggest wolf yet standing on a ledge above her, ready to pounce. It stared at her with cold, hungry eyes.

Belle braced, ready to defend herself until the end.

Then she heard a yelp and a thud, and there was a flurry of movement behind her.

Turning, she was shocked to see the Beast. He had leaped into the middle of the pack of wolves. Several of them had backed away and looked to be licking wounds. The largest of the wolves – the alpha – was still on his feet, hackles raised, teeth bared. The Beast's back was to

Belle and she could see where the wolves had bitten him.
One after another, the smaller of the wolves attacked. Each
time, the Beast managed to pick them up and hurl them
away. But Belle could tell that the Beast was growing tired.
The wounds on his back were bleeding and his head was
hanging lower and lower. She wasn't sure how much fight
he had left in him.

Then the alpha attacked.

The big grey wolf leaped up onto the Beast's back in
one fluid motion. The alpha's mouth opened as he went
for the Beast's neck. Roaring, the Beast dropped the
two smaller wolves he had been holding in his paws and
reached over his shoulder. Just as the alpha's jaws were
about to close, the Beast ripped the creature off his back.
The alpha's back legs dangled in the air as the Beast, for
one long moment, just held him in front of his face, their
eyes locked. And then the Beast, with the last of his energy,
hurled the alpha away from him. The wolf flew through
the air and slammed, with a crack, against a large stone.

Seeing their leader knocked unconscious, the rest of
the wolves took off in a panic.

The Beast waited until the wolves' yelps had all but

gone before letting out a whimper of pain. His shoulders, which had been tensed and high, slumped. And then he collapsed in the snow. Where his wounds touched the ground, the bright white powder turned red.

Belle stood, unable to move. She was as rooted to the ground as the trees around her. Looking down to where the Beast lay, she knew this was her chance to run. There was no way he could follow her or even try to stop her. Not in his condition. As she watched, he whimpered again and tried to clean one of the wounds on his arm. His blue eyes met hers for just the briefest of moments. But it was long enough for Belle to see the pain and vulnerability in them and for her to make a decision: she wasn't going to leave him there, hurt in the snow. She couldn't. Not after what he had just done for her.

Racing over, she kneeled down beside him, pulling off her cloak and laying it over him. "You have to help me," she whispered gently. "You have to stand...." Putting her body under his shoulder, she pushed up, letting the Beast lean on her like a crutch. He roared in pain and grew heavier as the sensation overtook him. Belle shivered. She needed to get the Beast back to the castle – before it was too late.

CHAPTER X

"LISTEN! WOLVES! WE MUST BE close to the haunted castle!"

Sitting in the back of Gaston's carriage, Gaston and LeFou were startled by Maurice's shout. The three men had been making their way through the forest for quite some time. The rest of the crowd had turned back, happy to return to the warmth of the tavern, once Gaston made it clear he was going into the woods. And while the forest wasn't exactly picturesque, it wasn't nearly as menacing as Maurice's wild tavern tale had led Gaston to believe.

"Maurice, enough is enough," Gaston said, turning to look at the older man. The carriage ride had made his wild white hair even more dishevelled and his eyes were whipping back and forth as he gazed around the forest desperately. "We have to turn back," Gaston added, not sure Maurice had even heard a word he said.

But apparently he had, because he quickly shook his head. "No! Look!" Maurice pointed up ahead.

Following the old man's finger, Gaston saw a tree on the side of the road. It was withered, its branches bent at odd angles, its trunk smooth with age. Over the course of their journey, Maurice had been telling them all about how he had first found the enchanted castle. He had mentioned something about a tree that looked like a cane and a hidden path.... Cocking his head to the side, Gaston narrowed his eyes. It *sort of* looked cane-like, but there was definitely no path behind it.

"That is the tree!" Maurice exclaimed, as if sensing Gaston's doubt. "I'm sure of it. Of course, it was downed by lightning at the time, but now it's been restored to an upright position. By magic, it seems...."

Leaning over, LeFou tapped Gaston on the shoulder. "You really want to marry into this family?" he whispered, rolling his eyes.

Gaston knew the smaller man was teasing him, but LeFou had a point. Enough was enough. He had let Maurice lead them out there with the sole intention of blackmailing him into giving Gaston Belle's hand in marriage. But if they couldn't find Belle, what was the point? "I'm done playing this game of yours," Gaston snapped, stopping the carriage. Jumping down, he put his hands on his hips. "Where is Belle?"

"The Beast took her!" Maurice said again.

Gaston's eyes narrowed. He was trying very hard not to lose his temper, but the old man was making it difficult. "There are no such things as beasts, or talking teacups, or ... whatever." As he spoke, his voice grew louder and his hands began to clench and unclench at his sides. "But there *are* wolves, frostbite and starvation."

Scrambling off the carriage, LeFou raced over to his friend's side. "Deep breaths, Gaston," he said. "Deep breaths."

Gaston's jaw clenched, and for a moment, it seemed a very good possibility that he was going to hit something. But then he took a deep breath, like LeFou had suggested. And another. And then one more, for good measure. "So," he started again when he was calmer, "why don't we just turn around and go back to Villeneuve? Belle's probably at home cooking up a lovely dinner...."

"You think I've made all this up?" Maurice asked,

seemingly unaware how close Gaston was to breaking. He looked up at the large man in confusion. "If you didn't believe me, why did you offer to help?"

"Because I want to marry your daughter," Gaston said, with no attempt to hide his plan any longer. "Now let's go home."

"I told you! She's not at home, she's with the –"

Rage flooded over Gaston and he erupted. *"If you say 'beast' one more time, I will feed you to the wolves!"* he screamed, all his composure gone. He stalked over to Maurice and raised his fists.

LeFou watched his friend go dark. He knew he had to do something. "Stop!" he cried, frantically trying to think of what to say next. When Gaston got angry, it was hard to pull him out of it. LeFou had really only seen him that way a few times – and it took a while to talk him down. Suddenly, LeFou knew exactly what to do. "Think happy thoughts," he said soothingly. "Go back to the war. Blood, explosions, more blood." As LeFou spoke, the red faded from Gaston's cheeks and his hands began to unclench. His eyes clouded over as he got lost in the memories of his glory days.

By the time LeFou finished speaking, Gaston was back in a good head space. "Please, forgive me," he said. "That's no way to talk to my future father-in-law, now is it?" He smiled at the old man. But the smile didn't reach Gaston's eyes.

That wasn't lost on Maurice. And neither was the fact that Gaston clearly had a dark side. "Captain," he said, backing up a step, "now that I've seen your true face, you'll *never* marry my daughter."

LeFou gulped. *I wouldn't have said that if I were you,* he thought. *Gaston might take it badly and if that happens ...* Gaston pulled back and hit Maurice. Hard. The old man sagged to the ground, unconscious.

You might just end up getting hit, LeFou finished his thought. He opened his mouth to try to once again calm his friend down, but it was too late. Gaston had given in to his rage, and there was no pulling him out of it. Not now, at least.

"If Maurice won't give me his blessing," Gaston said as he picked up the unconscious man and carried him over to a tree, "then he is in my way." He pulled a rope out of the carriage and tied Maurice's hands. He gave the knot a tug, checking to make sure it was secure. "Once the wolves are finished with him, Belle will have no one to take care of her but *me*." With an evil laugh, Gaston climbed back into the carriage.

LeFou swayed nervously on his feet as he looked back and forth between Gaston and Maurice. He understood his friend was upset. Gaston *hated it* when he didn't get his way. But leaving the old man out there to be eaten by wolves? The punishment seemed a bit severe. "For the sake of exhausting our options," he said nervously, "do we maybe want to consider a plan B?"

Gaston shot him a look. LeFou gulped and quickly got in the carriage, trying to ignore the pit in his stomach.

It looked as if they were sticking to plan A.

Belle had never had a patient who was as beastly as, well, the Beast. Granted, she had only ever tended her father's odd scratch or cut, but at least he had the common courtesy to be polite. Ever since she had got the Beast back to the castle, he had been nothing but cranky. And Belle was growing rather tired of it. He hadn't been the one who'd had to walk back through the snowy woods in thin shoes. Nor had *he* been the one who spent that entire journey fearing for his own life. No. The Beast had been unconscious through it all. It had been *Belle* who had anxiously looked over her shoulder at any little sound. It had been *Belle* who'd worried that, with each passing minute, the Beast grew weaker and closer to death.

She hadn't realized just how tense she had been until she and Philippe arrived back at the castle gates and Mrs Potts appeared at the front door, the staff in tow to help. Then, and only then, had Belle let out a huge breath and allowed herself to start shaking. And once she started, it had taken a long time – and a very hot bath – to stop.

But that was then and this was now. Now she had her hands full trying to treat the Beast, who was proving to be a big baby when it came to pain.

While Belle had recovered, Mrs Potts had ordered him to be taken up to his room in the West Wing. He now lay in his old bed, with members of the household staff gathered around to see if they might be of service. A pitcher of hot water and a bowl had been placed beside the bed. Pouring some of the water into the bowl, Belle added a pinch of salt before dipping a clean cloth into the mixture. She wrung out the cloth and then, ever so gently, dabbed it on a gash on the Beast's arm.

He roared, as though she had cut him anew. "That hurts!" he snarled, baring his fangs and trying to pull his arm out of reach.

"If you held still, it wouldn't hurt as much," Belle retorted, grabbing his arm and yanking it back.

"If *you* hadn't run away," the Beast said, his jaw clenched, "this wouldn't have happened."

"Well, if *you* hadn't frightened me, I wouldn't have run away."

Watching the pair bicker, Mrs Potts raised an eyebrow. Then she looked over at Lumiere, who hovered nervously by the door. They exchanged knowing glances but remained silent, both curious to see where this new sense of familiarity would lead.

"Well ..." the Beast went on, determined to get in the last word, "*you* shouldn't have been in the West Wing."

Belle wasn't going to back down. "Well ... *you* should learn to control your temper."

The Beast's mouth opened, then shut. Then opened

again. And shut again. Finally, he let out a small sigh. She had him there.

Smiling, Belle looked back down at the wound she was cleaning. The smile faded. Despite the bickering banter, she was honestly worried about the Beast. The wound was worse than she had initially thought. "Try and get some rest," she said, gently giving it one last dab with the towel. Standing up, she watched as the Beast's eyes slowly closed and his breath grew even. When she was sure he was asleep, and momentarily pain-free, she turned to leave the room. To her surprise, Mrs Potts and Lumiere were waiting by the door. She had completely forgotten they were there.

"Thank you, miss," Mrs Potts said, smiling gratefully up at Belle from where she sat perched on the serving tray.

Lumiere bowed. "We are eternally grateful," he added.

Belle nodded, surprised by the deep concern and worry she saw in their eyes. From everything she knew of the Beast, he wasn't a particularly kind master. Yet these two looked nearly as drained as the Beast himself. "Why do you care so much about him?" The question was out of her mouth before she could think to stop herself.

"We've looked after him all his life," Mrs Potts replied matter-of-factly.

"But he has cursed you somehow," Belle said. She *wanted* to understand why they had such loyalty. It just seemed so ... strange. When neither the teapot nor the candelabrum responded, she pressed on. "Why? You did nothing."

The Beast's cry from when she'd almost touched the glowing rose echoed in her ears: *You could have damned us all!* The castle was clearly under some sort of spell. And she couldn't imagine any of the castle's *staff* was responsible for their state.

"You're quite right there, dear," Mrs Potts said. "You see, when the master lost his mother, and his cruel father took that sweet, innocent lad and twisted him up to be just like him ... we did nothing." As if she had been waiting to tell their story for a long time, the words poured from Mrs Potts. She painted a sad picture of a young boy who loved his mother with all his heart. Back then, Mrs Potts told Belle, the castle had been a different place. It had been full of laughter and love, sunshine and innocence.

And then the boy's mother, the *Beast's* mother, Belle

clarified in her head, had grown ill. Belle's eyes grew wide as Mrs Potts explained that the boy had stayed by his mother's bedside day and night, watching as she withered away. He had begged the doctors to help her but they just shook their heads and offered up false promises.

The poor boy, Belle thought. *I never knew my mother, and I still feel the hole in my heart from where she should be.* She couldn't imagine what it must have been like for the Beast. To have known such love – and lost it.

As if sensing her thoughts, Mrs Potts went on with her sad tale. After the boy's mother had passed, nothing was ever the same again. The father was a cold, heartless man who tore the sunshine from his son and buried it deep down. As time had passed, all traces of happiness were taken from the castle, replaced with darkness and a sense of heartlessness – even before the curse.

Mrs Potts's voice trailed off as, on his bed, the Beast moaned in pain. The three watched, their breath held, until he once again settled. As she turned back to Mrs Potts and Lumiere, Belle's eyes fell on the glass jar and the rose that was slowly fading inside, the crimson petals gathered beneath it.

"What happens when the last petal falls?" she asked, afraid she already knew the answer.

"The master remains a beast forever," Lumiere replied. "And the rest of us become ..."

"Antiques," Mrs Potts finished.

"Knickknacks," Lumiere added.

Cogsworth, who had come to check on the patient midway through the conversation, cleared his throat. "Rubbish," he said harshly. "We become rubbish." Belle raised an eyebrow. The clock's voice was more severe than she had ever heard it.

All around her, the other members of the staff who had been helping tend to the Beast joined in, adding to the laundry list of what they would become. Belle listened, her heart growing sad. She knew what it felt like to be trapped. She felt that way living in Villeneuve, where every day was the same, every person like the others. The difference was, she *could* leave if she ever really wanted to get away. Mrs Potts? Lumiere? Cogsworth? They couldn't. They were stuck inside the castle walls and, she now knew, stuck inside the objects they had become, as well. She turned and looked at the sleeping Beast. Like his staff, he was trapped, too. He had been trapped for a long, long time – first by a cruel father and then by this curse.

"I want to help you," Belle said, surprising herself and the others. "There must be some way to lift the curse."

There was a heavy pause as the staff exchanged looks. Then Cogsworth spoke. "Well, there is *one* –"

"It's not for you to worry about, lamb," Mrs Potts said, stopping Cogsworth. "We've made our bed and we must lie in it." Her statement clear, Mrs Potts ushered the rest of the staff out of the room.

Belle watched them go. When she was alone with the Beast, she walked over to where he lay. She was surprised to see his eyes were open. He had heard everything. And the pain and shame Belle saw when their eyes met broke her heart. Before she could say anything, he closed his eyes and turned his back to her.

Sighing, Belle retreated and left him to sleep. But as she shut the door, she took one last look at the rose. As she watched, another petal fell. She wished there was something she could do to help the poor souls trapped there. But it all seemed a lost cause, as hopeless as turning back the hands of time.

CHAPTER XI

BELLE DECIDED THAT AS LONG AS she was in the castle, she would use her time productively, which for starters meant helping the Beast recover.

Adjusting her dress around her legs, Belle settled into the chair beside the Beast's bed. The Beast's eyes were closed, which gave Belle the chance to assess his wounds. It had been a few days since he'd saved her from the wolves, and with constant care, most of the cuts were beginning to heal. Still, the larger and deeper ones remained bandaged. Those would take longer to heal and were likely to leave scars. Gazing at him, Belle felt a surge of sadness for the creature. He already had so many invisible scars after growing up without a mother to protect him from a cruel father. It seemed unfair that he now had physical ones to match.

Belle sighed. It would do the Beast no good for *her* to sit there feeling sorry for him. Looking around for something she could do to entertain herself while he slept, Belle wasn't surprised to find very little in the way of entertainment. There were no books on the bedside table. The art was all torn and even the furniture was worse for wear. *It looks like I'll just have to make my own entertainment*, Belle thought.

Softly, she recited some of her favourite lines from one of her favourite works, *A Midsummer Night's Dream*. "Love can transpose to form and dignity. Love looks not with the eyes but with the mind."

To her surprise, the Beast's deep voice joined hers and they finished the verse in unison. "And therefore is winged Cupid painted blind."

Belle looked over, eyes wide. The Beast had apparently *not* been sleeping. He was gazing back at her, an amused expression on his hairy face.

"You know Shakespeare?" Belle asked. She knew her voice was filled with disbelief and she blushed. After what Mrs Potts had told her, she now knew the Beast had once been a human boy. A human *prince*. Still, she couldn't

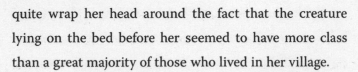

quite wrap her head around the fact that the creature lying on the bed before her seemed to have more class than a great majority of those who lived in her village.

The Beast shrugged. "I had an expensive education," he replied.

There was an awkward pause. "Actually, *Romeo and Juliet* is my favourite play," Belle finally offered.

"Why is that not a surprise?" the Beast replied, a hint of a smile in his eyes.

"Sorry?" Belle said, feigning offence.

"All that heartache and pining and –" The Beast shuddered dramatically. "There are so many better things to read."

"Like *what*?" Belle said, raising an eyebrow. She crossed her arms, the challenge thrown down.

The Beast smiled. Then he began to push himself up.

"Oh, no you don't!" Belle said, reaching out to stop him.

But even wounded, the Beast was far stronger than Belle. He brushed her off and got out of the bed. Then, without a word, he slowly made his way out of the room. Belle had no choice but to follow.

By the time they made it down the West Wing's long hallway, turned several corners, and climbed one smaller staircase, Belle was nearly bubbling over with curiosity. The Beast had not said a word or given a hint as to where they were going. He just walked slowly, pausing every now and then to catch his breath.

Finally, they came to a stop in front of a pair of grand doors, which soared at least two storeys high and were intricately carved with reliefs depicting various scenes. Standing next to the Beast, Belle tried to make out some of the larger ones, but before she could, the Beast pushed open the doors. "There are a couple of things in here you can start with," he said.

Belle gasped.

In front of her was the most beautiful thing she had ever seen. It was a library. But this was not just any library. This had to be the biggest, grandest library in all of France. The ceiling soared above her, shelves full of books going all the way to the very top. A massive fireplace dominated one wall, and even on the mantel, books were displayed. On another wall, a large window let in plenty of light to read by, but even so, candles were lit throughout the chamber. Despite its immense size, the room was comfortable, cosy. Belle looked around at the multitude of deep cushioned chairs and imagined how peaceful it would be to curl up in one with a book in hand.

"Are you all right?" the Beast asked, his voice laced with genuine concern.

Belle imagined she looked like a fish gaping in water for how shocked and awestruck she felt. She turned and smiled up at him. "It's wonderful," she said, knowing that was not grand enough a response to a room such as this.

"Why, yes, I suppose it is," the Beast said thoughtfully, as though noticing this for the first time. "Well, then it is yours. You can be master here." He bowed and turned to leave.

Belle's voice stopped him. Her neck was craned back as she looked to the shelves at the very top of the room. "Have you really read every one of these books?"

"Not all of them," the Beast replied. "Some are in Greek."

Belle's mouth dropped open. "Was that a joke?" she said, beginning to smile. "Are you making jokes now?"

The Beast tried not to smile as he replied, "Maybe...."

Without another word, the Beast turned and left the room. Belle remained where she was, shaking her head as he made his exit. What had just happened?

As the days passed, Belle found more and more reason to ask herself that same question. Instead of what *had* happened, however, it quickly became what *was* happening? Because there was no denying it – something had changed between Belle and the Beast. She wasn't sure if it had started when he rescued her in the woods or when she had turned around and rescued *him*. Or perhaps it had been the afternoon he shared the library with her and she first saw the softer side of him. It might have even started somewhere in between all that – when Mrs Potts had told her the story of the Beast's youth. *When* it had happened didn't matter. What mattered, what Belle could not deny, was the simple truth that there was a spark of something between them that hadn't been there before. Something that made the days at the castle feel less like a prison sentence and more – well, more like fun.

And the Beast had become less like her captor and more of a friend.

Belle no longer sneaked down to the kitchen to get her meals. Instead, she and the Beast shared the dining room table – he at one end, she at the other. Sometimes they would each bring a book and read at the table in companionable silence. At other meals, they would talk about the books, sharing their favourite parts or what they would have changed. So caught up in their mutual love of reading was she that Belle stopped noticing when the Beast slurped his soup straight from the bowl and ignored the silverware entirely. Sometimes she even went so far as to sip the soup the same way, to make the Beast feel more comfortable.

Meals and books were not the only things they shared. When the weather permitted, Belle would join the Beast outside as he showed her around the grounds, or they would walk Philippe. And even when the weather wasn't perfect, they found ways to enjoy themselves outside the castle walls. Snowy days led to snowball fights; sunny days led to picnics.

Belle even encouraged the Beast to help her and the castle staff clean up the castle – the two of them scrubbing the floors until the old gleaming marble shone through, wiping the years of grime off the windows until they saw sparkling sunlight. They transformed the West Wing, removing the shattered columns and debris and replacing the torn bits of fabric with cosy blankets to make a proper bed for the Beast.

With each moment and adventure they shared, Belle grew more and more comfortable around the Beast. She no longer shuddered if he accidentally brushed her with his paw. Nor did her smile fade when his flashed, revealing sharp fangs.

In fact, Belle realized with a start at lunch one afternoon, she didn't even really see those parts of him any more. She saw the kindness in his eyes when he looked at her. She heard the intelligence in his voice when they debated literature. And she saw the pride he had in his home when he looked around.

I'm seeing the man inside the Beast, she wrote one afternoon in a diary she'd started keeping. If her current experiences didn't warrant a journal, she didn't know what did. *I'm seeing what Mrs Potts and Lumiere and Cogsworth and all the others have seen all along. It just took me some time....* Closing the pages, Belle stood up and went to the window of her elegant room. Outside, the last of the day's light was fading. A nearly full moon was beginning to peek over the horizon, illuminating the snowy gardens below in a pale, ethereal light. Looking out, Belle was struck once again by the beauty of the castle. Since her friendship with the Beast had grown stronger, and they had made the effort to return the estate to its former glory, the whole castle had become brighter and cheerier right before her very eyes. She saw the beauty in the lines of the stone that made up the castle walls and appreciated the towering turrets. It was not the quaint and picturesque architecture of Villeneuve but it was enchanting nonetheless.

Spotting the Beast making his way towards the colonnade, book in hand, Belle turned and grabbed her own book from the bedside table. Making her way downstairs and outside, she went to join him.

"What are you reading?" she asked when she, too, had entered the colonnade.

The Beast looked up, startled to see her. He dropped the book to his side. "Nothing," he said, trying to hide it from Belle.

It was too late. Belle had already seen the title. "Guinevere and Lancelot," she observed.

The Beast shrugged. "King Arthur and the round table," he clarified. "Swords, fighting...." His attempt to focus on the more action-packed parts of the book was not lost on Belle.

"Still ... it's a romance," she pointed out, trying not to smile as the Beast shrugged and looked sheepish.

"Felt like a change," he finally said.

For a moment, the pair just stood there in somewhat awkward silence. Despite all the time they had been spending together, this felt different to Belle. Maybe it was the moonlight. Maybe it was the Beast's admission of change. Maybe it was just a shift in the air. Whatever the reason, Belle felt a sudden compulsion to say something she had not said before. "I never thanked you for saving my life," she finally said softly.

"I never thanked you for not leaving me to die," he responded without hesitation, as though he, too, had been wanting to say the words for a long while but had never found the right time.

The air crackled between them as they stood, eyes

locked, their words lingering in the air. Just when Belle was sure it couldn't get any more tense, they heard shouts followed by laughter coming from inside the castle. The servants, it seemed, were having a nice evening. The noise broke the tension and both Belle and the Beast smiled in relief.

"Well ... they know how to have a good time," Belle said.

The Beast nodded. "Sometimes, when I take my dinner, I listen to their laughter and pretend I am eating with them."

"You should!" Belle said, impressed he would admit such a thing. "They'd love that."

"No, I've tried," he replied, the moment of levity gone as quickly as it had come. "When I enter a room, laughter dies."

Belle's mouth opened and shut. That was *exactly* how she felt whenever she went into town. She said as much to the Beast. Then she added, "The villagers say that I'm a funny girl, but I don't think they mean it as a compliment." To her surprise, she felt tears prick at the backs of her eyes. She had never admitted to anyone that it hurt her feelings – not even her father.

"I'm sorry," the Beast said, his tone genuine. "Your village sounds terrible."

"Almost as lonely as your castle," Belle said.

Once again the Beast nodded, not offended by her statement. Over the past few days, Belle's presence – and the life she breathed into the castle – had shown him just how lonely a place the castle had been. "It wasn't always like this," he said. He paused as an idea came to him, then gave her a smile. "What do you say we run away?"

Belle cocked her head, surprised by the suggestion. That was the *last* thing she had expected to hear come out of the Beast's mouth. Intrigued, she nodded and followed as he led her out of the colonnade and back into the castle. And despite the many questions she had forming in the back of her mind, she remained quiet as he led her down now familiar hallways and up a flight of stairs to the library.

With purpose, the Beast walked over to a simple desk that was tucked against one of the library's walls. Pulling a key out of his pocket, he unlocked one of the cabinets.

Belle peered over his shoulder. Resting on a pillow

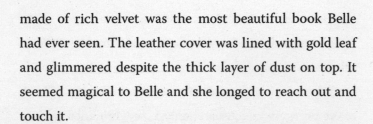

made of rich velvet was the most beautiful book Belle had ever seen. The leather cover was lined with gold leaf and glimmered despite the thick layer of dust on top. It seemed magical to Belle and she longed to reach out and touch it.

"The Enchantress gave me this," the Beast said, turning and seeing Belle's wide eyes. "Another of her many curses." He slowly opened it, the spine cracking with lack of use. There was no writing, no title page or dedication. Instead, the first page opened to reveal an antique world atlas. Unlike ordinary atlases, this one did not show countries or capitals. It just showed land and sea. Belle looked up at the Beast, a questioning look in her eye. "A book that truly allows you to escape," he answered.

Stepping forward, Belle's eyes grew still wider as she saw the art come to life. Waves lapped against beaches. Green trees swayed in invisible winds. A soft golden dust seemed to rise from the pages and swirl slowly over the landmasses on the map. "How amazing," she breathed, her heart pounding in her chest.

The Beast did not seem as impressed. "It was the

Enchantress's cruellest trick of all," he said softly. "The outside world has no place for a monster like me. But it can for you." Slowly, he reached out and took Belle's hand in his. Then he gently moved it to the book. "Think of the place you've most wanted to see. First see it in your mind's eye. Now feel it in your heart."

Belle closed her eyes. She didn't need to think of a place she wanted to see. She knew it instinctively. Reaching out her fingers, Belle placed them on the page. Instantly, the room around them began to spin and the library walls seemed to fade away.

When Belle opened her eyes, she was no longer looking at the floor-to-ceiling bookshelves. The snow-covered peaceful gardens had vanished and the stars had faded. They were standing in a small dusty apartment with a view of glittering lights shining from a city skyline.

The Beast gazed out of the window and saw the wooden blade of a windmill move past. "Where did you take us?"

"Paris," Belle said, her whisper barely audible over the sound of the Montmartre windmill's blades rushing by.

"Oh, I love Paris," the Beast exclaimed. "What would you like to see first? Notre Dame? The Champs-Élysées? Too touristy?"

But Belle was absorbed in her own thoughts, looking around the little dim room they were standing in. She had thought about this particular apartment for so many years, had pictured it in her mind's eye. But she had never dared dream she would see it for real. Her eyes brimmed with tears. "It's so much smaller than I imagined," she said after a moment, blinking back the tears.

They had been transported to the dusty attic where Belle had lived with her father and mother so many years before. It looked abandoned, a small crib and broken easel the only reminders that the place had once been a home. As Belle walked forward, the sadness she had felt earlier returned with a vengeance. For some reason, she had imagined that the enchanted book would reveal her childhood home as it had been, not as it was now. But what she was looking at was clearly an empty shell of a place. No one had lived there for years – not since Maurice had moved himself and Belle to the country.

Beside her, the Beast kept silent, letting her have the moment and the memories. But as she picked up a rattle that had been caught in the corner of the crib, he finally spoke. "What happened to your mother?" he asked softly.

"That's the only story Papa could never bring himself to tell," Belle said, clutching the rattle in her hand. The wood was old, but the detail was still exquisite. It was a perfectly carved rose. "And I knew well enough not to ask."

As she spoke, the Beast's eyes travelled to the corner of the room. He moved to pick up a black mask that resembled a bird's beak, his expression pained. That mask meant only one thing: it was what doctors used to prevent catching their patients' dreadful disease. Belle followed his gaze, and as she saw the mask, tears brimmed anew in her eyes. The plague. That was what had taken her mother. That was what had sent her father fleeing for the safety of the country.

All these years, she had resented him for keeping her trapped in Villeneuve. But now she knew what he must have endured. She could picture her mother insisting he take Belle away, insisting they leave her there before they, too, were infected. She could not imagine how it must have felt to watch his beloved slowly die and not be able to save her. Belle's knuckles turned white as her grip on the rose-shaped rattle tightened.

"I am sorry I ever called your father a thief," the Beast said.

Lost in her thoughts, Belle was surprised by the Beast's deep voice. She turned her face up to him. He was staring down at her, concern etched in his features. Wiping the tears from her eyes, Belle took one last look around the room. She had seen enough. She put the rattle in the pocket of her apron, not wanting to part with it.

Reaching out, she took the Beast's hand. "Let's go home," she said. "To the castle."

The Beast nodded, and together, they placed their hands once more on the pages of the enchanted book, closed their eyes ... and pictured home.

CHAPTER XII

GASTON WAS GROWING RESTLESS. He had spent the past few weeks doing what he normally did – hunting, participating in eating contests, taking one of the local girls out for dinner. But he was wondering when Belle would finally return.

Maurice was no doubt long gone. He wasn't going to return to bother Gaston, and when Belle came back from wherever it was she had run off to, the path to their marriage would be clear. Yes, it was all going to work out just fine, Gaston thought as he made his way towards the tavern for his evening dose of adoration and grog. He just needed his future wife to hurry home.

And he needed LeFou to stop talking.

Gaston's constant companion was, once again, babbling on about Maurice – which was making it rather difficult for Gaston to completely put the moment in his past. "Wow, this is some storm," the smaller man was saying. "At least we're not tied to a tree in the middle of nowhere, right? You know, it's not too late. We could just go get him...."

Gaston didn't respond.

LeFou pressed on. "It's just, every time I close my eyes, I picture Maurice stranded out there. And then when I open them, he's...."

His voice trailed off as Gaston swung open the doors to the tavern, revealing Maurice.

"Oh, that's funny, I was going to say 'dead'," LeFou finished, his voice squeaking.

Maurice was surrounded by the usual tavern goers, including Jean the potter and Pére Robert. Other than a red nose, he seemed no worse for wear, and it was clear from the daggers the villagers were shooting at Gaston that he had felt well enough after his ordeal to tell them all about what had happened.

"Gaston," Jean said, his voice serious, "did you try to kill Maurice?"

Gaston knew he had only a few options. He could

fight, which was his usual answer. He could run, but that option was weak and made his skin crawl. So after a quick glance around the room, he decided to go with another option: deny, deny, deny. Plastering a warm smile on his face, he walked quickly to Maurice, who had his arms crossed. "Oh, Maurice," he began. "Thank heavens. I've spent the last five days trying to find you. Why did you run off into the forest in your condition?"

As his words bounced around the room, the villagers who had gathered shuffled, unsure of who to believe.

"What?" Maurice said in disbelief. Then he shook his head. "No! You tried to kill me! You left me for the wolves!"

Gaston put a hand to his chest as though Maurice's words had hurt him. "Wolves? What are you talking about?" he asked. He looked at the villagers and rolled his eyes as if to say, *Are we really going back down this road again? Are you really going to believe him over me?* He tried not to smile smugly when the majority of them returned his eye roll.

"The wolves near the Beast's castle," Maurice answered, his voice rising and adding to his manic appearance.

"That's right," Gaston said condescendingly. "There's a beast with a castle that somehow none of us have ever seen?"

Maurice hesitated. Looking around the room, he saw that everyone was waiting for his answer. "Well ... yes," he finally said.

Gaston had Maurice – and everyone else – just where he wanted him. Like when he cornered his prey on the hunt, he had Maurice on the defensive, as if Maurice knew his time was running out. Slowly, Gaston shook his head. "It's one thing to rave about your delusions," he said. "It's another to accuse me of murder."

To his surprise, it was Pére Robert, not Maurice, who spoke up. The priest stepped in front of Maurice defensively. Then he looked at the gathered crowd. "Listen to me, all of you," he pleaded. "This is Maurice, our neighbour. Our friend. He is a good man."

Gaston tried not to smile. He could not have set the situation up for the final blow better if he had tried. "Are you suggesting that I am not?" he said, sounding hurt. "Did I not save this village from the savagery of the Portuguese marauders? Am I not the only reason you people are gathered here this evening and not buried up on the hillside?"

His words, like an arrow shot from his bow, struck home. The villagers mumbled to each other, their growing doubt in Maurice clear.

"Maurice," Jean the potter said, turning to look at the old man, "do you have any proof of what you're saying?"

"Ask Agathe!" he replied, frantically trying to keep the room with him. "She rescued me!" Turning, he pointed to the far dark corner of the tavern where the old beggar woman had been watching everything silently. Feeling everyone's eyes on her, Agathe cowered and pulled her tattered hood tighter around her face.

Gaston raised an eyebrow. "You'd hang your accusation on the testimony of a filthy beggar woman?" he said.

Realizing that might not have been the best of moves, Maurice looked around. He needed to change tactics. Spotting Gaston's ever-present companion, Maurice let out a cry. "Monsieur LeFou! He was there. He saw it all!"

"Me?" LeFou said, gulping as the attention turned to him.

"You're right. Don't take my word for it," Gaston said, once again thrilled by how the whole scene was playing out in his favour. He walked over and put his arm around his friend. "LeFou, my dearest companion, did you and I, *Le Duo*" – he used the nickname, his voice oozing false sincerity – "find any beasts or haunted castles on our search?"

LeFou's head swung back and forth. On his shoulder, Gaston's grip tightened. It was clear what answer *he* wanted to hear. But looking at Maurice, LeFou remembered how bad he had felt as they drove away, leaving him in the cold and dark. Gaston's grip tightened further. "It's a complicated question on a number of accounts, but ... no?" he finally answered.

"And did I, your oldest friend and most loyal compatriot," Gaston continued, laying it on thick, "try to kill the father of the only woman I've ever loved?"

"Well ..." LeFou hedged. "'Kill' is such a strong word. No. No, you didn't."

That was all the crowd needed to hear. Instantly, the tide of good feeling shifted from Maurice to Gaston.

As the old man's face fell, a smirk tugged at the corner of Gaston's mouth. He had won. "Maurice, it pains me to say this," he said insincerely, "but you've become a danger to yourself and others. You need help, sir. A place to heal your troubled mind." He walked over and put a large hand on Maurice's shoulder. Then he squeezed, hard. "Everything's going to be fine." But while his words were nice, his tone was as cold as ice.

Maurice gulped. He knew, without a doubt, that nothing was going to be fine. Nothing at all.

Inside the castle, the Beast was having similar thoughts. Time was running out and he was not even remotely sure that things would be all right. And clearly he wasn't the only one. While he had hoped to get ready for that evening alone, an audience had gathered – an audience with an opinion.

"This is it, master," Mrs Potts said as she entered the West Wing. The Beast was in the large bathroom, immersed in a huge tub of soapy hot water. "Now or never."

"The clock is ticking," Cogsworth added.

"The rose has only four petals left," Lumiere added.

"Which means tonight ... you *must* tell her how you feel."

The Beast sighed. He knew that his staff was just trying to help. Nothing they were saying was a surprise. He *knew* time was running out. He *knew* that night was important. He *knew* Belle was his one chance – the castle's one chance. Hearing it out loud did nothing to ease his growing anxiety. And he did not care to admit how especially nervous he was about the upcoming evening. He had made an offhanded comment to Belle about how beautiful the ballroom looked after all her hard work, and how they should celebrate it with a dance. He'd never thought she would say yes.

He signalled the others to give him a moment of privacy and finished his bath. A curtain had been drawn in front of the tub. He stood and shook himself dry. Finally, he spoke. "She will never love me," he said.

"Do not be discouraged," Lumiere said to the shadow of the Beast behind the curtain. "She is the one."

"There is no *one*," the Beast retorted. He pulled back the curtain and stepped into the light provided by Lumiere's candles. "Look at me. She deserves so much more than a beast."

To Lumiere's credit, he didn't cringe on seeing the Beast, who, at that particular moment, was looking rather, well, silly. His hair was sticking out in every direction from his shaking himself dry, and the towel he had wrapped around his waist only made his large shoulders seem wider and hairier. Lumiere cleared his throat and pressed on. "You care for her, don't you?"

The Beast nodded. He did care for Belle, more than he ever would have thought possible. The past few days and their trip to Paris had only solidified those feelings. But he was no fool. While he might have come to care for her, and she might have learned to be around him without cringing, that did not mean she loved him in return. He was a beast, after all. No matter how many baths he took, no matter the clothes he wore or if he managed to eat his soup with a spoon, that wasn't going to change – unless she *did* somehow love him as he was. But that was unlikely.

Lumiere saw the doubt and fear in his master's eyes but forged ahead, propelled by his nod. "Well then, woo her with beautiful music and romantic candlelight...."

"Yes," Plumette added, "and when the moment's just right...."

The Beast cocked his head. "How will I know?"

Cogsworth, who until that point had been purposely keeping himself out of the conversation, cleared his throat. "In my experience," he said, "you will feel slightly nauseous."

Lumiere shot him a look, silencing the clock. "Don't worry, master," he said, turning back to the Beast. "You'll do fine. The problem has been that until now, the girl could not see the real you."

"No," Mrs Potts said, disagreeing. "The problem was ... she *could*."

Instantly, the room grew silent. Tension filled the air as the staff turned and looked at the teapot. Some, like Lumiere, hoped to see a glint of humour in her eye. Others, like Cogsworth, were unsurprised by her sudden announcement. Either way, everyone's attention finally turned to the Beast, whom they watched, with eyes wide, as Mrs Potts went on.

"For years," she said, "we have hoped against hope that this curse would make you a better man. But you have remained angry and selfish and cruel, and we are all running out of time. And there is one more thing your

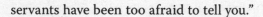

servants have been too afraid to tell you."

"What?" the Beast asked. He was surprised to discover that he feared her answer. Was she going to tell him exactly how hated he was? Was she going to tell him how miserable they had been and for how long? Was it possible she was going to find a way to make him feel even worse than he already did?

"We love you," Mrs Potts said.

The Beast nearly staggered back with the weight of her words. Of all the things he had imagined she might say....

Mrs Potts went on. "Until now, we have loved you in spite of how you were. But since that girl arrived, we love you *because* of it." Around her, the servants nodded in agreement. "So stop being a coward and tell Belle how you feel. And if you don't, I promise you'll be drinking cold tea for the rest of your life."

"In the dark," Lumiere added.

"Covered in dust," Plumette chimed in.

In silence, the staff looked up at the Beast and waited for his response.

And then the Beast smiled. Slowly at first, it spread across his face until it took over. And it wasn't the scary

smile he had first flashed at Belle. It was a warm smile. It was a genuine smile. It was the smile of a beast who no longer felt alone. It was the smile of a *man* who finally felt hope.

As Belle stood in her room letting Garderobe primp and pamper her, she was struck again by a case of nerves. Ever since she'd agreed to celebrate the restoration of the ballroom with a dance, butterflies had been firmly lodged in her belly. Now, as the moment to go downstairs grew closer, the feeling grew stronger.

Ever since they had returned from Paris, Belle had felt another serious shift in her relationship with the Beast. He had seen her at her most vulnerable and he had been a source of strength for her. Their conversations now went far beyond books. Their walks in the gardens were longer, neither wanting them to end. Belle found herself anticipating dinner, no longer just for the scrumptious food but for the company. If she'd had a friend to talk to, she probably would have admitted that her feelings for the Beast, as unlikely as it seemed, had become deeper than she had ever thought possible.

And now she was about to go and spend an evening with him, dancing in the ballroom. She sighed. How had she got here?

Garderobe gave Belle's dress one last adjustment and then turned her around so she was facing the full-length mirror.

Belle gasped. After her first day in the castle, she had been slightly hesitant to let the wardrobe dress her. They had talked about Belle's preference for clothes without frills, for outfits that had practical elements, like hemlines that didn't drag on the floor and pockets – much to Garderobe's chagrin.

But slowly, Garderobe had begun to create ensembles that fitted Belle to a tee. And that night, she had outdone herself. Belle didn't even recognize the girl staring back at her with wide brown eyes. Her hair had been pulled back halfway, accenting her cheeks, which had been ever so lightly dusted with blusher. The dress was something out of Belle's wildest fantasies. It floated around her like a golden halo. With every movement she made, it shone, catching the light and casting it back into the room. Garderobe stretched out one of her drawers, and suddenly, a layer of gold dust magically fell from the ceiling, coating the dress and making it, if possible, still more beautiful. Plus, it was easy to move in, light as a feather.

Pleased with her work, Garderobe pushed Belle out of the door.

Belle stood still for a long moment. Her heart pounded. *It is just a night,* she thought. *Stop dilly-dallying and get down those stairs.*

Taking a deep breath, Belle began the long walk down the hall towards the staircase. Reaching the top, she looked across to the top of the West Wing's stairs. To her surprise, the Beast was standing there – clad in his best formal wear, looking as nervous as she felt. Their eyes met. They walked towards each other, meeting on the centre landing. Then he bowed his head and extended his arm, inviting her, without words, to join him. She didn't hesitate to take it.

Together, they descended the staircase. With each step, Belle's anxiety faded. It felt normal to be walking with the Beast. And when he started to lead her into the dining room, it was *her* decision to turn to the ballroom instead.

She sensed his hesitation as she led him to the middle of the dance floor. But as quickly as that hesitation had appeared, it disappeared as music magically began to play. The room had been scrubbed clean and lit with hundreds of candles so that everything glowed like the golden dress Belle wore. The stage was set.

And then they began to dance. They waltzed in perfect time, Belle's feet following the Beast's automatically. They moved in a series of steps and delicate spins, each partner in tune with the other. It was as though they had been dancing together for years, not minutes, and once again, Belle was struck by how comfortable she felt around the Beast. As Cadenza reached a crescendo in the music, the Beast lifted Belle so she floated at his side, and then swept her into a thrilling dip. When the music finally came to an end and the ballroom fell into silence, Belle felt a strange tug of sadness that it was over.

As if sensing this, the Beast did not release her hand. Instead, he led her out to the large terrace that circled the ballroom. A companionable silence fell over the pair as they both stared up at the starry sky. The air was crisp, as it always was around the enchanted castle, but not uncomfortable. Belle felt as though the Beast's arms were still wrapped around her, the warmth from the ballroom somehow finding its way outside.

"I haven't danced in years," the Beast said, breaking the silence. "I'd almost forgotten the feeling." He dragged his eyes from the stars and looked down at Belle. His gaze was full of warmth – and something else. He shifted nervously on his feet as though not sure whether to go on. Belle waited, trying to encourage him silently. Then he spoke again. "It's foolish, I suppose, for a creature like me to hope that one day he might earn your affection."

Belle hesitated. It wasn't foolish. At least, moments earlier it hadn't seemed foolish. "I don't know...." she said softly.

Hope flared in the Beast's eyes. "Really?" he asked. "You think you could be happy here?"

"Can anybody be happy if they aren't free?" Belle asked softly.

The Beast blinked guiltily, knowing she was right.

An image of Maurice flashed through Belle's mind. "My father taught me to dance. Our house was always filled with music."

"You must miss him," the Beast said, the tone of her voice not lost on him.

Belle nodded. "Very much."

Seeing the tears rise in Belle's eyes, the Beast felt his heart tighten. He hated to see her in pain, especially when he knew there was a way he could ease it. "Come with me," he said, taking her hand.

Silently, he led her off the terrace and back through the ballroom. He didn't answer when she asked where they were going and didn't explain when he brought her into his room and lifted a small hand mirror up to her. All he said was "Show me Maurice." Then he handed the mirror to Belle and waited.

The face of the mirror swirled magically, and within moments, Belle's reflection had been replaced by an image of Maurice. With growing horror, she watched her father being dragged through the village square. Terror was etched on his face and he was calling out to someone to help him.

"Papa!" she cried. "What are they doing to him?"

The Beast had hoped to make Belle happy by showing her Maurice. Her reaction was not what he had anticipated. He peered over her shoulder, and his eyes grew wide as he, too, saw what was happening to the old man. Pain for Belle, for what was happening to her father, overcame him. Then, as Belle continued to watch her father through the mirror, the Beast's gaze shifted to the rose jar.

Another petal dropped.

Mrs Potts's words echoed in his head. The feeling of Belle's hand in his burned through him. He pictured his staff, their hopeful faces as he had finally got dressed for the evening. Then he looked back at Belle and saw the sorrow in her eyes. He knew this was a moment of choice. But he also knew there was no choice to be made. He had to start righting the wrongdoings that he *could* right.

"You must go to him," he said, trying to keep his own pain from his voice.

Belle looked up. "What did you say?" she asked, shocked.

"You are no longer a prisoner here," he went on. "No time to waste."

Tears of gratitude and appreciation replaced her tears of sadness as Belle looked up at the Beast. There was so much she wanted to say. So much she *needed* to say.

But she didn't know where to begin. She started to return the mirror, but he shook his head.

"Keep it with you," he said, "so you will have a way to look back on me."

"Thank you," Belle said in a whisper. *Thank you for everything*, she added silently.

And then, before she could change her mind, Belle turned and ran.

CHAPTER XIII

THE BEAST DIDN'T GO BACK downstairs. He couldn't bear the thought of seeing the expectant, hopeful faces of his staff. Instead, he walked out onto the West Wing balcony, not daring to glance at the bell jar to see how many petals were left on the enchanted rose. From there, he watched Belle race off on Philippe, heard the clanging of the castle gate as it shut behind her, listened until the sound of the horse's hooves faded into silence as it galloped through the woods. And still he did not move. Not even as the clear sky clouded over and the air grew uncomfortably chilly. He just stood there, the increasing wind whipping at his coat, his blue eyes troubled.

His last chance was gone – for good. While they might have just shared a magical evening, he knew somehow that Belle would never return.

After a while, he returned to his room, unclasping his beautiful coat and letting it fall to the ground. Behind him, he heard the unmistakable sound of Cogsworth's waddle.

"Well, master," the majordomo said, his voice chipper, "I may have had my doubts, but everything is moving like clockwork." He smiled at his own wordplay. "True love really does win the day!"

"I let her go," the Beast said, his tone flat. What good was delaying the inevitable? It was a large castle, true, but news spread fast. It would be better just to get it out in the open and deal with the fallout.

Cogsworth's mouth dropped open. "You ... *what*?"

As if on cue, Lumiere and Plumette entered the room. Mrs Potts followed on her trolley. From the looks on their faces, the Beast could tell they had heard everything.

"Master ..." Lumiere said, the flames on his candles growing dim. "How could you do that?"

"I had to," the Beast replied simply.

"But why?" Lumiere and Cogsworth asked in unison. They were both looking at the Beast in confusion. His behaviour was so odd. It was as though the Beast had suddenly become a different person.

"Because he loves her," Mrs Potts answered for the Beast.

Everyone turned to the teapot. Her voice was soft, her eyes sad as she looked at the Beast. His shoulders slumped, but he did not deny what Mrs Potts had said. She was right. He did love Belle.

"Then why are we not human?" Lumiere asked, still confused.

Cogsworth, unfortunately, was no longer confused. Now he was mad. "Because *she* doesn't love *him*!" he snapped. "And now it's too late!"

"But she might still come back...?" Plumette suggested hopefully.

The Beast shook his head. "No. I've set her free." He turned his back to the staff. "I'm sorry I couldn't do the same for all of you," he said, meaning it with every fibre of his being.

Then, stepping out onto his balcony, he looked at the empty stable. Belle's leading Philippe out of the stable had been the hardest thing the Beast had ever had to witness. The pain he had felt in those first few years after the Enchantress had cursed him paled in comparison to the pain he had felt as Belle urged Philippe away. He had let his heart, which had been closed for so long, open, and the result? A deeper wound than he could bear. Because he knew the memory of Belle, like the curse, would now be with him forever.

He left the balcony and began to climb the castle's highest turret. The wind blew against him, threatening to whip him right off the stones, but still he climbed. The menacing gusts were a welcome distraction. But even that wasn't enough to keep images of Belle from flitting across his mind. Reaching the top of the turret, he peered through the woods, hoping for one last glimpse of her. But all he saw were trees. With a groan, he collapsed to the ground. There was no denying it any longer: she was gone for good. All he had left of her, all he would ever have of her, were memories that would fade over time, leaving him alone – and a beast – forever.

Belle urged Philippe on, her heels digging into his sides. She knew the horse was fading, but she needed to get back to Villeneuve. Her father was in danger.

At first, the woods were strange to her and all she could

do was hope Philippe remembered where he was going. But soon she began to recognize familiar landmarks. A patch of blueberries here, a small pond there. As the moon rose higher in the sky, she finally burst out of the woods and into the clearing at the edge of the village. She made sure her most prized possessions – the magic mirror and a small satin pouch she'd taken from the castle – were still safely in her lap.

Then, hearing a commotion near the square, Belle steered Philippe in that direction. To her surprise, a crowd had gathered around a horse-drawn wagon, which looked like a small metal prison with its steel frame and tiny barred window. She spotted Gaston and LeFou standing nearby. Gaston looked smug, as always, while LeFou looked uncomfortable. She continued to scan the scene, and then her breath caught in her throat.

Maurice was slumped inside the wagon's cage.

As Belle watched, Pére Robert ran up to the man locking Maurice inside – Monsieur D'Arque, the head of the town asylum. "This man is hurt!" Pére Robert said. "Please! He needs a hospital, not an asylum!"

Ignoring him, D'Arque finished his task and headed up to the driver's perch. Gaston walked over and leaned against the wagon, seeming to whisper something to Maurice.

Belle had seen enough. That wagon wasn't going anywhere. Kicking Philippe forward, she made her way into the middle of the crowd. "Stop!" she cried.

Her voice cut through the crowd, silencing everyone instantly. The people turned in her direction, eyes wide. Her ball gown flowed around her, the gold glitter catching the moonlight and making the dress sparkle magically. She could hear the whispers of the villagers beginning like a slow wave. Some wondered where she had come from. Others wondered if it was really her. Others muttered "that dress" with envy and awe.

Ignoring them, Belle dismounted. She kept her head high, her eyes seeking support in the crowd of villagers. She didn't find much. Most of the villagers were eyeing her with open distrust now that their initial shock had faded. Still, there were a few friendly faces. Pére Robert was standing close by, his expression bewildered and a bit defeated. And Jean the potter was there, too, though he looked puzzled and helpless, as usual.

Pushing down the slew of unkind words she wanted to hurl at the villagers, Belle stepped in front of the wagon.

"Stop this right now!" she ordered, causing the horses to startle. She ran to the back of the wagon and peered through the locked door. Her father lay on the floor, clutching his side in pain. "Open this door! He's hurt!"

Monsieur D'Arque climbed down from his perch. As he walked towards her, Belle couldn't help cringing. There was something dark and cruel in his eyes, and his pale skin reminded her of the monsters in some of her stories. "I'm afraid we can't do that, miss," he said. "But we'll take good care of him." While his words were meant to sound reassuring, they came across as a threat.

"My father's not crazy!" Belle protested. She turned and looked around the crowd, hoping for help. No one stepped forward. Finally, she turned to the one man she thought might advocate for her. "Gaston ... tell him!" she pleaded.

Gaston stepped out of the shadows where he had been waiting quietly. He had been worried that Belle had witnessed his part in Maurice's incarceration. He knew that if she had, any chance of marrying her would truly be over. But luck, as usual, was with him. She seemed completely unaware. Puffing out his chest, he put on his most sympathetic expression and walked to her. "Belle, you know how loyal I am to your family," he said, laying on the sincerity, "but your father has been making some unbelievable claims."

"It's true," Jean said. "He's been raving about a beast in a castle."

Belle looked back and forth between the two men. *That* was why Maurice was being hauled off to an asylum? She nearly laughed out loud in relief. "But I have just come from the castle," she said quickly. "There *is* a beast!"

Reaching out, Gaston put a hand on her shoulder. Then he gave her a condescending smile. Ever the showman, he spoke as much to the crowd as to her. "We all admire your devotion to your father," he said, "but you'd say anything to free him. Your word is hardly proof."

Panic gripped Belle's heart. She needed something to show them that she wasn't making it up. But what? In the pocket of her dress, her hand closed around the mirror. "You want proof?" she asked. She pulled out the mirror and held it up to face the villagers. *"Show me the Beast!"*

Once again, the mirror face swirled magically. The reflection of the village faded away and was replaced by an image of the Beast. He sat slumped against the turret wall, the picture of dejection. "There is your proof!" Belle cried. Gaston's face grew pale with shock.

"Well, it *is* hard to argue with that," LeFou said, turning to look at his friend.

"This is sorcery!" Gaston shouted, snatching the mirror from Belle's hand. He held it up for all the villagers to see. "Look at this beast. Look at his fangs! His claws!"

The villagers craned their necks, hoping to get a better look, then recoiled when they caught sight of the Beast. Watching their reactions, Belle bit her lip nervously. She hadn't thought things through when she pulled out the mirror. She had been so desperate to save her father that it hadn't occurred to her what actually seeing the Beast would do to the villagers. She hadn't thought that they would see only the Beast's appearance, not the man inside she had grown to care for. "No!" she cried out, trying to fix the situation. "Don't be afraid. He is gentle and kind."

"She is clearly under a spell," Gaston called out, shooting Belle a look. "If I didn't know better, I'd say she even *cared* for this monster."

Belle felt his words like a slap across the face. After

all he had done, *he* dared call the *Beast* a monster? "The Beast would never hurt anyone," she said, turning and pleading with the villagers. They looked back at her, their expressions wary, and the unease in the pit of her stomach grew. She should have known better. The villagers loved their Gaston. He was their war hero, their unofficial leader. He was their one small claim to fame. And Belle? She was an odd girl who liked to read.

As Gaston continued to rile the villagers into a frenzy against the Beast, Belle backed away. She had lost all hope of turning the tide in her favour. Catching sight of her, Gaston shouted to three of his henchmen. "We can't have her running off to warn the Beast," he said. "Lock her up."

Before she could turn and run, one of the men grabbed Belle roughly by the arm. Belle kicked and shouted, but it was no use. As Gaston called for his horse, she was dragged and tossed into the wagon cell where her father was being held. Monsieur D'Arque moved to stand guard.

Throwing his leg over his big black stallion, Gaston turned once more to the villagers. Shouts of approval rang out as he lifted his hand to the night sky. "That creature will curse us all if we don't stop him!" he hollered, riling

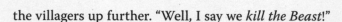

the villagers up further. "Well, I say we *kill the Beast!*"

The village erupted in bloodthirsty cries as Belle watched in horror behind the iron bars. Gaston was in his element. *This* was what he lived for – chaos and destruction, mindless violence. The Beast wasn't just a scary monster to him; he was an enemy, and *this* was battle. As Gaston led the mob from the village, he stoked their fears until they were burning as bright and hot as the torches some of the men carried. He painted a picture of a slobbering creature that lived in the dark and shadows. A beast with razor-sharp fangs and massive paws. A monster that roared and foamed. A living nightmare that needed to be destroyed. By the time the mob had disappeared into the woods, they were carrying weapons of all shapes and sizes. Some held shovels; others seized pitchforks. A few found axes and hefted them over their shoulders. And *all* of them – armed or not – looked ready to follow Gaston in his wild plan to kill the Beast.

Unable to do anything else, Belle stood still, her hands clutching the iron bars. The Beast, Mrs Potts, Lumiere ... everyone she had grown to love ... they were in serious danger. And it was all her fault.

CHAPTER XIV

INSIDE THE BEAST'S CASTLE, THE STAFF members felt as though they were already dead. Their one hope of salvation – Belle – had fled, and now the Beast was back to brooding, the rose was still wilting, and they had no chance of reversing the curse before it was too late.

As the night had grown darker, they had gathered in the foyer, taking solace in all they had left – each other. Mrs Potts and Chip nuzzled together on the serving trolley while Plumette rested her head on Lumiere's shoulder. His flames had grown dim and his expression was as drawn and serious as that of Cogsworth, who stood off to the side.

"He has finally learned to love," Lumiere said sadly, gazing towards the window that looked out on the turret where the Beast sat.

"A lot of good that does us if she doesn't love him in return," Cogsworth pointed out. He crossed his arms and pouted.

Shaking her head, Mrs Potts wheeled her trolley closer to the grumpy clock. "No," she said. "This is the first time I've had any real hope she would."

Cogsworth opened his mouth to make a snippy retort but was stopped by Chip. The young teacup had turned towards the door and was listening intently to something. "Did you hear that, Mama? Is it her?" he asked, jumping down from the serving trolley and hopping over to the window.

The rest of the staff rushed to join Chip at the window. They strained against the windowpane, trying to hear whatever the young teacup had heard. In the distance, they saw light from torches flash through the trees.

Lumiere's flames erupted in excitement. "Could it be?" he asked, pushing through the other staff. It was hard to see outside through the frost that covered the window. He held up a flame, warming the window until the frost melted. Then he shouted, "*Sacre bleu!* Invaders!"

The others peered through the cleared window.

Lumiere was right. It wasn't Belle coming through the woods, returning to the Beast. It was a mob! And from the looks of it, a very angry mob. The villagers pushed through the castle gate and made their way across the bridge up to the colonnade. Leading the charge was a tall, broad man on a black stallion. As the staff watched, he turned and addressed the mob.

"Take whatever treasures you want!" he cried. "But the Beast is *mine!*"

The staff collectively gasped in fear. What were they going to do?

Cogsworth knew exactly what *he* had to do. He had to warn the Beast. Leaving the others to form a small, sad barricade at the front door, Cogsworth headed to the turret. He hopped and wobbled his way up a dozen flights of stairs and down long halls before finally waddling out onto the balcony. Peering around, he tried to spot the Beast among the stone gargoyles that lined the balcony. He finally saw him perched near the far end. His head was down, his shoulders hunched.

Cogsworth cleared his throat. "Oh, pardon me,

master," he said nervously.

"Leave me in peace," the Beast said, not bothering to look up.

"But the castle is under attack," Cogsworth said urgently.

The Beast still did not look up, his face cloaked in darkness. When he spoke next, his voice rippled with pain. "It doesn't matter now," he said sadly, finally raising his head. His piercing blue eyes were stormy and full of held-back tears. "Just let them come."

Cogsworth had had enough. Gone was the calm, patient, loyal majordomo. He had spent too many years stuck in his clock body to have his master give up now. He had watched the Beast throw away his only chance at happiness and he had silently let him. But not any more. Now he was going to speak his mind. "Why fight?" he snapped. "Why indeed! Why do any thing at all?" Finishing, Cogsworth caught his breath and waited for the Beast to say something, anything, in return. But all he did was once again lower his head.

With a sigh, Cogsworth turned and began the long walk back to the foyer. It looked like the staff members were on their own.

"I have to warn the Beast...."

Belle looked around frantically. Her hands were clenched by her sides, and her eyes were wild as she desperately searched the small space for any means of escape. There wasn't one. The window was too tiny – and covered by bars – and the wagon had been locked from the outside.

"*Warn* him?" Maurice asked in confusion. He sat slumped in a corner. He looked worse than he had when he was a prisoner in the Beast's castle. His clothes were dishevelled and his hair was sticking up in every direction. He had scrapes on his palms from falling on them, and exhaustion hung heavy on his shoulders. "How did you get away from him?" The last he had known, Belle was being held prisoner by the very beast she now wanted to protect.

Belle stopped pacing. She turned to her father and took his hands in hers. "He let me go, Papa," she said. "He sent me back to you."

"I don't understand."

Reaching into the small pouch she had taken from the castle, Belle pulled out the rose-shaped rattle.

Maurice recognized it instantly. His hands began to shake as Belle told him how the Beast had taken her to Montmartre and had shown her their old home. Maurice took the rattle and moved it from one hand to the other as the realization of what it meant, what Belle now knew, hit hard.

"Belle," he began, "I had to leave your mother there. I had no choice, I had to save you –"

"I know, Papa. I understand." Belle's kind eyes met Maurice's. "Will you help me now?"

Maurice struggled to hold back tears that threatened to spill out of his eyes. His daughter had always been so caring and so forgiving. He just hadn't known until now how much *he* had needed her forgiveness.

"But ... it's dangerous," Maurice said.

"Yes, it is," Belle answered bravely. She waited for him to argue. But her father simply smiled and nodded. Then he clapped his hands.

"Well, then," he said as he looked around the tiny wagon cell, "it looks like we need to find a way to get out of here so you can go and save your beast."

Belle smiled. "Thank you, Papa." Then her smile

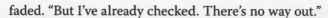

faded. "But I've already checked. There's no way out."

Maurice shook his head. If he had learned anything over the years, it was that there was always a way out. He peered through the small window at the lock on the wagon door. Its make-up didn't look unlike some of his music boxes.

"I think I might be able to pick the lock, if only I had –"

Maurice suddenly saw the hairpin Belle was holding up in front of him. There she was, anticipating his every need again. They shared a grin.

Then Maurice got to work picking the lock. When it finally clicked free, they slowly pushed the wagon door open.

"What are you waiting for?" Maurice whispered to his daughter. "Go!"

Giving him a grateful smile, Belle took off across the town square, not stopping to see if Monsieur D'Arque had spotted her.

She made it to Philippe and hopped on the horse's back. Giving the big animal a strong kick, she pulled on the reins and steered them out of the village. Behind her she could hear D'Arque's angry shout and her father's happy cheer. Leaning forward, Belle urged Philippe on. They didn't have time to celebrate this minor victory. They needed to get back to the castle.

As they galloped through the thickening trees, Belle could only hope that they would get back in time. She didn't want to imagine what Gaston and his bloodthirsty mob might do when they came face to face with a beast larger than anything they had ever seen before. Then her thoughts turned to Mrs Potts, Lumiere, Cogsworth and little Chip. They would be defenceless against the mob.

CHAPTER XV

"**A**TTACK!"

Mrs Potts's voice rang out through the foyer. On her command, the furniture around her came to life.

Despite Belle's fear, the staff members of the castle were far from defenceless. Or rather they were trying to be. As soon as they had seen the approaching mob, they had sprung into action. While Cogsworth had been trying, and failing, to get the master to stop wallowing and fight, Mrs Potts, Lumiere and Plumette had come up with a plan. It was simple – barricade the door – but it was a plan nonetheless.

They had tried to block the door, but when the villagers started breaking it down with a battering ram, they knew it was fruitless.

So they had decided to flee their post at the door

and play to their strength, lying in wait, as still as real furniture, while the unsuspecting villagers poured in. Finally, Mrs Potts yelled the signal, and the objects sprang into their surprise attack.

Chairs kicked. Plumette and the other dusters waved their feathers in villagers' faces until they started to sneeze. Candles shot their flames high into the air, blinding some and giving the backsides of several unsuspecting villagers quite the burn. As the furniture advanced, the mob shrieked in fear and the villagers tried to defend themselves. But the castle staff had the element of surprise.

Standing amid the chaos, Gaston tried to make sense of what was going on. He knew how to fight other men. He had done that plenty of times. He knew how to hunt animals. That, too, he had done. But a roomful of furniture that could walk and talk? That was something he had never encountered before.

"Gaston!"

Hearing LeFou's warning cry, Gaston turned to see a tall coatrack pulling back one of its 'arms', preparing to hit him. Gaston didn't think. He just acted. Grabbing LeFou

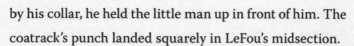

by his collar, he held the little man up in front of him. The coatrack's punch landed squarely in LeFou's midsection.

LeFou grunted. A moment later, things got worse as a large harpsichord stood on its back legs and fell forward. Once again, Gaston used LeFou as a human shield. There was a muffled shout as the harpsichord fell onto LeFou.

"Sorry, old friend," Gaston said, not bothering to help LeFou up, "but it's hero time."

"But ... we're *Le Duo*...." LeFou's voice grew weaker as the weight of the harpsichord bore down on him. A moment later, he passed out.

Gaston took one last look at LeFou. Then he looked down at the mirror he still had clutched in his hand. He could see the Beast sitting on a turret somewhere high above the foyer. "Hero time," he repeated under his breath. He turned and raced through the furniture. He ducked out of the way as a small teacup blasted by him on the back of a serving trolley. He moved to the side as a sideboard tried to trip him, and he avoided falling over a small foot stool that barked at him like a dog.

Moments later, he was bounding up the grand staircase as the noise of battle faded behind him. He kept climbing. His battle was somewhere ahead; he knew it.

Then, as if to prove him right, Cogsworth appeared at the top of the stairs. The small clock was descending from one of the turrets, his expression glum.

"My, my, what are *you* doing all the way up here, clock?" Gaston said. "Is there a beast up there?"

Cogsworth gulped. He had just inadvertently given away the Beast's position. Before Cogsworth could do anything to stop him, Gaston swung his leg back and kicked Cogsworth down the stairs. As Cogsworth thudded away, Gaston once again set his sights on the top of the turret stairs. Now that he knew the Beast was somewhere up there, it was only a matter of time before he had another trophy to mount on his wall.

Far below the turret, the household furniture continued to push back the villagers. Mrs Potts poured boiling tea out of her spout while Chip, riding Froufrou, drew a dozen annoyed villagers towards the kitchen, where Cuisinier was waiting, pots of grease also ready to be poured. As soon as Chip was safely past, Cuisinier dumped the grease on the floor. A moment later, the villagers entered the room and instantly began to slip and slide. They fell into a pile on the floor.

Unbeknownst to anyone, a new figure was making her way through the chaos: Agathe the beggar woman. Though she wore her usual rags, she looked different from how she normally did in the village. Her face was clean and the hair underneath her hood was formed into soft curls. She walked calmly past the droves of fighting villagers and objects, and ascended the staircase that led to the Beast's lair.

Meanwhile, Chip headed back to the foyer. He arrived just in time to see villagers flooding out of the front door, screaming in fright. He was about to let out a triumphant shout when, out of the corner of his eye, he saw his mother swinging on the chandelier. Hot water continued to pour from her spout, spraying the fleeing villagers.

Suddenly, she slipped and fell through the air.

Mrs Potts yelled.

Chip gasped.

And then, just when it looked as if Mrs Potts was going to shatter against the hard ground, a hand reached out and snatched her from midair.

It was LeFou! The little man had saved her! They stared at each other, both surprised by the sudden turn of events. "I used to be on Gaston's side," he said, shrugging apologetically. "But I'm just tired of being treated like an object, you know?"

"I do know, yes," Mrs Potts said, smiling. "Now, shall we get back to it?"

As Mrs Potts hobbled off to help the others, LeFou, feeling lighter now that he had finally shaken off his abusive partner, peered around the foyer. Only a few villagers remained inside. Most had run away, and those who had stayed were being funnelled out through the front door by a large talking candelabrum and his army of candles. LeFou watched as the front door slammed behind them. A moment later, the castle staff shouted triumphantly. The castle was saved!

And then Belle burst through the door.

The girl was breathing hard. Her brown hair fell about her face in waves, and her cheeks were red. But her eyes were cold and hard. Instantly, LeFou knew exactly who she was looking for. "He's upstairs," he called. Turning, Belle gave him the slightest of nods. Then she raced towards the grand staircase. "Oh, and when you see him, let him know that *Le Duo* is over," LeFou shouted at her back. "I'm Le Single now!"

When Belle had ridden through the castle's gate, she had been sure she was too late. She heard people shouting and saw villagers running. But she suddenly realized that they were running *out* of the castle. Hope had flared in her chest, and when she had finally made it through the front door, she had been thrilled to see that the castle staff, her friends, had won. They stood around the foyer, cheering and congratulating each other, as the villagers fled, proverbial tails tucked between their legs.

Then she had realized something was missing: the Beast was nowhere to be seen.

And the bad feeling in her stomach had rushed back.

Now, as she raced up the stairs, her heart pounded. All she could think about was getting to Gaston and stopping him before he could do something awful to the Beast. What-ifs flooded through her mind: *What if I had never left? What if I had just kept the mirror hidden? What if I'm too late? What if I never get to see the Beast again?* Her eyes filled with tears and she stumbled on the top step. She knew that if the Beast was gone, she would have no one to blame but herself.

She had seen where the Beast was when she flashed the mirror in front of Gaston. She had recognized the large stone statues that lined the castle's highest turret. Since he hadn't been downstairs, and since LeFou had seemed confident Gaston was up there somewhere, Belle had a pretty strong feeling that she would find both Gaston and the Beast on that turret. Picking up the pace, she plunged down the long hallway and onto the walkway that led to the tower. Then she skidded to a stop.

She had been right. The Beast and Gaston were on the balcony. Their backs were to her, so they didn't see her arrive.

"Hello, Beast. I am Gaston," the hunter said smugly. "Belle sent me." He was holding a large gun, the barrel pointed straight at the Beast. Gaston's finger tightened on the trigger. "Were you in love with her?" Gaston asked,

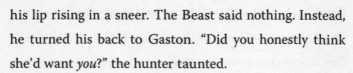

his lip rising in a sneer. The Beast said nothing. Instead, he turned his back to Gaston. "Did you honestly think she'd want *you*?" the hunter taunted.

Still the Beast said nothing.

And then Gaston fired.

Belle cried out as the Beast dropped over the edge of the turret. "What have you done?" She ran over and tried to push past Gaston. The large man reached out and grabbed her arm. She struggled to free herself, but his grip was too strong.

Staring down at her, he asked, his voice full of disbelief, "You prefer that misshapen thing to me ... *when I offered you everything*?" His fingers dug into her skin, turning it red. Belle cringed. Gone was the patriotic war hero. The man standing in front of her had finally revealed himself as the true monster he was. "When we return to the village, you will marry me. And the Beast's head will hang on our wall!"

"*Never!*" Belle shouted. Perhaps Gaston's hand slackened for just one moment. Or perhaps shock made him temporarily weaker. Or perhaps it was something more magical than any of that. But whatever the reason,

Belle was able to yank her arm free. Pivoting on her heel, she grabbed the barrel of Gaston's gun. Then she kicked him in the shin and yanked the weapon from him – hard.

Gaston wasn't about to let go of his gun, even if the person on the other end was his supposed future wife. He hung on to it as Belle swung it closer to the turret's edge. His feet slipped and slid as he struggled to find his footing on the cold surface. But the stones were slick from the snow that usually blanketed the castle, and some were even loose. Gaston cried out as his foot landed on one loose stone. Releasing the rifle, his hands flew into the air as he stumbled backwards over the edge of the turret. Belle gasped, sure that she had just sent Gaston plummeting to his death.

But Gaston hadn't survived the war by sheer luck. The man had lightning-fast reflexes. Just in time, he managed to swing himself to safety through a window below. With a grunt, he landed on the spiral staircase that led to the turret. His rifle, in the meantime, continued to fall and finally came to rest on a stone footbridge a few storeys down.

Instantly, Gaston was on his feet. He glanced out of the window. He saw Belle running towards the spiral staircase. For the briefest of moments, he thought the worry and fear he saw in her eyes was for him. But following her gaze, he saw the real reason for her fear: the Beast. The hulking creature had survived his own fall and was climbing slowly down around a slightly lower turret than the one Gaston had just been on.

A fresh wave of anger washed over Gaston and he quickly began to run down the stairs. He heard Belle shout as she gave chase, but he ignored her, pulling his bow and arrow out of the quiver strapped to his back. Pausing at another window, he took aim and fired.

The arrow struck the Beast's thigh, burrowing deep.

The Beast roared in pain. Gaston started to smile, pleased his arrow had hit home. But his pleasure was short-lived, as the Beast reached down and pulled the arrow out. Then he disappeared around the turret and out of Gaston's view.

Suddenly, Gaston felt something – or rather, someone – tugging at his back. His attention momentarily distracted from the Beast, he whipped around to find Belle tearing at the quiver. Her thin fingers pulled at the leather holder as she desperately tried to break it free. When that didn't work, she resorted to grabbing the arrows. She began to snap them in half one by one.

Gaston raised his hand to strike Belle away but stopped himself. Out of the corner of his eye he saw that the Beast had reappeared and was leaping down from one parapet to another. His going was slow due to the wounds Gaston had inflicted. Each time he landed on one of the low stone walls, he groaned in pain. Still, he kept going.

Shoving Belle away, Gaston once again took up the chase. His footfalls echoed off the stone walls as he raced down the rest of the staircase. When he reached the bottom, he ran onto a bridge. Across the way he saw the Beast, paused, ready to swing himself onto another parapet. If he made it, he would be as far away from Gaston as the mazelike roof of the castle allowed.

The Beast reared back on his haunches ... and leaped.

At the same time, Belle reached the Beast's lair. Racing out onto the balcony, she frantically searched the roofline for the Beast. She found him just as he jumped.

He flew through the air, his arms stretched out in front of him to grab the side of the stone wall. He barely made it. His grip started to slip.

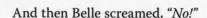

And then Belle screamed, *"No!"*

"Belle?" the Beast said, turning as her cry echoed over the castle's roof. Their eyes met, and in that instant, the Beast was filled with a strength he didn't know he still had. He pulled himself to safety, then made his way towards Belle, leaping from parapet to parapet.

Unfortunately, he was also making his way back towards Gaston, who was lying in wait. The hunter had ducked between the gargoyles that lined a landing not too far from the Beast's rooms. He watched with disgust as Belle called out to the Beast, and he sneered when the Beast seemed to revive suddenly at the sight of Belle. Wrapping his hands around a thin stone spire, he pulled it until it broke off. Once again armed, Gaston waited for the Beast to come to him.

He didn't have to wait long. Focused on reaching Belle, the Beast didn't even bother to look around as he landed on the gargoyle-lined walkway. His long legs swept him across the stones, his eyes locked on the terrace where Belle stood.

Gaston waited until the Beast was just past him, and then he roared. Jumping out of the shadows, he brought the spire down on the Beast's back.

The Beast roared in pain but kept going.

Seeing the Beast's determination, Gaston felt another rush of anger. "Fight me, Beast!" he shouted, following him. He hit him again and again. With every blow, Gaston managed to slow the Beast, but no matter what he did, he could not stop him. It made him furious and he swung the spire harder. Finally, he managed to knock the Beast off balance. The Beast staggered down a small set of stairs and out onto another stone footbridge.

Gaston jumped down behind him and continued his assault.

Under the combined weight of Gaston and the Beast, the footbridge, which had not been used in years and had fallen into disrepair, began to shake and crumble. Neither man nor beast paid any attention. Gaston had seen something lying at the far corner of the footbridge – his rifle. And the Beast had seen how very close he was to Belle. If he could make it to the end of the footbridge, he would be on the cupola that stood parallel to his rooms. From there it was just one giant leap between him and Belle.

"Gaston! *No!*"

Belle's cry warned the Beast. He turned to see Gaston, spire lifted high, readying to strike the death blow. The Beast had had enough. He was not going to let Gaston stop him from reaching Belle, not when he was that close. In one swift move, he reached up and yanked the spire from Gaston's hands. Then he hurled it against the far wall. It shattered into a thousand pieces. Snarling, the Beast wrapped his paw around Gaston's throat and swung him over the edge of the crumbling footbridge.

"No," Gaston pleaded as his legs dangled in open air. "Please. Don't hurt me, Beast. I'll do anything."

For a long, tense moment, the Beast just stared at Gaston. The Beast's features were twisted with rage and hate – for all the years he had been trapped in that form; for the man in front of him, who could see him only as a beast; for the time he had already lost with Belle and the fear that he might lose still more.

Then his rage and hate began to fade. Turning, he saw Belle looking at them, hope in her eyes. It seemed she believed he could do the right thing, that he could be the best version of himself. And suddenly, the rage and hate were gone. Slowly, he swung Gaston back over the bridge's wall and set him down. "Go," he said. "Get out."

As Gaston scrambled away, the Beast turned and locked eyes with Belle. In that moment, he didn't need to hear her to know she was proud of him. All he wanted, more than anything in the world, was to be next to Belle. Dropping down on all fours, he took a deep breath. He had just enough distance to get his speed up to make a leap from the bridge to the balcony – and Belle.

Seeing what he was about to do, Belle shouted, "No! It's too far!"

But she was too late. The Beast's hind claws dug into the stone and he pushed off. Gaining speed, his four paws pounded over the stone. And then ... he leaped.

For a moment, he seemed to hover in the air, suspended over the abyss of emptiness between the castle's roofs. Then time sped up, and with a thud he landed safely on the balcony. Looking at Belle, he smiled. He had made it! Nothing could keep him from Belle now....

Boom!

The Beast roared in agony as the sound of gunfire echoed over the castle.

On the crumbling footbridge, Gaston reloaded the rifle. He had grabbed it from where it had been hidden among the rubble. As Belle watched, hopeless, he aimed the gun once more, an evil grin spreading across his face.

Boom! He fired again. The bullet flew through the air and slammed into the Beast, who fell to the ground.

But Gaston's luck had just run out. His weight, the decay of the footbridge, and the heavy recoil of the rifle proved too much. Before he could even let out a triumphant shout, the stones beneath his feet gave way completely. In an instant, there was only empty air – and a long drop into nothingness – under him.

Lifting her head, Belle saw Gaston – and his horrible rifle – disappear in a cascade of stones.

CHAPTER XVI

BELLE WANTED TO BELIEVE everything would be okay, that the Beast would be okay. But as she sat, his head cradled in her lap, she knew time was running out. It had already run out for Gaston, though that had caused her only a momentary pang of regret. He had been a horrible man. While she never would have wished his fate on anyone, she would not bother to waste tears or time on his memory.

The Beast, though, was another story. She didn't want him to become a memory. She wanted him to stay there, with her, alive and well. She wanted to tell him how much he meant to her. She wanted to tell him how sorry she was for inadvertently sending Gaston to the castle in the first place. Yet looking down at him, she knew that her chance to do that was quickly slipping away. The Beast's breathing was laboured and his eyes were shut tight, the pain clearly overwhelming his body. Softly, Belle reached down and ran her fingers along his cheek.

When the Beast felt her touch, his eyes opened. "You came back," he said, looking at her with pure love. He lifted his paw and brushed back a lock of Belle's hair.

"Of course I came back," she said, trying to fight the tears that threatened to spill onto her cheeks. "I'll never leave you again."

The Beast lifted his shoulders in the slightest shrug. Then he sighed. "I'm afraid it's my turn to leave," he said, his voice weak.

Belle shook her head. *No!* she wanted to shout. *Fight! Don't just give up! Not after all we've been through. It took me so long to find you.* Despite her best efforts, the tears began to fall. The Beast's head was growing heavier in her lap. As she stared down at him, she felt her heart already breaking. Against the odds, the Beast had shown her true beauty. He had shown her it was okay to be different. He had shown her it was okay to feel lost and made her realize how desperately she had wanted to be found. She had learned that things were not always what they seemed, that people could surprise you. He had given her the one thing she had always longed for – something more. And now? Now he was dying in her arms.

Struggling for words, Belle choked back a sob. "We're together now," she said. "It's going to be fine. You'll see."

"At least I got to see you one last time," he said. As he spoke, his paw dropped from Belle's hair. His eyes closed. His breathing grew slower, and then it stopped altogether.

With another sob, Belle threw herself over the Beast's still body. He was gone. And she had never told him she loved him.

As the Beast took his last breath on the terrace above, his staff members, unaware of what had happened between their master and Gaston, were in the middle of a celebration. They had all gathered on one of the lower terraces to watch as the villagers ran off through the woods. Lumiere's flames were shining bright, buoyed by victory. Plumette had fluffed her feathers, and Cogsworth was ticking and tocking at a much faster rate than usual. Even the larger pieces of furniture, like Garderobe and her long-lost love, Cadenza, had made their way out to celebrate.

Lumiere turned to Plumette and took her in his arms. The feather duster giggled flirtatiously. "We did it, Plumette," he said, dipping her. "Victory is ours!" He leaned down to kiss her and gasped. She had grown still and silent in his arms. She was no longer alive. With the Beast gone, the curse had taken full effect.

One by one, the once animate objects grew inanimate. As Lumiere watched in horror, Garderobe froze in the middle of a theatrical flourish. Letting out a shout, Cadenza began to play his keys, frantic to keep them moving. But there was nothing he could do. They, too, slowed until, finally, they stopped and Cadenza became still. The curse swept through the castle like a wind, and no matter how they tried to escape it, the staff could not get away.

Froufrou barked one last time before turning back into a piano stool. Mrs Potts frantically approached Lumiere and Cogsworth, searching for her son. But before she could find him, her face disappeared in the painted ornamentation of the teapot. Chip became still next, his features fading away until he no longer resembled a precocious little boy and was just a chipped teacup.

"Lumiere...."

Hearing Cogsworth's voice, Lumiere turned, dreading the inevitable. The little clock was struggling against the curse, trying his hardest to keep ticking. "No!" Lumiere cried. "Hang on, Cogsworth."

"I ... can't ..." Cogsworth said, his voice growing weak. He gave a long, slow tick and an even slower tock. "My friend, it was an honour to serve with you."

Lumiere lowered his flames as Cogsworth's voice faded completely. The only sound he made now was the ticktock of a small clock. He was no longer the majordomo. He was an object. And as Lumiere looked around, he saw that they were *all* objects now. No one but him was left. Lumiere knew that up in the master's lair, the last rose petal had fallen. A moment later he, too, stiffened and the light faded from his candles as his final transformation took place.

Soon the terrace was quiet except for the ticking of the clock that had once been Cogsworth. A soft snow began to fall, covering the objects and making them look like ghosts.

Up on the balcony, Belle barely noticed the snow falling on her head and shoulders. She didn't know that the curse had been enacted. All she could think about was the Beast, lying in her arms. His body still felt warm, and for a desperate moment, she wanted to believe that he was still there. She cradled his head in her hands. His fur felt soft in her palms and she wanted to force his eyes open so she could once again see them, the most beautiful blue she had ever known, staring back at her. "Please, don't leave me. Come back," she begged. Overcome with emotion, she slowly leaned over and placed a soft kiss on his forehead. And then, because she had never said it to him while he was alive, she whispered the words she had been carrying in her heart: "I love you."

Though Belle did not know it, Agathe had silently entered the room and was standing on the balcony next to what was left of the enchanted rose. The woman lowered the hood of her cloak and extended her hand towards the bell jar. In an instant, the jar disappeared, leaving behind the crimson petals and a trace of golden dust. Agathe swirled her hand and the petals rose. The golden dust seemed to multiply, moving rapidly towards the Beast, enveloping him entirely before lifting him off the ground.

Feeling the weight of the Beast's body lift from her lap, Belle looked up and gasped, seeing the golden haze swirling around him. She noticed that the air felt warmer, thicker. Then, quite suddenly, there was a flash of light, and one of the Beast's paws turned into a hand. Belle stood, watching intently.

More bursts of light followed as the rest of the Beast's features turned into human ones. Finally, he landed softly on the ground, the transformation complete.

Silence fell over the balcony.

For a long moment, Belle stood where she was, her head spinning with what she had just witnessed. She stared in awe at the man standing in front of her. He was still wearing the clothes he had worn as the Beast. He had the same piercing blue eyes, though they were now wide and filled with concern as they looked upon her tear-stained face.

Belle's heart felt as if it would burst with joy. She knew, deep in her soul, that this was the Beast she had grown to love, once again in his human form. And she knew, without hesitation, that she didn't want to waste another moment not being close to the one she loved.

Blue eyes met brown, and then, as dawn broke over the horizon, they leaned forward and kissed.

It was a kiss Belle would never forget – one better than any in all the books she had read. It was a kiss full of apology, full of thankfulness, and full of deep, deep love. It was a kiss full of enchantment. And as their lips met, that magic exploded from them to the rest of the castle.

As the sun rose higher into the sky, the castle began to transform. The cold grey stone became awash with gold. The snow faded from the ground, giving way to bright green grass. Colourful flowers burst forth, and in the colonnade, the white roses turned red. Up on the parapets of the castle, the gargoyle statues, their faces so long stuck in frightening sneers, returned to their original forms of noble beasts and men. Even the sky seemed touched by the magical transformation. Clouds disappeared, revealing a sky almost as brilliant blue as the Prince's eyes.

Inside the castle, the transformation continued. As the light from the dawn filtered through the large windows, it illuminated the objects that had, only moments before, been rendered immobile. Froufrou turned from a foot

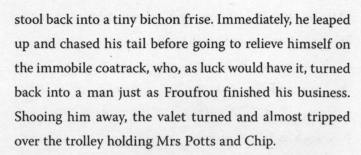

stool back into a tiny bichon frise. Immediately, he leaped up and chased his tail before going to relieve himself on the immobile coatrack, who, as luck would have it, turned back into a man just as Froufrou finished his business. Shooing him away, the valet turned and almost tripped over the trolley holding Mrs Potts and Chip.

He shouted as it started to roll away, barely missing Garderobe, who was waddling in and out of the sunlight. As she did, she turned from wardrobe to human to wardrobe again until, finally, she landed with a thud right next to Cadenza. Moments later, they both transformed once and for all back into the diva and the maestro.

And so it continued. Throughout the castle, excited cries could be heard coming from all over as the curse was lifted. Maids giggled as their feathers turned back into legs, and candles shouted happily as their wicks turned back into fingers. In the kitchen the stove became the chef again and immediately began giving orders to prepare a feast.

Cogsworth's ticks became a series of coughs as he, too, transformed back into his human shape. Brushing off his coat, he looked around for Lumiere and smiled when he saw that the candelabrum was once more head footman – but still up to his old tricks. He was chasing Plumette around the dining-room table. Catching her, he dipped her back and kissed her passionately.

Cogsworth was saved from witnessing how long the kiss went on by the rattling sound of china. He looked up to see the trolley carrying Mrs Potts and Chip barrelling towards the top of the staircase. For a tense moment, it looked as if they might tumble to their doom. But as Cogsworth watched, the trolley jerked to a stop, sending Mrs Potts and Chip flying forwards. Midair, as their fragile bodies hit the sun, they transformed, and they slid down the rest of the stairs on their very human posteriors.

"Oh, Chip!" Mrs Potts cried happily. "Look at you – you're a little boy again!" Reaching out, she tried to give his cheek a squeeze. He ducked out of the way, like any little human boy would, and raced towards the front door. As he flung it open, the sun poured in – and so did some of the villagers.

For truth be told, they had been under the enchantment, too. Now, with every moment that passed, they were beginning to remember all they had forgotten: the castle with the cruel king and the haughty prince, the lavish parties that had once been thrown, their loved ones who had worked there.

Approaching the front door, Jean the potter took in the castle, which now glowed with happiness and warmth. And then his eyes fell on Chip in the doorway and, beyond, Mrs Potts. He shouted happily, "Darling?"

Mrs Potts smiled back. "Hello, Mr. Potts," she said, running towards him.

"Beatrice, Chip," he said as his wife and son fell into his arms. "I've found you."

The reunions continued. And standing in front of the castle, smiling to herself, was Agathe. She had only ever wanted to see the Prince become a kinder man. And as she watched his happy staff members run about the castle, calling out to one another, hugging one another, she knew that he had found a way to be kind. He had found his heart. It had taken some time and one particularly stubborn young woman to help him do it, but nevertheless, he had found his way.

Seeing that her work was done, Agathe smiled and turned, leaving as silently and mysteriously as she had arrived.

Meanwhile, Plumette let out a shout. Everyone turned towards the staircase. At the top, as if on cue, stood the Prince. Belle was beside him, and their eyes were locked in a look of pure love. The staff rushed to greet them.

"Hello, old friend." The Prince addressed Lumiere happily. Belle watched the Prince embrace each member of the staff – of his family, really – allowing him the moment that had been so long in the making. She sighed contentedly. All was as it should be.

EPILOGUE

BELLE HAD NOT THOUGHT IT POSSIBLE to be that happy. But she was that happy. Deliriously, wonderfully, blissfully happy.

Gliding across the ballroom in her prince's arms, she smiled as they passed faces now so familiar to her. She saw her father, free and healthy. She caught sight of Lumiere and Plumette dancing nearby. She saw Chip, wedged between his mother and father, pretending to be annoyed but clearly loving the attention. Cogsworth was there, as was the diva, Belle's former wardrobe. She waltzed happily with her maestro. *This,* Belle thought as she gazed around the room, *is my family.*

She lifted her head, and her eyes met the Prince's piercing blue ones. He smiled down at her and she felt the now familiar warmth of love shoot through her whole body, starting at her toes and travelling to the tips of her ears. Over the past few weeks, she had found herself loving the Prince more with each passing day as she watched him embrace the life that had been denied him for so long.

I'm living my own adventure, she thought as he swung her around. She had found a life outside the village, and there were still so many places to visit and experiences to be had. What's more, she had found a partner who wanted to travel, as well, a partner with whom she could share all these adventures. *And there is nothing more I could ever want. Except....*

Feeling Belle tense in his arms, the Prince looked at her, his eyes narrow with worry. "Belle ..." he said. "What are you thinking?"

Belle took a moment to consider her answer and tried not to smile as the Prince's expression grew more worried. Then, reaching up, she ran a hand down his smooth cheek. "How would you feel about growing a beard?"

Letting out a roar of laughter, the Prince pulled Belle closer. His eyes locked with hers and he nodded, an unspoken promise to always try to be the best version of himself, the version she had believed was possible before he had. Then, leaning in, he kissed her. And as she closed her eyes and gave in to the magic of the kiss, the world faded away until it felt as if it were just the two of them, caught up in a tale as old as time. Belle thought about the future – about the reading classes she could teach in the castle library for all the village students, the travelling she and the Prince would make time for, the friendships with those in the castle that would undoubtedly be lifelong. A tale that had begun once upon a time and would end, Belle knew, happily ever after.